THE REIGN OF THE

FORTUNATE KING

1495-1521

Other Books by Elaine Sanceau

Indies Adventure (Career of Afonso de Albuquerque)
The Land of Prester John
Henry the Navigator
Knight of the Renaissance (D.João de Castro)
Good Hope (Voyage of Vasco da Gama)
Captains of Brazil
The Perfect Prince (Biography of King João II)

In Portuguese
Castelos em Africa (Portuguese in Morocco)
Casos e Curiosidades
Recortes de Pequena História

História de Portugal

CASAMENTO DE D. MANUEL COM D. LEONOR
(Século XVI)

(Museu da Misericórdia de Lisboa)

THE REIGN OF THE

FORTUNATE KING

1495-1521

By

Elaine Sanceau

ARCHON BOOKS
1969

ISBN:0 208 00968 X

Library of Congress Catalog Card Number: 70-105396

PRINTED IN THE UNITED STATES OF AMERICA

Contents

Geneological Table of the Dynasty
    founded by D. João   XI
Forward   VIII

I.	Improbable Inheritance	1
II.	The New King	8
III.	Iberian Throne	17
IV.	Gates of the East	26
V.	First Fruits	35
VI.	Repercussions	43
VII.	Latter-Day Crusade	48
VIII.	India	57
IX.	The Dark Kingdom of Africa	70
X.	The Forests of Brazil	80
XI.	North African Mirage	85
XII.	Apogee	95
XIII.	Dropping the Pilot	104
XIV.	Afternoon Shadows and Sunshine	116
XV.	The Little Kingdom	122
XVI.	The Family and the Court	135
XVII.	Mainly Matrimonial	147
XVIII.	1521	156

Chronology   168
Bibliography   171
Index   174

Genealogical Table of Dynasty founded by D. Joao, Master of Aviz illegitimate son of D. Pedro I of Portugal

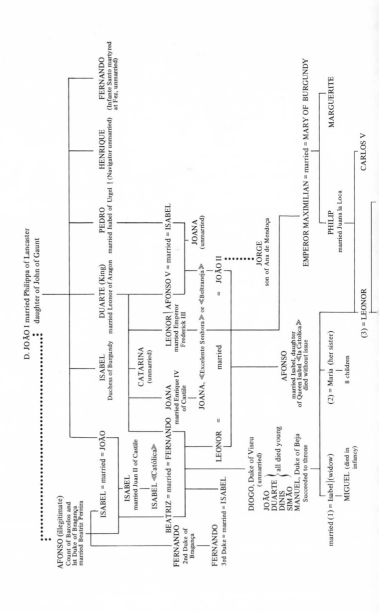

Foreword

This book is an attempt to give an all-over picture of a reign that was in many ways unique in history. It was an age of flowering and fulfilment in which the world beheld the unprecedented spectacle of a small nation, implemented exclusively by its own resources and on its sole initiative, projecting its aegis over continents and oceans hitherto unknown. The like had not been seen before, nor has it been seen since. All previous empires had radiated overland around their centres. The expansion of Portugal, wider than any achieved in the past, extended overseas and to the far ends of the earth. As will be clear to readers of this book, it is not to the man who gave his name to this astounding reign that we may attribute its glory; the glory was earned by a nation trained to sacrifice by great leaders who had gone before and who died without seeing the harvest of their labours.

Those who have read my other books will find here episodes which I have treated at greater length elsewhere, and I make no apology for this. My present aim has been to correlate them all, to fit them into their background, and to give a general view of the great age of Portugal as it might look to those who stayed at home. The aspects are so varied and so multiple that I can hardly hope to have succeeded, and here is where I feel I should apologize for having failed to fill so vast a canvas.

The radiant years soon passed; it could not have been otherwise. A nation of less than two million souls had aimed at the impossible and for a while achieved it. And it would be untrue to say that nothing remains today of the great effort. Portugal has left her imprint indelibly on many distant lands throughout the world, where we still find vestiges of her speech, her names upon the map, her buildings in cities and wilderness, and where live descendants of her sons who were the first to bring the races of the earth together.

I

Improbable Inheritance

A boy of fourteen knelt before a young man of twenty-six. Both were in tears. The inconceivable had come to pass. The mighty figure that had dominated both their lives and disposed of their destinies had vanished from the scene. The great king, D.João II – that brilliant overwhelming personality, unbending will and hand of iron seldom concealed in velvet glove, relentless, unpredictable, but withal strangely lovable – was dead.

And Manuel, his cousin, now was king, and young D.Jorge, the late king's sole surviving son, was kneeling at his feet.

It might so easily have been the other way about. Everyone knew that since the tragic accident four years earlier, in which the lawful heir had lost his life, the King had dreamed of bequeathing his kingdom to his only other child – D.Jorge, son of his former mistress, D.Ana de Mendoça. He even had attempted to put through a petition to Rome to have the boy legitimated.

Such a solution would have been wholly unjust. After Prince Afonso's death, in 1491, the legal claimant to the throne could only be the King's first cousin, Manuel, then Duke of Beja.

This was obvious to everybody, as the King must have known, but D.João, accustomed to bend men and events to his will, could not believe that he might not impose it once again in this, and while he lived few dared gainsay him.

It was a weary broken-hearted woman who fought to the last for Manuel's right. His sister, the Queen Leonor, bereaved of her adored and only son, expended all her love and loyalty defending her brother's cause – her last remaining brother out of six.

Some stormy arguments were overheard between the King and Queen. For many days the atmosphere at court was tense and grim.

Although the firm hand on the rein never relaxed, although the King was no more than forty years old, everyone knew his days were numbered. The question of the succession loomed sombrely. Nobody but the Queen would dare discuss the subject with the King, though the burden was felt by all.

By all except, apparently, the parties most concerned. So far as we can gather neither Manuel nor Jorge had anything to say upon the matter. They formed no factions and made no comments. They stood aloof letting their champions fight. They even seem to have remained on perfectly good terms with one another. Of course D.Jorge was still a child, and Manuel had been well disciplined. The impression at court was that, if his lord and master so ordained, D.Manuel was quite prepared to step aside and recognize D.Jorge as heir.

But that would have meant civil war. It was unlikely that the great fidalgos whose pretensions had been crushed with a relentless hand by the late king, would bow the knee before his bastard son. Most certainly they would proclaim Manuel as their rightful lord, their opponents would rally round D.Jorge, and so the peace and order in which D.João had left his realm would in a short time be replaced by chaos.

He was far too intelligent not to see that, even without his wife to point it out, to say nothing of the respectful hints dropped by his private secretary, and the advice of his Father Confessor. He loved his son, but he had loved his lifework too – the welding of a little kingdom into a world power. He could not bear to think that strife and faction should undo all his hopes and plans. So the Queen won. Quite suddenly, the King made up his mind. Before leaving for the baths of Monchique in the Algarve, whose healing waters were his one remaining hope, he sat up all night with his confessor making his will, in which D.Manuel – "our esteemed and beloved cousin" – is named heir to the throne. The next morning D.João went and told the Queen what he had done. Husband and wife made peace and parted friends. The King then left for the Algarve where he died three weeks later.

Thus it was that, on October 26th 1495, the day after his death, D.Manuel was proclaimed King of Portugal and the Algarves, Hither and Beyond the Sea in Africa, and Lord of Guinea.

There came to him D.Diogo de Almeida, Prior of the Hospital, leading his pupil D.Jorge by the hand. Both of them were dressed in the white sackcloth of mourning. In the name of the dead, D.Diogo begged the young king to take charge of the orphan, remembering the many benefits he had received from Jorge's father: "As I promised the King, your cousin, I bring him to you, and hand him over to your care, to be honoured and nurtured as becomes his birth, that all men in your kingdom and all foreigners may praise your gratitude for what the King, his father did for you."

D.Manuel listened and he wept. He raised the kneeling boy and clasped him to his heart. In a voice choked by sobs he promised to treat him like a son. Thereafter D.Jorge became a member of the royal household, spending his days beside the King, and sleeping with him in his bed by night.

Had Manuel then sincerely loved his formidable predecessor? It is not easy to pronounce upon the question. Certainly his recorded reactions suggest more than purely official grief. There is no doubt that the late king had always been kind to this young cousin, whatever the rigour shown towards other members of the family.

Manuel's path to the throne is a complicated and tragic story. When, on May 31st 1469, he was born in his father's palace at Alcochete, as many as eight lives stood before him in the line of succession. He was the last child of six sons and three daughters born to the Infante D.Fernando, paternal uncle of D.João II. In after years the chroniclers complacently related auguries and happy portents that had marked his birth. Had not his mother laboured for several days until upon the sacred feast of Corpus Christi, she brought forth this son? Exactly at the moment when the Host was carried in procession past her door! So they gave her baby the blessed name of the Saviour – Emanuel, or rather Manuel as was the usual and more popular version.

However that may be, the fact remains that no special excitement shook the land when the number of the Infante D.Fernando's sons reached the half dozen. One more or less – what difference did it make? He was in a position to maintain them all.

The Infante D.Fernando, only brother of the King Afonso V, had been adopted son of his unmarried uncle, D.Henrique, generally called The Navigator. His other uncle and namesake, the martyred Infante D.Fernando, also made this nephew his heir. From both the younger Fernando inherited titles and lands. He was Duke of Viseu and Lord of Covilhã, Serpa, and Moura, Constable of Portugal, governor of the Order of Christ and Santiago, and ruler of the archipelagoes of the

Atlantic Ocean. He had been married at the age of sixteen to his first
cousin Beatriz, daughter of yet another uncle already deceased, who
brought with her an ample dowry further to increase his fortune.
    The Infante D.Fernando, impulsive, mercurial, and not a little spoilt
between his brother who refused him nothing, and his indulgent uncle
D.Henrique, held greater state than any uncrowned prince in the Peninsula. His household was magnificent, his generosity was lavish.
    Undermined by tuberculosis, he lived eagerly and feverishly. He
dabbled in colonization of Atlantic islands and he fought the Moors. He
assaulted Tangier and failed resoundingly, but shortly after raided and
destroyed Anfa, further to the southwest, returning with an aureole of
glory and with ruined health, to die at Setubal, aged thirty-seven.
    His widow, D.Beatriz, a woman of both character and brains, man-
aged her late husband's estate and brought up her large family under
the kindly protection of King Afonso. The King had dearly loved his
brother and was anxious to help in every way. Already, to console
Fernando during his last illness, D.Afonso had promised him that the
heir to the throne, the young Prince D.João, should marry the Infante's
elder daughter, Leonor. A year after this wedding, he gave Leonor's
sister, then thirteen years old, to the great Duke of Bragança, the King's
intimate friend and cousin, a middle-aged man. Thus two more consan-
guineous marriages were added to the tangled geneology of the royal
House, and King Afonso felt quite satisfied that he had done the best
he could for his two nieces.
    As for the nephews – four of the six had died within the next few
years, leaving only D.Diogo, the second son, and little Manuel the
youngest, whom the Prince D.João, fourteen years older than himself,
took under his special protection.
    It was an uncomfortable family atmosphere in which Manuel grew
up. He stood at the crossways of the opposing currents of two powerful
rivalries. On the one hand was D.João, the heir, his patron and his
brother-in-law, a young man wise beyond his years, a personality whose
dynamism all could feel although its power was still held in reserve.
Over against him stood the mighty Duke of Bragança, the greatest lord
in all the realm, who maintained royal estate and ruled some fifty
towns and castles up and down the land. Ambitious, proud, beloved of
the King, the great duke was superbly confident and threw his weight
about. The young Prince D.João, already jealous for the royal author-

ity, did not approve of this, and personally he did not like the man. And João was adored by his good-natured father – his pride, his joy, the apple of his eye, the son of the wife of his youth whom he had never ceased to mourn.

Such was the picture of the court in which D.Manuel's boyhood was spent. The Duke and the great nobles, like bees humming around a honey pot, gathering benefits from their open-handed king, while the young Prince, aloof and hostile, looked on, biding his time as all could see. Meanwhile, the Princess and the Duchess, the sisters Leonor and Isabel, loving each other intensely, yet remained loyal wives, and both were quite devoted to their little brother Manuel.

As for their mother, the widowed Infanta D.Beatriz, she pursued her uneasy way with great precaution. She would have liked to act as mediator between her sons-in-law, but there is no doubt which one she preferred. The husband of her younger daughter, some years older than herself, to Beatriz was guide and mentor. On every problem she sought his advice, and it was his opinion that – always with perfect tact – she tried to recommend to her young son-in-law. With this boy D.Beatriz could never feel entirely happy. D.João listened reverently to all she had to say. How kind his Lady Mother was to take interest in his affairs! And he continued to act just as he thought fit.

D.Beatriz was really a most remarkable woman. Her self-control amazes us. She never quarrelled with D.João, either as Prince or King – not even when she saw her dear friend the Duke tried and executed for High Treason – not even when her elder son, D.Diogo, discovered to be plotting regicide, was stabbed to death by order of the King, if not by his own hand. Through both these tragedies the Infanta remains in the background, silently suffering no doubt, but calm and unprotesting and withal loyal to the Crown. She must have been fully aware that there was justice in the sentences. The Duke of Bragança, though probably not designing murder, was carrying on a correspondence with his cousin the Queen of Castile the purpose of which was to cross his sovereign's policy, at home and overseas; while as for her son, D.Diogo, Duke of Viseu, a vain and foolish youth led astray by unprincipled counsellors, he was the centre of a plot to kill the King and her grandson, Prince Afonso the heir, with a view to occupying the throne himself.

Whatever anguish she endured, the mother of the criminal made no attempt to raise her voice, but devoted her life to her remaining children: the young Queen Leonor, the widowed Duchess Isabel, and the boy Manuel, then fifteen years old.

"Forget you had a brother," the King is said to have told the trembling lad summoned before him just after D.Diogo's death, "and remember that I regard you as a son." With tears, D.João explained why D.Diogo had been executed. And so, since his estate was forfeit to the Crown, the King proposed to give it all to Manuel. He would not be Duke of Viseu — that was a traitor's title! Henceforward he would be styled Duke of Beja. The heritage of the Infante D.Henrique was also to pass to him during his lifetime. Afterwards it must revert to the Crown — but then, who could tell? If the young Prince Afonso died without heirs, D.Manuel would be his sole successor!

Silently and on bended knee D.Manuel kissed the royal hand. What were his feelings? None can guess. He seems to have been as reserved and tactful as his mother, who accepted the King's condolences without recrimination, and herself wrote to the wardens of her dead son's castles, ordering them to surrender the keys to their sovereign.

D.João, as good as his word, showered D.Manuel with grace and favour. Throughout his reign we see the Duke of Beja by the formidable King. Silent and obedient, he comes and goes; he takes part in festivities at court and receives embassies from overseas. He it was who went to escort young Afonso's bride when she came from Castile in 1490. Some people think he fell in love with her himself. Yet six months later when the Prince was killed by a fall from his horse, leaving Manuel as only lawful heir, we are told he wept and lamented as if his heart was broken.

When D.João II died, it seems that he shed bitter tears, although by then there could be no need to dissemble. He took all the late King's servants into his special care, and respected nearly all of the dead man's wishes.

Nearly all — his mother and sisters saw to it that one clause in D.João's will was disregarded: "Item — Because I have seen and I know what harm is brought to kingdoms and dominions by the return of those who have erred against the kings and lords thereof, I enjoin and command the said Duke, my cousin, not to receive back to these realms those who are now abroad because of errors thus committed against me, nor yet their sons . . . ."

The late King was mistaken if he thought D.Manuel could feel as he did on the subject. The Duke of Bragança's execution had taken place when he was still a child, and he had nothing personal against him. Moreover, at his side were his mother and sister, the Duchess Isabel, both weeping and imploring. D.Beatriz longed to see her grandchildren return from exile, restored to the titles and dignities enjoyed by their father. The Duchess of Bragança was pining for her sons whom she had sent away to the protection of Castile when they were small. The Castilian sovereigns, who had welcomed the refugees — most useful hostages! — and brought them up, now wrote to Manuel, urging him to lift the ban.

King Manuel lent a willing ear. He would begin his reign by amnesty to all political exiles! He sent a cordial invitiation to the late Duke's children and his brother to come home and have their confiscated property restored.

With feasting and rejoicing the Braganças came, welcomed like conquering heroes in every Castilian village they passed on their way to the frontier. D.Jaime, a dashing youth of seventeen, already was honoured as Duke; his younger brother, D.Diniz, who hardly could remember Portugal, rode by his side. Both were under the guardianship of their uncle, the Senhor D.Alvaro, brother of the beheaded Duke and sole survivor of the elder generation.

It was a triumphant progress, and tongues were freely wagged, abusing the late King who had banished the Bragança family. D.Manuel heard of that and disapproved.

"Honoured Cousin," he wrote to the Senhor D.Alvaro, "Some people tell me that certain servants of the Duke, your brother, speak of the King, my Lord — whom may God assoil — in a manner that is unseemly. I charge you and my nephew to advise them all that this will greatly displease me, and any who do so will surely receive severe punishment at my hands, as is only right."

The exiles could come home, their lands and titles were to be restored, the family was to be reunited. But neither they nor anyone was to speak evil of the dead. The late King had always been Manuel's friend. At the last he had entrusted him with all that he held dear: his kingdom, his son and everything he had prepared and planned. D.Manuel refused to have his memory vilified.

II

The New King

King Manuel, first of the name in Portugal, was a very presentable young man. Fair and good-looking, with brown hair growing well back from a high forehead, his smiling grey-blue eyes lighted a pleasant face. Always impeccably groomed and elegantly dressed, he was slender and tall, with long and shapely legs. His arms alone were disproportionate, for we are told his fingers reached down to his knees. There was great strength in those long arms which handled a lance more dextrously than any man. Brought up by King João II who had loved manly exercise, D.Manuel excelled in every game and sport. He shot with the crossbow, hunted the boar, hawking was his delight, and like his cousin he was a splendid horseman.

At the same time his mind had not been neglected. Culture was in the family tradition, and in that humanistic age, D.Manuel passed for a good Latinist, able to appreciate the niceties of style; he had a genuine love for letters and all learning. Like D.João, he gathered scholars around his table at meals, for conversation and discussion, and he especially enjoyed talking to foreigners and travellers returned from distant lands. Such things he had grown up with in the air he breathed; in every other way, however, the new king could not have been more different from his predecessor.

After the restless, dynamic, unexpected D.João, who kept his counsellors and courtiers on their toes and made everyone jump, D.Manuel must have been very soothing. He was benign and calm — a mild man, slow to anger and easily placated. He would not actually prevent justice taking its course, but his good nature often brought about confusion of conflicting orders.

There seems to have been none the less a definite vein of obstinacy in his character. Manuel had enormous faith in his own judgment and once his mind was made up, his council could not easily dissuade him. This king knew what he wanted and he meant to get it, but at the same time there is a strange and rather baffling negativeness about Manuel. It is much easier to see what he was not than to establish what he really was. He was not violent nor cruel, nor licentious, nor intemperate in any way. There was no scandal in his private life; he ate in moderation and he drank no wine; however late he went to bed he always got up early. A decent clean-lived man, evidently, and a conscientious ruler not given to sloth. Fond of his family — at the time of his accession D.Manuel was unmarried still, but we know that his mother and sisters — especially the widowed Queen Leonor — did what they liked with him, and to his household he seems to have been a kindly master. That is about as near as we can get to Manuel's personality. His soul and spirit are remote. Perhaps the inhibitions of his youth and upbringing built up an ivory tower around his inner man — obviously he had learned in early life to observe and keep his mouth shut. We are told that he never spoke a hasty word.

One positive feature stands out, however, from the blurred outline of his image, and that is his passion for music. As Duke of Beja in his youth, and later on as king, he lived surrounded by musicians. He lured them to his service at any price from all the lands of Christendom. Needless to say, his chapel boasted of the finest choir in Europe; and not only in church but everywhere, from dawn to dusk, he never wanted the music to stop. Whether attending to despatches, or resting in the afternoon, or riding out, or sailing in the royal barge, or having meals, or when he went to bed at night, his orchestra was always at his side, with sackbuts, cornets, harps, fiddles and tambourines, and every other instrument, performing solo or in unison, or in accompaniment to song.

They also say that he liked to have jesters in the royal household — not for their jokes, which did not really amuse him much, but because their quips might often serve as wholesome rebuke to the courtiers' follies, for Manuel did not command the astringent tongue of his predecessor with which to chastise them.

Like every king and prince of the royal house of Portugal, D.Manuel dreamed of leading a crusade to Africa one day to fight the Moors, but there was really little of the fiery warrior about him. He was essentially a man of peace. We wonder how he would have coped with the situation of fourteen years before, when D.João had come to reign, for things were then chaotic. Afonso V's easy-going rule and open-handed generosity, prolonged for nearly forty years, had left the higher ranks of the nobility considerably above themselves. Led by the Duke of Bragança, each landed lord aspired to be a petty sovereign, with right of justice over all his tenants. When the King proposed sending the Crown Magistrate to visit all estates and verify local administration, a great howl had arisen, which swelled to danger point when every owner of privileged lands was intimated to present his title deeds for confirmation — each one, not even excepting the mighty Duke of Bragança! The fat was in the fire. A tyrant come to reign! they cried, and conspiracies had followed to be suppressed by blood. The Duke was sentenced and beheaded; his family and followers were banished, their property was confiscated. The noble lords were brought to heel. The King had won. From that time on he ruled absolutely, paternally, *pola ley e pola grey* — for the law and for the people.

All this had come about some ten years before D.Manuel succeeded to the throne. He came into no heritage of trouble — not even when he recalled the Braganças and restored their lands and titles. They were no longer dangerous, D.João II had drawn their teeth, they were no more than inoffensive princes of the realm, whose state was mainly ornamental. As for the fidalgos — they now revolved in the King's orbit, loyal to a man, ready at his command to do or die. All were as proud as Lucifer, but service and obedience had become a matter of pride. To them "the King our Lord" appeared a father figure, disposing of their destinies as their actual fathers had done upon a smaller scale when they were young. Royal grace and favour was the fountainhead from which all blessings flowed, and more than that, the sovereign was the symbol of their nation and their race and the glory of Portugal for which a man of honour would gladly lay down his life.

Nothing stirs human loyalty like an ideal and a sense of mission. The strength that Manuel brought to his throne was the quest he took over from his predecessor, who in his time had held it from their great-uncle, Henry the Navigator. The Infante had inspired Portugal to seek the far ends of the earth, to bear the Cross of Christ to pagan lands and — incidentally — bring home the glittering treasures of the East. Mixed motives, it may well be said, but is not the same true of almost every human undertaking? For Portugal the Quest was sanctified by blessing of the Holy See. Successive Bulls entitled her to claim possession of lands hitherto unvisited, there to make the light of the Gospel shine before peoples unknown, around the world – *usque ad Indios*, as far as the Indians.

This was the mission to which Manuel had been brought up, although he never had been destined for the throne. D.João II, on making the boy heir to all that his condemned brother had owned, did not forget the legacy of the Infante D.Henrique. The Navigator, a childless man, had adopted his nephew D.Fernando as his heir – "my grandchildren" – is what he calls Fernando's children in official documents. D.Manuel, born after the Infante's death, was last surviving son of these, and the King D.João had made over to him the islands discovered by their great-uncle. He passed to him not only islands, but the Quest. In this D.Fernando had been no more than moderately interested. D.João as a youth had taken it wholeheartedly upon himself, and he had trained D.Manuel to carry on.

From the age of fourteen the King had set this youngest cousin at the window of the world. The boy was at his side in every council concerning Discovery; he heard instructions given to pilots sailing for unknown seas, and helped receive ambassadors sent by exotic kings. When Bemoi, refugee prince from Senegal, arrived suing for aid from Portugal, it was the young Duke of Beja who embraced him at the palace door, who took him by the hand and led him to the King. The day that Pero da Covilham set forth on his adventurous journey overland, across the Middle East to India and to seek the land of Prester John, D.Manuel was present when the King wished him godspeed and the Bishop of Ceuta gave the traveller the most recently drawn world map. At that time D.João's well-beloved son and heir still lived, but obviously the King was preparing Manuel to take over the plan and purpose of the Infante, and that is why he gave him for device the armillary sphere.

Africa and India had been to Manuel familiar words since childhood. Ivory and gold dust, leopards' hides and scented woods and serpents' skins were everyday objects at court. Lions could be seen in Lisbon at the royal palace of Alcaçova, and camels at Evora, and with the royal pages around the King were little Africans, dark and bejewelled, the sons of princes sent by their fathers to Portugal, to study and to be instructed in the Christian faith.

Traders and explorers from day to day returned with their reports of expeditions towards the heart of Africa — across the sands to the desert city of Timbuktu, or by the waters of the Senegal to the Songhoi and Mandinga realms of Cantor and Mali, or further south through the dark forests where black pepper grew, to the mud walls of the mysterious city of Benin. The King of Benin had exchanged ambassadors with Portugal; the King of Congo asked for preachers and teachers, for he would be a Christian. And when he and his family were finally baptized, the King's uncle would have no name but Manuel, for he too was a Duke, he said, and must be called after the Duke of Beja!

During the late King's reign league after league of African coast had been added to the map, southward from Cape Catherine, and far below the Congo river along those desert lands where — Duarte Pacheco says — nothing was found "that could delight a man." Sometimes following the shore, at others sweeping out to sea, the Portuguese pilots had learned Atlantic winds and currents like a book, and so at last had found the way around the end of Africa, the fearsome Cape of Storms, which became the Cape of Good Hope.

D.Manuel had seen Bartolomeu Dias return with his report of having reached the Indian Ocean. If that were so indeed, the problem of the ages had been solved, and the sea route to India was no more a wishful dream.

But how much shorter it would be to reach the East by sailing from the West around the world! cried a foreign visionary who hung about the court thrusting before the King his fixed idea. D.João had shrugged his shoulders. He and his cosmographers knew quite well that the earth was round, but not so small as Columbus imagined. The man then withdrew his plan to Queen Isabel of Castile. She believed, and she financed him, and he discovered for Castile some islands in the western ocean that he said were Cathay or Zipangu.

The canny D.João II again shrugged his shoulders. Let his rivals go west, but leave the Orient to him! Diplomacy was brought to bear, and so in 1494 was signed the famous Treaty of Tordesillas, in which Castile and Portugal, with sanction of the Holy See, divided the terrestrial globe between them according to a line traced 375 leagues west of the Azores.

Quite satisfied with his share of the bargain — for after all those "Indies of Castile" were very far from Asia! — D.João at once set

about making ready for the great voyage that was to crown The Navigator's Quest. He blew no trumpets but he worked intensively, and
Bartolomeu Dias superintended preparations. Wood was felled in the
royal forests and ships were built, especially designed by the best naval
architects; pilots and cosmographers got together and discussed their
findings. All things were nearly ready and the fleet was expected to sail
in 1496 — but in October 1495 D.João II died. And what should happen next?

Nothing at all! declared the more reactionary among the young
King's counsellors. Let us be realists! This was a small country of
limited manpower, and with a long land frontier to defend. Had it not
been adventurous enough to conquer and occupy three Moorish fortresses beside the Straits of Gibraltar? To hold in fee the wealthy
towns of Azamor and Safi by the Atlantic coast of Morocco, to colonize the islands of the Ocean, to have explored the whole length of
West Africa, negotiating with African kingdoms inland and founding
the fortress settlement of São Jorge da Mina to trade in ivory, slaves
and gold, after turning the caravans of the Sahara down to the sea
coast? Did not the King of Portugal entitle himself Lord of Guinea?
Surely he should be satisfied with all these things! As it was, they
already caused much sacrifice and trouble. The King must not forget
that he had envious and ambitious neighbours. Think of the bother
there had been about the Guinea coast alone! How hard it was to keep
away foreign corsairs, whose rulers might publicly apologize, but pri-
vately encouraged such incursions.

This little realm was up against great powers. As if Castile and Aragon united were not menacing enough, they now had Granada to swell
their strength! There was no doubt that Portuguese discoveries were
exciting their envy and emulation. Had not Columbus led them to the
Antilles — and naturally they did not mean to stop there! If Portugal
once got to India and brought home the jewels and spices of the East,
who knew what hornets nests might not be raised?

So spoke the cautious and the elderly, but there were young adventurous spirits who were all for going on — and with them was the King,
for all his calm self-possession still a young man. This quest was his
inheritance, he said, and it came with the kingdom. It was a sacred trust
left by his great-uncle, the Infante D.Henrique. Manuel would press on
and leave the result in the hands of God. If it were the Lord's will that

India be discovered, He would provide the means and would protect the Realm that undertook such great risks to further His purpose.

D.Manuel's choice was made — the great choice of his life and reign. His orders were that preparations should proceed. They must have been already far advanced or it would hardly have been possible to have things ready and complete by July 1497.

As indeed they were. The three ships, designed to the instructions of Bartolomeu Dias, were seaworthy and strong, solidly built in oak and pine from the royal forests. Small ships they were — it seems that none exceeded 120 tons — square-rigged to bear up against the great seas that roll from the Antarctic. The voyage destined was far and would take months. Where provisions might be renewed was quite uncertain. Therefore the King bought a fourth ship to be loaded with stores, an old vessel that could be beached and burned when it was empty.

The pilots were furnished with all the most up-to-date devices of nautical science. We are told that D.Manuel had many conferences with Abraham Zacuto, the great Hebrew astronomer from Salamanca, who had been living in Portugal since 1492, when the sovereigns of Castile had expelled all the Jews from their kingdoms. D.João II had gladly welcomed so valuable an assistant, and Abraham Zacuto brought with him his Perpetual Almanach, a work of erudition from which his pupils, José Vizinho and others, compiled simplified Tables of Declination by which sailors could reckon latitudes on the high seas. Astrolabes, wooden and metal, and all the most perfect instruments available were supplied to the captains and navigators. These were picked men, already chosen, it would seem, by the unerring judgment of D.Manuel's predecessor.

Vasco da Gama, Captain-General of the fleet, was a man of some thirty years and much experience of the sea. He was unmarried still, a born leader of men, afraid of nothing in the world, straight as a die, as hard as nails, of unshaken tenacity in all his undertakings. His brother Paulo, gentler and more human, but with equal steadfastness of purpose, would be second in command, and Nicolau Coelho, friend of both, adventurous, light-hearted, careless of his life, made up the team. The pilots, Pero de Alenquer, Pero de Escolar, and João de Coimbra, were famous in their calling; 170 good men composed the crew of the three ships, and with them interpreters of Arabic and all African languages then known.

Sailing orders were precise. This was no hit-or-miss excursion into the blue. Not for nothing had the rulers of Portugal been co-relating information, direct and indirect, about the East for nearly seventy years. Not for nothing had Pero da Covilham journeyed by land to India. It seems certain that he reported home before losing himself in Abyssinia. The King had some idea of what kingdoms and ports existed by the Indian coast. There was nothing haphazard about the voyage planned for Vasco da Gama.

He was to lead his ships across the equator, in mid-ocean, down to the South Atlantic and round the Cape of Good Hope into the Indian Ocean. From the east coast of Africa they were to follow the route of the Arab dhows over to India. Where landfall should be made was duly determined — they were to seek the trading port of Calicut. There Vasco da Gama would visit the reigning prince, known as the Samorin (Lord of the Sea) on behalf of D.Manuel, greeting him with a friendly message from his European brother: The King of Portugal, having heard that the Samorin was one of the greatest Christian kings of India, desired his friendship and commercial intercourse. On what grounds was based the assumption of the Samorin's Christianity is not quite clear. Presumably because it was known that the natives of the Indian coast were not Moslem. In that case, what were they? Not being savages as were the African tribes, they surely were not heathen — so what else could they be but Christian? Of the rival religions of the Orient — Hinduism and Budhism — few yet suspected the existence. Upon the other hand, everybody was well aware that the apostle St. Thomas had preached the Gospel in Asia and founded Christian churches in the East. Was it not likely therefore that the Samorin of Calicut was a good Christian? In which case, cut off as he was by the Moslem world, he naturally would welcome an ally and co-religionist from overseas.

Thus far Vasco da Gama's functions were diplomatic and peaceful. None the less the fleet must be prepared for defence or attack. That the Indians themselves should show hostility seemed unlikely; trouble, if any, would come from the "Moors." Moslems, whether North African, Egyptian, or Arabian, were all "Moors" to the Portuguese — the hereditary foemen of the Faith, from whose hold their peninsula had been reconquered inch by inch at cost of blood. The holy war had recently been carried across the Straits to Africa where it was raging still. The Arab world — one language and one faith, extending from the western ocean to the Far East — for centuries had been a threat to Christendom. And it was well known that the spice trade of the Indian seas was all in Moslem hands. The arrival of a Christian power within these enclosed preserves would obviously arouse resentment. Though Vasco da Gama was to do nothing to provoke a clash, there was no doubt that one might easily occur. Therefore the fleet must carry armaments and artillery. Only three ships to run the gauntlet of an age-old monopoly in countries to be reached by sea routes hitherto unsailed by man, at the ends of the earth, was certainly a great gamble. D.Manuel's chosen captains must have known their chances of survival were fifty-fifty.

But glad and proud, they bowed the knee before their king, and thanked him for the great honour conferred them. Reverently their commander took the sacred banner of the Cross in hand and vowed to bear it high before all foemen of the Faith and defend it unto death.

The July sun shone on the little village of Restelo by the Tagus mouth, upon the ships São Gabriel, São Rafael and Berrio — or São Miguel — preparing to weigh anchor.

Blessed by a night of vigil in the chapel on the hill above, the three captains embarked, watched by a multitude that wept to see husbands and brothers, sweethearts and friends, borne so far away — how far or for how long? None could guess, nor if the parting might not be for ever.

In high heart they embarked. Were not they the elect? To them was entrusted the fulfilment of an age old dream, the crowning of the quest in which three generations had laid down their lives. And what of theirs? They too might die, but none the less they were certain of glory.

The new king watched them go. He knew he must possess his soul in patience for the silence of the next few years. For good or ill, the die was cast. Under his leadership Portugal would achieve her destiny and fulfil her mission.

III

Iberian Throne

At home, meanwhile, were many questions to be solved. First and foremost was one that touched the King closely. At twenty-six, D.Manuel was still a bachelor. This must be remedied without delay. Shortage of direct heirs had been a source of concern in the realm for a number of years. Afonso V had had only one son and one daughter, and she retired into a convent at an early age — to the disgust of her brother who did not like to feel alone in the line of succession. He himself had only one legitimate heir, killed in an accident at the age of sixteen. As for collaterals, death had eliminated one by one the numerous sons of the Infante D.Fernando, until D.Manuel came to the throne as the last of them all.

A king, young and unmarried, is an interesting person to parents of nubile princesses, and the sovereigns of Castile and Aragon had several on their hands. Therefore it was not many days after Manuel's accession to the throne that he received a message of hearty congratulations from Fernando and Isabel, together with the offer of their third daughter, the thirteen-year-old Infanta Maria.

D.Manuel politely postponed decision, although his mind already was made up. In marriage, as in most other things, he intended to continue his predecessor's policy. Matrimonial alliance with Castile had always seemed desirable to D. João II. Portugal, isolated at the extreme end of the European continent, between the Spanish mountains and the sea, could incur danger from no other side, and therefore had no axe to grind in the imbroglio of European politics. Peace with Castile meant freedom to devote all efforts towards the ocean paths and the lands overseas. At sea, as on the home frontiers, hostility with Castile would mean complications. Then, let the dynasties unite as closely as might be, and breed if possible an heir to all the kingdoms.

With this in mind, D.João II had married his son to the eldest Infanta of Castile and Aragon. She had only one sickly brother who not improbably might die, leaving his sister sole heiress. The match was made to everyone's content, not least to that of the young people. Feasting and rejoicing had been prolonged for six months before the fatal ride at Santarem had wrecked all hopes, sending the brokenhearted bride back to her parents' arms.

D.Manuel was quite resolved to marry in Castile, but it was the sad-eyed young widow of his cousin he proposed to wed, and not the child Maria. Expediency or inclination? Both, it appears. Isabel was pretty and good, and it is generally believed that Manuel had loved her from the time that he escorted her, a radiant bride, from the frontier to Evora, to marry Prince Afonso. A silent figure in the background, he had observed that brief idyll, and − quite sincerely, it would seem − had mourned its tragic end. Strange fate it was that now left Manuel in Afonso's place, ruling the kingdom that would have been his, and free to woo his widow!

Her parents were quite ready to accept his suit, but the girl was not easily persuaded. Five years had passed but Isabel still mourned. Marriage was not for her, she sobbed. For only six months she had lived and loved before her happiness was wrecked forever! Since then her sole desire had been to retire with her sorrow into a convent. And why would they not let her?

They reasoned with her gently but firmly. A princess could not choose her way of life. She had a duty to the nation. She was not free to take the veil, not even when her heart was broken. To reinforce the argument Isabel's spiritual directors were called in. They told her she would be serving God by marrying the King of Portugal, so ensuring peace between the kingdoms.

Then she gave way. The marriage settlement was signed, proxy vows were exchanged, and Manuel impatiently awaited the arrival of his bride.

His eagerness was evident. Fernando and Isabel, always archbargainers, saw here a chance for further concessions. A holy opportunity, in fact, which Mother Church would surely bless!

The pious sovereigns of Castile and Aragon had more than once been pained by the lax attitude of the Portuguese Crown towards the Jews. When Fernando and Isabel, in fervent gratitude for the fall of Granada,

had expelled all Jews and Moors out of their Christian realms, they
noted disapprovingly that D.João II did not seem inclined to follow
their example. Not only did he tolerate the Jews already living in his
lands, but against a capitation tax, he granted six months' asylum to
refugees from Castile. He even suffered those with wealth or skills to
remain in his country. True, those who could not pay and did not leave
within the period specified were rounded up and cast into captivity —
the 15th century version of the modern concentration camp. Damião
de Gois says it was generally believed that the King, who was no fanatic, would presently have let these prisoners go, but his death intervened.

Neither was Manuel, although devout, fanatical by nature. One of
the first things that he did was to free Jewish captives, and he refused
the handsome sum of money offered by the grateful Jews — which
indicates that his motives were humanitarian rather than interested. His
cousins over the frontier observed and disapproved.

They wrote to say that happy though they were to have D.Manuel
for son-in-law, their daughter did not feel she could enter a realm where
enemies of the True Faith were tolerated! How could she go to join
her bridegroom while the evil seed had not been extirpated?

D.Manuel was determined at all costs to have Isabel. He bore no ill
will to the Jews, but they would have to go!

"Judges, Aldermen, Attorney, and Good Men," he wrote to the cities
of the realm, "we would have you know that, feeling it to be for the
service of God, and our own, and the welfare of our realms, on the
advice of our Council and learned men, we have ordained that within a
certain time, all the Jews living in our realms must leave." But this was
not to be made a pretext for hounding them out with persecutions —
"our will is that they should be unmolested, honoured, and well-treated
in word and deed, even more than they were before . . . let no man
make bold to do them any harm . . . for whosoever disobey I shall
punish forthwith! "

That the expulsion of the Jews was a praiseworthy act pleasing to
God, it is unlikely that D.Manuel ventured to doubt. At the same time,
so far as can be seen, we gather that he did not really like it. For one
thing, Jews were very useful. His own physician, Mestre Dionisio, was a
Jew, so also was the invaluable cosmographer, Abraham Zacuto! Could
not some means be found to make the Jews profess Christianity?

The King then thought out a cold-hearted plan. All Jewish children under fourteen years old were to be taken from their parents to be brought up in the Christian faith! The parents would no doubt cry out at this, but the remedy was in their hands: Let them but be baptized, and they would be permitted to remain in Portugal and keep their offspring!

The spiritual advisers of the King applauded this godly decree. What did it matter if the children lost mother and father if their souls were saved? At the moment if might seem harsh and cruel, but it was really kindness in the long run.

Meantime, how horrible! most Christian parents cried, embracing their own little ones. The human heart spoke louder than the age old prejudice. Mothers and fathers, out of pity for the Jews, braved the authorities and helped them hide their children.

Perhaps if Manuel had been a father at the time he might have been less callous. As it was, his conscience seems to have been quite unperturbed. Why should it not be since the Church approved? But what he really wanted was to prevent the departure of the Jews. If they would but profess the Christian faith in baptism, he promised them, not only could they keep their children and their homes, but no enquiry would be made for twenty years as to how they were practising their new religion. A more deliberate invitation to nominal conversion cannot be imagined.

Many accepted it and kept their children, while practising in secrecy Jewish rites. Those too high-minded for hypocrisy went sorrowing into exile, or yielding to despair, killed themselves and their little ones.

The sovereigns of Castile and Aragon egged on their son-in-law. They urged him to make haste. Their daughter would not join him till his realm was decontaminated. They gave him to the end of September 1497 to cast out the accursed thing. The girl herself wrote – or was made to write – that she but awaited his letter declaring that the deed was done, to fulfil her part of the contract.

September came and ended. The sorrowful outcasts went their way. The bridegroom waiting eagerly at Castelo de Vide, was informed that he could proceed to Valença and claim his bride.

He was told to come without pomp, followed by a small retinue. This would have to be a quiet wedding. The heir to the Castilian throne had fallen very ill at Salamanca where he lay at point of death. His father, who was with him at the time, could not stir from his side. His mother, the elder Isabel, with anguish in her soul came dry-eyed to her daughter's marriage, and even when news of the fatal issue came, she showed no sign. Let this be kept a secret, she enjoined, until the bridal pair had left. The Prince's illness was sufficient excuse for no display of joy or feasting.

The bride, absorbed doubtless in wistful memories of that happy wedding feast at Evora six years before, seems to have noticed nothing wrong, but Manuel found out the truth and talked it over with his mother-in-law. He must take Isabel away, he said, before she suspected her brother's death, and when they were in Portugal, he would himself break the sad news.

So Isabel returned a second time to the country she once had entered with such joy. The shadow that had fallen so soon after had not lifted from her life. It followed her through villages where she was welcomed with sober warmth, to Evora of poignant memory — Evora of the tournament and festival, and dancing and the flowering of young love. So long had Isabel lived in a world of melancholy dreams that probably she did not notice the strained faces and subdued voices around her.

At last, at Evora, her husband told her of her beloved and only brother's death, and all semblance of joy was quenched. The court went into mourning and attended solemn exequies. Such was the strange sad marriage for which Manuel had sacrificed the Jews. At least he had his love, and it appeared that his ambition too was soon to be fulfilled.

Only one life — that of a child unborn — now lay between the Queen of Portugal and heirdom to her parents' thrones. That one frail obstacle was soon removed. The widow of the young Castilian prince miscarried, giving birth to a dead baby.

Let Isabel and Manuel come back to Castile at once, the sovereigns wrote. They must be solemnly acclaimed Crown Prince and Princess, heirs to the kingdoms of Castile, Leon and Aragon.

So the dynastic dream was really coming true! We may suppose that Manuel rejoiced. His Portuguese subjects were less enchanted. Hegemony of the Peninsula was not their aspiration. All that really interested them was to have Portugal remain an independent kingdom. Association with a Castile united to Aragon might be too much of a bear's hug!

As for the journey projected, a number of the councillors disapproved. To have their king "outside his kingdom in the power of another king" did not seem good to them. Opinions expressed in the council were many and divergent. Cortes had to be summoned to consent to the King's absence abroad, and be persuaded that the journey was "very necessary."

At last, on March 29th 1498, the King and Queen set forth across the frontier for Toledo. They travelled with only a small escort, as both parties agreed was best. Officially Portugal and Castile loved one another dearly. Were not their rulers kinsmen and allies? None the less everybody felt, the less their subjects got together the better. Sooner or later somebody was sure to start an argument and sparks would fly. So Manuel and Isabel set out with no more than 300 followers, all carefully selected.

It was a long and tiring journey for the frail young Queen, already four months pregnant and undermined by grief and tuberculosis. She bore up bravely none the less and played her part with dignity the whole weary way — from Elvas to Badajoz, to Toledo, on into Aragon her father's kingdom right across to Saragossa.

The party rode all dressed in black, and all in black likewise the sporting Duke of Medina Sidonia pranced forth to greet his sovereigns' heirs. Thirty-eight liveried falconers that followed him caught every furred and feathered creature as they passed. The Duke of Alva and the Bishop of Placencia met the procession on the road to Badajoz where they were received with great pomp and led beneath an awning of brocade to the cathedral. Thence they went on to Guadelupe for the Easter festival, and meanwhile fresh and salted fish was brought each day in relays from the sea until the Lenten fast was over.

At Toledo there was at least one joy for Isabel, for there she found her parents waiting. Her father and husband embraced with "much love and courtesy" and with killing politeness each stood back to let the other pass first through every door. D.Manuel and his mother-in-law dropped on their knees at the same time before each other, as high-breeding prescribed between crowned heads. The younger Isabel tried to kiss her mother's hand, but that was not permitted her. Her mother blessed her, but received her as a queen and equal.

Cortes were held at Toledo to proclaim the young couple heirs to the Castilian throne. Mass was said in the cathedral, after which the

Queen of Castile handed her daughter to a chair at her side before the
altar. King Fernando led Manuel to a seat between her and him. Facing
them were the delegates of the Cortes sitting on benches while the
grandees and noblemen squatted on cushions and carpets on the steps
of the altar. The kings had begged them thus to take their place without
observing any order of precedence, and so avoid the usual arguments
and quarrels. The Archbishop of Seville held out a golden cross upon
which Manuel and Isabel took their solemn oath to govern Castile faithfully and well, observing all its laws and ancient privileges. Then, each
man in his turn, the lords and delegates of all the realm knelt and did
homage. This rite took several hours, after which the royal procession
adjourned to the archbishop's palace for the state banquet at which the
kings sat at one table and the queens at another. All went off very well
but it was an exhausting day for Isabel, and worse was to come − the
long ride over the harsh mountains of Aragon, to Saragossa on the
burning plain, where the royal party was received with even greater
ceremony and pomp.

Great ceremony, but cold looks, and quarrelling between the citizens
and clergy as to whose the right of bearing the royal canopy. They well
nigh came to blows, which − says the chronicler − "looked very bad to
everyone," but had to be left unpunished not to offend the city.

These haughty citizens of Aragon were difficult to manage. They
refused to swear allegiance to their king's daughter. A woman could not
succeed to the throne of Aragon, they said. Failing a male heir, the
States of the Realm were entitled to choose one for themselves.
D.Fernando insisted, and then they tried to bargain: Let him restore
the privileges of which he had deprived them in the past, they said, if he
would have them acknowledge his daughter's rights. The King declared
he would do nothing of the kind, and there followed a prolonged
wrangle. In any case, the citizens of Saragossa declared, they could
reach no conclusion before their colleagues of Valença and Barcelons
had arrived. Why should His Highness thus condescend with them?
asked the King's daughter with a touch of her mother's imperiousness.
Better leave Aragon and return with force of arms to take the kingdom.
Then he could make what laws he liked!

But meanwhile she was weary of it all. Worn out and ill, her disease
gaining on her day by day, Isabel waited and made her will. Grief was
her sole inheritance upon this earth, she felt. She did not expect to
survive her coming ordeal.

At least that ended the deadlock. On the 24th of August 1497, surrounded by her father, mother, husband, and — since privacy was not for a 15th century queen — supported in the arms of D.Francisco de Almeida, knight of D.Manuel's Council, with great labour and anguish Isabel brought forth a son.

A boy! Praise be to God! Delirious with delight, King Fernando rushed from the room, crying exultantly to the crowd that seethed outside: "Rejoice and thank the Lord, we have a man child! "

All in a moment bells began to peal from all the churches of the town. Salvoes were fired and revelry began at once. Meanwhile the happy grandfather returned to his daughter's bedside — to find her life blood was ebbing away.

She should not, must not die! Distractedly her father took her in his arms. "Daughter, have faith in God! " he cried, shouting so loud that everybody heard outside the door. He almost shook her as he tried to make her move. "Oh Daughter! Call upon Our Lady and the Saints! " But Isabel lay white and still. Her father put her down upon the bed, while the poor mother who so bravely and so recently had mourned an only son, sank to the ground as if felled by this last bitter blow. Her husband picked her up and carried her away to her own room where he left her lying as if dead, while he returned to speak "many and prudent words" of consolation to his sorrowing son-in-law.

With a presence of mind which never seems to have deserted him, D.Fernando ordered the laying out of the dead queen upon black pillows, with uncovered face for all to see. Dressed in the same garments in which she had given birth, Isabel lay there till midnight and then they carried her to the convent of Jeronimos outside the town where she was laid to rest.

The baby, motherless from birth, was christened Miguel. Here at last was a true heir to the thrones of Castile, Leon and Portugal, and one which Aragon could not disclaim, for he was grandson of their king. So the problem was solved, albeit in sorrow.

As for the widower — "The King, our Lord was very sad," writes Garcia de Resende, "and very grieved by the loss of such a wife and so great a dominion as he had lost." Wife or dominion? Which counted most? We have no clue. It is not often possible to see into D.Manuel's heart. On this occasion as on many others he leaves us guessing. The twelve days he remained before returning home were devoted to the

execution of his dead wife's will and last wishes. Then, leaving his
orphan son in the care of the broken-hearted grandparents, "with much
love," Manuel bade them farewell, and so journeyed back to his own
realm to the relief of his subjects who could not help feeling anxious
about their king – so far away, surrounded by Castilians! His mother
and sisters welcomed him with open arms. After the last hectic six
months ending in tragedy, it really was a good thing to be home!

Already in Castile the baby Miguel had been proclaimed Crown
Prince of his grandparents' kingdoms. Let Manuel now have him sworn
heir to the throne of Portugal, wrote Fernando and Isabel. The Portuguese people, however, viewed with no special enthusiasm the prospect
of a dual monarchy. They insisted upon conditions. Their king must
promise them that no post of administration or finance or justice
should ever be filled but by a true-born Portuguese, in the next reign
nor for all time. D.Manuel was himself Portuguese and understood their
sentiments, so he agreed. On this condition little Miguel was proclaimed
heir. Thus it would seem that the whole of the Iberian Peninsula was
soon to be united – a prospect pleasing to dynasts.

One wonders if it really was. Damião de Gois tells us that Manuel
showed little grief when, less than two years later, in July 1500, he
heard that the baby Miguel was dead. No public mourning was decreed
in either realm, nor any "of the ceremonies customary on the death of
such persons." Perhaps, with Garcia de Resende, many people felt that
"God did not wish to see the Portuguese and Castilians united."

However that may be, it is certain that at this time D.Manuel's
attention was engrossed by something far more exciting than pan-
Iberianism.

IV

Gates of the East

The summer of 1499 as usual saw the court at Sintra. Here, but a few hours ride from Lisbon sweltering in the sun, was everything the heart of man could wish: cool forests, green and leafy, clothed the hills. Fountains gurgled in mosaic courtyards of the fair fantastic palace that D.Manuel's great-grandfather had built over the ruins of some ancient Moorish Alhambra. A dream palace this was, all Gothic arabesque, with windows opening on surprising vistas of blue sky and sea, beyond the arid purple plain, like magic casements looking to some distant fairyland.

At Sintra kings relaxed, far from the heat and noise and smells of the medieval city, and in the happy hunting grounds of the dense woods chased the wild boar through mottled glades, or stalked the gentle deer.

In this deep peace D.Manuel was spending the hot months of 1499 — a far more restful summer, we suppose, than that of the previous year, with all those wearying journeys across dusty Spain that had been started full of hope, only to end in sorrow and frustration. But what about that other hope – the Quest for which D.Manuel had been brought up? Would that also fade out? Two years had passed since Vasco da Gama had sailed and yet there was no sign.

No sign till the 10th of July, and then a little battered ship hove to and anchored in the harbour of Cascais. The captain disembarked at once, and without lingering to speak to anyone, rode up the hills to Sintra, and craved audience with the King. In travel-stained and faded clothes, haggard and gaunt and deeply bronzed, this seemed to be the ghost of Nicolau Coelho.

But it was Nicolau Coelho in the flesh! The brave little "Berrio" had sailed home out of the storms and distant seas. Sailed home from whence? the King asked eagerly, and Nicolau proudly replied: "From India!"

And where was Vasco da Gama with the flagship São Gabriel? And where was the São Rafael commanded by his brother Paulo?

Vasco was hale and well a month ago when Nicolau Coelho saw him last near Cape Verde, but the good ship São Rafael had been burnt on a sandbank in the Indian seas, and Paulo da Gama, on board his brother's ship, lay dying. Vasco hoped to get him to the Azores in time to save his life, and meanwhile Nicolau Coelho had sailed home to bring the news.

Wonderful news, world-shaking news! The sea route to India was found to be open to navigation! The King left Sintra and rushed down to Lisbon. Immediately he wrote to his parents-in-law: It had pleased the Lord in His mercy to guide the captains of his ships, and one of them had just returned, informing him "that they have found and discovered India and other kingdoms and domains nearby."

From Nicolau Coelho already he had heard the whole thrilling story — the story of the greatest voyage yet recorded in human history. For ninety days the ships had sailed south and southwest in mid-Atlantic, far from any sight of land, before turning east to touch the savage coast beside the Cape of Good Hope that Bartolomeu Dias had found, where penguins strutted on the shore and small wild herdsmen drove fat cattle over lonely pastures.

Around the Cape and northward they had sailed, by forest-covered hills out of which nameless rivers wound to join the ocean. Populous shores these were, teeming with very tall black men who lived in a manner much like those of the familiar Guinea Coast. They responded to friendly gestures and were willing to barter fresh food for beads and cloths. And by that time fresh food was badly needed by the seamen in the agonies of scurvy. By the "River of Good People," as they called it, they had beached their ships and caulked and careened them before proceeding further.

Wearily they went on. The mighty Cape lay far behind, but still there seemed to be no sign of India.

No sign until one day beside a swampy shore, amid the seething naked crowd that gathered round them in canoes, there came a man who looked upon the strangers' ships without surprise. He had seen such before, he said, in havens further up the coast, at which the worn-out seafarers rejoiced. The terminus of Arab navigation could not be far off!

And indeed it was not. Some ten days later Nicolau Coelho was taking soundings round the Island of Mozambique. It hardly was a town that they saw there, only a cluster of straw shacks beside a swampy shore, but rising high above, the tower of a minaret struck a familiar note, and a white Arab house with courtyards and terraces indicated the presence of a Moslem lord. Ashore were turbaned men, all speaking Arabic, and in the port were four ships belonging to "white Moors," laden with gold and silver, pearls, rubies, cloves, ginger and pepper.

The golden East at last! The trials of the long voyage were nearly over. So it appeared at first. The Portuguese in their exotic clothes were taken to be Turks, and therefore the Sultan of Mozambique made them welcome as brother Moslems. Turks coming down from Egypt through the Red Sea sometimes appeared in those waters although they seldom sailed so far south as Mozambique. When, however, it was found out that the newcomers were Christians, trouble began and followed them all up the coast. Pilots, for which they asked, were only given to betray. The sultan passed the word to other ports frequented by Arab shipping, and though Mombasa — a real town with tall stone-built houses — was a fair sight for weary eyes, and though the travellers heard with joy that there were Christians living there, these could not help against the local lord, who responded to friendly overtures by treason.

Still seeking for a pilot to guide them across the Indian Ocean, the travellers came on Easter day to Malindi, and there at last they found good faith and friendship.

Nicolau Coelho had much to tell of Malindi — a pretty little town, shaded by palms and fragrant with orange trees — to some people it looked like Alcochete, beside the Tagus facing Lisbon. At Malindi the Portuguese were entertained and regaled with good things. The Sultan, who had quarrelled with Mombasa, wished to be the friend and ally of D.Manuel. He visited Vasco da Gama on his ship and gave him beautiful and curious gifts. Best of all, he found him a good pilot — Malemo Canaqua was this man's name. He was the best known pilot of these parts. He and Vasco da Gama got on very well, discussing navigation and comparing instruments.

They crossed the Indian Ocean in twenty-three days before the wind. With joy and emotion at last they sighted the mountains of

Malabar and hove to off the coast of Calicut. "There is the land you seek! " the Arab pilot said, and falling on their knees, the Portuguese recited the Salve Regina. A man was sent ashore and he had the good luck to meet a "Moor" from Oran who spoke a jargon of Venetian and Castilian. He was a friendly soul, for he had met and liked Portuguese traders at Oran. He now became their guide and adviser.

A strange city was Calicut, straggling beside the shore, all milling with a multitude such as no European town had ever seen. Brown men, men almost black or nearly white, some with long hair and beard, others with shaven head, some wearing turbans, all with gold earrings, and all naked to the waist. The women, dusky and small, bejewelled with necklaces and earrings and bracelets jangling on their arms and ankles, did not seem very beautiful to the strangers. But these people were gentle and amiable. The seamen when they went ashore frater- nized happily with them, exchanging goods and tasting one another's food. The Indians found ship's biscuits delicious, and wheaten bread a luxury almost unknown. Fruit was abundant in this land, but quite different from European fruit — except for cucumbers, oranges and lemons. There was no wine saving a drink made from palm juice, only palm oil was known, and meat was never eaten.

By European standards Calicut could hardly be called a city. It was a labyrinth of narrow winding lanes between thatched houses that were more like shacks. The only stone buildings to be seen were the royal palace and the churches.

Christian churches, of course? One hoped they were! But Nicolau Coelho was perplexed. The buildings were very beautiful and richly carved on the outside. Within was rather dark, but through the gloom, Vasco da Gama had seen an image of Our Lady with the holy Child. Quite happily he and his followers had entered to say their prayers. As their eyes got used to the half light, they saw that the walls were covered with paintings of saints. They must have been saints because they had diadems, but for heavenly beings they were strangely hideous, with four or five arms each and monstrous teeth protruding over their lips.

The King's palace stood in a garden perfumed by flowers and aro- matic herbs, and shaded by tall trees. It was a long low building into which one passed through several doors before reaching the inner court where the sovereign (the Samorin, Lord of the Sea, was his title) sat cross-legged upon cushions underneath a golden canopy, chewing with scarlet teeth some herbs and spitting them into a bowl. He was a tall dusky man, bare-footed and bare-legged, wearing a sleeveless jacket embroidered with golden flowers, a jewelled mitre on his head, jewelled earrings glistening on his cheeks, gold bracelets on his arms and ankles, and precious rings for each finger and toe.

What manner of man had the Portuguese found him for dealing with? Difficult, it would seem, and changeable — a man who might blow hot and cold from one day to another. And he expected to be approached with a splendid gift! The travellers had heard that with dismay. They had done what they could and got together of the best they had: striped cloths and scarlet caps, six hats, strings of coral, a set of brass basins, some sugar, oil, and honey. Admittedly these things were not impressive. The courtiers laughed and the King had despised their offering.

All might have yet gone well, were it not for the "Moors" — the Arab traders who frequented Calicut to fetch the pepper that they carried every year to the Red Sea to reach Europe via Alexandria and Venice. These merchants feared for their ancient monopoly. They knew where the strangers came from and that they were men to be reckoned with. Familiar as the Arabs were with the court of Calicut, it was not difficult for them to discredit Vasco da Gama with the sovereign and sow seeds of suspicion in his mind.

Owing to their intrigues the Portuguese had spent a hazardous three months at Calicut, part of which time their captain was detained ashore virtually under arrest. Only his tact and good sense had saved the situation. He got off at last on relatively good terms with the Samorin, who even wrote a letter to D.Manuel. All the while that the ships lay off the coast it had rained hard and heavily — much harder and more heavily than winter rain in Portugal, in spite of which it was much hotter than a Portuguese July!

The return journey had been difficult. For weeks becalmed, in the Indian Ocean, drifting far from all islands over an unknown sea, with water and provisions running short and scurvy ravaging, there had been a very bad patch, and many men had died. On each ship there hardly remained seven or eight able to heave or haul. Fifteen more days of such weather and all would have been lost. But the blessed east wind had come at last. It blew them to the coast of Africa, to Malindi, and welcoming friends, and oranges and healing.

After four blissful days the decimated crew had sailed again, but they no longer had man power to navigate three ships. Paulo da Gama's ship, São Rafael, had been burnt on a solitary sandbank, and her commander, a very sick man, transferred to his brother's ship. So round the Cape, to the Atlantic once again, and northward to the Cape Verde Islands. There the two captains separated. Vasco still hoped that Paulo could reach the Azores alive and there might be restored to health. Thus Nicolau Coelho in the "Berrio" returned alone.

D.Manuel heard him with joy. He lost no time in writing to Castile of the great cities and great peoples his captains had found and the riches that Vasco da Gama would be bringing back: cinnamon, ginger, nutmeg, pepper, to say nothing of precious stones.

As for the Christian souls living in Indian lands, D.Manuel admits they do not seem to be so grounded in the faith as was to be desired, but he does not doubt they will be "converted and wholly conformed, to the advancement of God's kingdom and destruction of the Moors in those parts." From the material point of view, the King now "hoped in God" that the spices, which hitherto had been wholly in Moslem hands, "through our ordinance, with our men and ships, should henceforward be sent to furnish Christendom in Europe with spices and precious stones." All of which would redound in furtherance of the holy war against the Moors which was the earnest aim of both kingdoms.

So wrote the King in faith and hope, while Lisbon, whispering, wondered. Could it be true? Had the sea route to India really been found? Had these few lean, weather-beaten men, with empty hands and faded clothes, really come back from the realms of the golden East? A supercilious young Italian merchant, Girolamo Sernigi, sniffed and shrugged his shoulders. Where were the treasures of those fabled lands? And where – the people asked each other, tragically wide-eyed – where was Vasco da Gama? Dead, it was naturally to be assumed!

There passed several weeks of suspense while by the Tagus bar caravels posted by the King kept anxious watch. Towards the end of August, off Belem, was seen at last the very ship São Gabriel, which had sailed bright and new two years before, now battered and weary but gaily beflagged. No, the commander had not come as yet. It was João de Sá, his secretary, who had been charged to take the ship, while

Vasco da Gama lingered at Terceira to bury his brother.

João de Sá confirmed Nicolau Coelho's tale at every point. São Gabriel was bringing samples of all the things promised – spices and scented wood, and precious stones. And there were human specimens as well: six Indians all natives of Calicut – less black than men of Guinea, rather of a reddish hue, noted the King, with straight black hair and features like Europeans. A Moor from Tunis (or Oran) had come too – a very knowledgeable man – and, most remarkable of all, a Jew of Alexandria, captured in India and converted on the voyage, christened by the name of Gaspar da Gama, after the captain who had sponsored him.

D.Manuel wrote enthusiastically about this man to D.Jorge da Costa, the ninety-year-old Portuguese cardinal at the papal court of Rome. How clearly the Lord's hand was shown in this! Having ordained that India be discovered for His holy service and the good of Christendom, "at the same time He has sent us this man, whom we value as much as all the rest! " Through him more had been learnt about the newly discovered lands than could have been found out in many years. The Jew knew Hebrew, Chaldean, Arabic and German, and "he also speaks Italian mixed with Spanish so clearly that he can be understood like a Portuguese, and he understands us too."

This intriguing person was by origin a Polish Jew whose parents migrated to Alexandria where he had grown up and become an expert in precious stones. Later, he had travelled to Tartary and by the shores of the Black Sea. Thence to India where he had lived for thirty years and visited the Far East before taking service with Adil Khan of Bijapur in the island of Goa. When the Portuguese fleet had reached the island of Angediva on the return voyage, his master had sent him to spy upon the new arrivals. Vasco da Gama, however, had captured him and certainly would have put him to death if the versatile Hebrew had not shown himself so pleasant and informative, and begged so earnestly to be permitted to become a Christian.

D.Manuel enjoyed long and interesting talks with this man. Gaspar told him that there were thirty-eight kings reigning in India. Of these the Samorin was chief ruler by the coast, but inland the great King of Vijayanagar commanded wide domains and vast armies of men, horses, and elephants, and owned the diamond mines. He told of the ships, great and small, from Cambay and the Red Sea, which sailed around the

Indian Ocean carrying merchandise, and the corsairs who frequented those shores, armed with bombards and bows and arrows.

Of the religion — or religions — of these countries Gaspar da Gama seems to have said little, for Manuel informs the Cardinal that most of the kings and nations of India "are Christian — more or less after the manner of Calicut." It would be a great thing for Holy Church to lead them to full knowledge of the Faith!

The King had written to the Pope of all these things, but he felt certain that the Cardinal — Portuguese-born — must surely rejoice to have been spared to see this day. Yet this was more than a mere national triumph; its repercussions would echo through time and space. Let D.Jorge speak of all this to the Pope and stir up the College of Cardinals to celebrate in fitting manner!

Perhaps also the Holy Father might be glad to make some gesture of recognition of the great service rendered Christendom. Already from time to time Bulls had been issued commending the Portuguese effort and confirming possession of the lands discovered. Nothing more seemed necessary — "but none the less we should be glad, and beg you most affectionately, after our letters have been given to the Holy Father and College, to speak as if upon your own initiative" that some new token of approval should be manifested, "in whatever manner may seem best to Your Reverence."

Meanwhile, in Lisbon, King and people waited breathlessly for the arrival of Vasco da Gama to set seal upon the triumph. He came sadly and without haste. The death of Paulo at the end of the long weary quest — just within sight of home and the crowning reward — had destroyed all his pleasure. He lingered at Belem to meditate and pray, and there his friends and many courtiers came to find him. Let him put his mourning aside, they said, and go to meet the welcome of the King.

Vasco da Gama dressed himself simply in leather cuirasses and put a round cap on his head. With the long beard he had brought back from the voyage still untrimmed, he disembarked at the Terreiro do Paço. The courtiers and fidalgos all were gathered there to greet him enthusiastically, and a vast multitude filled the great square, gazing enthralled upon the man who had led his ships to the far ends of the earth. The King rose from his chair when the captain approached and Vasco da Gama fell upon his knees. He had fulfilled his charge, he said. The Lord had brought him home and he was satisfied.

Wonderful days followed, delirious days. King and people rejoiced together. Throughout the land church bells were pealed, solemn processions walked the streets, sermons were preached, and there were tournaments and feasts and games.

Before the King and his sister, the dowager Queen Leonor, Vasco da Gama – *Dom* Vasco by royal favour now – displayed the choicest things that he had brought: jewels, necklaces and sumptuous oriental cloths, silver trumpets sent by the Sultan of Malindi, benzoin and musk and amber, and porcelain from China purchased at Calicut.

All Lisbon gaped upon the human specimens from overseas, who walked gaping in their turn. The King had clothed them in fine raiment and he treated them as honoured guests. A cicerone was detailed to show them everything and explain the wonders they saw: the palaces of Lisbon and the cathedral, the rich churches, and ceremonies of the court. And they were taken far afield to see the Gothic Abbey of Batalha. Next year the King would send them home to tell the story to their friends.

Already the second Indian fleet was preparing to sail. Next year another one would go, and so on forever. A splendid present would this time be sent to the Samorin, and useful merchandise to be exchanged for pepper. The golden gates were open, they must never close again! Henry the Navigator's quest had ended in triumph.

A great thank-offering must be offered to the Lord. D.João I's abbey of Batalha already commemorated the nation's victory on land that had ensured its independence. D.Manuel would raise an abbey at Belem to mark victory over the sea.

From that time on he styled himself, not only King of Portugal and the Algarves, on this side and Beyond the Sea, and Lord of Guinea, but also Lord of the Conquest, Navigation and Commerce of Ethiopia, Persia, and India.

V

First Fruits

Of course it was urgent to go back. Immediately! While enthusiasm
still was high and all voices acclaimed the glory of the enterprise and his
subjects extolled D.Manuel as the most fortunate of Christian kings. To
think that within two years of his accession there should have been
discovered for the Crown a wider sphere of influence than the world
had seen! What other prince of the Penınsula, or indeed all Europe,
had been so blessed?

Yet, amid the thundering applause, both king and counsellors were
well aware that things had not gone wholly according to plan. The
peaceful trade and happy intercourse with co-religionists to which the
Portuguese aspired, had somehow failed to be established. The Moslem
powers, so long before them in the East, clearly had no intention of
surrendering their advantage, and they had great riches and prestige to
support them. Quite evidently Vasco da Gama's three ships, his few
men and his paltry present had failed to impress. Polite greetings and
friendly offers would not be enough. Material strength must show behind fair words, and wealth must be displayed.

The second expedition to India should be carefully organized
with a view to reetifying past errors. Time was short for the next fleet
to be ready to sail in the spring of 1500, as was desirable it should.
Experience had shown that July — the month in which Vasco da Gama
had left — was too late for reaching Mozambique in time to catch the
westerly monsoon across the Indian Ocean. In order to do this it would
be necessary to sail from Portugal in March. This gave no more than six
months for the equipment of an expedition on a scale before unimag-
ined.

While making ready thirteen ships, D. Manuel prepared a letter for
the Samorin, composed by Duarte Galvão, distinguished historian,

diplomat, and literary stylist. It was a pious and sententious document, written as from one Christian ruler to another:

"Great and powerful Prince Samorin, by God's mercy King of Calicut, We Dom Manuel, by His divine grace, King of Portugal and the Algarves, on this side and Beyond the Sea, Lord of Guinea in Africa, give you warm greeting as one whom we greatly esteem and love. God Almighty, beginning, middle, and end of all things, Who orders days and times and human events, Who by His infinite mercy created the world and redeemed it through Jesus Christ, Our Saviour, has ordained many things for the welfare and profit of the human kind in times to come . . . ." D.Manuel hopes that the Samorin will "consider with sound and sincere judgment the greatness, novelty, and mystery of the voyage of our people who went to you and your lands," so surely he would "do as we here in the West are doing, giving great praise to the Lord God that in your time and ours He should have granted so great a blessing to the world, permitting us to know and see each other . . . ."

Recapitulating past history, the King informs the Samorin how, over sixty years ago, "the Infante D.Henrique, a prince of Portugal, of virtuous life and holy customs," had been divinely inspired to promote this navigation. The quest, continued after the Infante's death, had been at last brought to a glorious conclusion. The hand of God was obvious in all this! D.Manuel was quite convinced that "Our Lord God never ordained so marvellous a thing as this our navigation for the sole benefit of trade and temporal profit, but for the spiritual welfare and salvation of souls, which we should value more, in which He may be served and His holy faith communicated."

Now that the way was open, in order to fulfil what was so manifestly the Lord's will, "we are sending our captain with ships and merchandise, and our factor to remain there at your pleasure. And we are sending religious persons, learned in the Christian faith, to celebrate the divine office and minister the Sacraments that you may see our faith and religion instituted by Jesus Christ Our Saviour...." The Samorin, of course, was well aware how two of the apostles "St Thomas and St Bartholomew, preached in your parts, performing great miracles, and leading people from the error of paganism and idolatry in which the whole world used to be...." D.Manuel "as a brother" begged the Samorin "to be conformed to the Lord's will and wish, and to be pleased to receive our friendship and give us yours as well as trade and intercourse

which we offer you peacefully, for the service of the Lord." Surely the
Samorin must be overjoyed that "people from so far away should come
to seek your friendship!" Admittedly, as always happened in the
wicked world, there would be evilly-disposed persons who might try to
wreck happy relations, but the King trusted the Samorin's virtue not to
lend ears to such. However that might be, "our purpose is to follow the
will of God rather than that of man," and he felt confident there were
many who would welcome his people and their friendship. God knew
he only wished for peace — "May he give you His grace to carry out His
will!"

Thus Duarte Galvão, with deep conviction and sincerity of heart,
interpreted D.Manuel's sentiments and the King signed in great good
faith. How little all this pious exposition might mean to the Samorin
did not occur to either. The Indian ruler was a Christian, was he not —
at least in a relative way? To thrash out doctrinal differences as yet
would surely be untimely.

At the same time both king and counsellors admitted that something
more concrete than edifying thoughts should pave the way to happy
understanding. Together with the letter went a worthy present.

A silver wash-hand basin, gilt embossed, with a ewer to match; a
silver goblet and two silver truncheons; four costly cushions, two of
crimson velvet, two in brocaded silk; a rich brocaded canopy with
golden fringes; and finally two Arras tapestries, one showing figures and
the other one green leaves. This was an offering that the Samorin could
hardly scorn.

The Captain-General of the fleet, Pedro Alvares Cabral, had been
chosen with care. Handsome and tall he cut a most imposing figure as
ambassador, and as a warrior he was impressive. He was tactful and
prudent, both brave and mild, and was liked by his men. D.Manuel felt
he was the right person to face all perils and smooth past resentments.

The captains and officers for each one of the thirteen ships were also
picked men. Among them was Bartolomeu Dias, discoverer of the Cape
of Good Hope, and Diogo Dias, his brother. Nicolau Coelho, who had
sailed with Vasco da Gama, cheerful and adventurous as ever, was ready
to return to India after no more than seven months at home. The
general Commander's secretary was Pero Vaz de Caminha, whose literary style has been admired by generations. The factor to be left in
charge of the trading post at Calicut was Aires Correa, an influential

business man of noble birth, who could speak fluent Arabic. Although he was a family man with a young wife and small children whom he was loth to leave, Aires Correa was delighted to be sent to India. And his two eldest boys, eleven or twelve years old, could come with him, thus he would not be parted from all his children.

As D.Manuel had promised the Samorin, "religious persons, learned in the Christian faith," accompanied the fleet. Frei Henrique de Coimbra, a Franciscan friar and confidant of the King, was leader of a band as zealous as himself to gather souls into the fold of Holy Mother Church.

But travellers to unfamiliar lands must be prepared for all eventualities. Diplomacy, religion and trade might not be successful, and then what was there to fall back upon but a display of force? The fleet of Pedro Alvares Cabral was fully armed, with artillery and all weapons of war.

By the 8th of March, 1500, everything was ready. The send-off was more splendid than anything seen before. The King and all his court heard Mass that morning at Belem. The white and crimson banner of the Knights of Christ was carried to the altar to be blessed and solemnly returned to the hands of the captain. The King walked beside Pedro Alvares Cabral down to the riverside and there bade his captains farewell. The green hills round Belem were covered with a colourful and seething crowd; small boats bedecked with flags and manned by oarsmen gaily dressed, plied between the shore and the fleet which also was fluttering with colour. The sea appeared a field of flowers, writes the chronicler. From the ships sounded a merry fanfare of trumpets, fifes and drums and flutes that blended with the reedy skirl of bagpipes such as shepherds play on the mountains to gather their flocks. These instruments had been brought down for the seamen to distract the tedium of long hours upon the empty ocean.

An auspicious departure, the happy presage of which appeared to be confirmed a few months later when one of the smaller ships returned, bearing letters and exciting news.

And here we fall into a controversy. Was it of deliberate intent that the fleet had set its course so far southwest? Vasco da Gama had sailed into mid-ocean many miles west of Africa to pick up the trade winds that blow around the Cape. So Cabral had doubtlessly been instructed to do — but why had he led his ships by a still wider curve? Generations of historians have argued over this. All that is certain is that he exceeded by far the necessary deviation and that the result was sensational.

A new land – island or continent – had been revealed under the southern stars! A land of lush forests and running streams and mighty rivers. Beneath the leafy shades roamed men and women, naked and unashamed as Adam and Eve in Paradise. Great parrots, bright crimson and electric blue screamed in the trees; strange scented fruits grew in the woods; the air was fresh and gentle, as sweet as summer breezes in Entre-Douro-e-Minho. "This is a gracious land," wrote Pero Vaz de Caminha, "and could be made to produce anything." Already they had noted groves of brazil-wood – that tree which gave the lovely scarlet dye so eagerly sought by the textile industry. "Land of the True Cross" was the name the captain chose for these enchanting shores, discovered during the happy Easter week.

The fleet lingered there for some days, taking on wood and water, and fraternizing with the simple savages. Before setting sail for the Cape and India, Cabral despatched Gaspar de Lemos home with the interesting news.

More lands in the West – the general public was not deeply moved. It is noteworthy that in Portugal no one suggested that these might be the outskirts of Asia.

But D.Manuel was delighted. Everything fitted in so well! "It seems Our Lord miraculously caused this land to be discovered because it is most convenient and necessary for the navigation to India." A useful port of call for taking on supplies. So he informed his Castilian parents-in-law.

As usual he wrote to them at once. The tie that had bound him to Fernando and Isabel, so prematurely cut by death was being renewed by Manuel's betrothal to the younger sister of his first ill-fated queen. Whatever romance has been woven around Manuel's courtship of the star-crossed Isabel, his offer for the hand of young Maria seems to have been dictated by expediency alone. It is not even apparent that the initiative came from him. Isabel and Fernando had decided that to marry their daughter in Portugal was the best match they could make for her. It was a kingdom in expansion and ascension. Vasco da Gama's successful voyage to India convinced them of this. This time any reluctance shown seems to have been on Manuel's part. It was not till his baby son Miguel died, on July 19th 1500, that he decided to close with the Castilian offer, and this time it is he who makes conditions. Some years before they had obliged him — against his better judgment — to expel the Jews. Now he insists that all mosques in the newly-conquered kingdom of Granada should be demolished, and all Moslems banished from the Castilian realms. Thus he and the "catholic sovereigns," his parents-in-law, would stand side by side with drawn swords against all foemen of the Christian faith. The "catholic" couple had no objection to so godly a proposal. The mosques were overthrown and all the Moors sent packing overseas as an alternative to baptism, while the Infanta travelled over the frontier to meet her pious bridegroom. Maria, third daughter of Fernando and Isabel, had not her dead sister's romantic charm, nor — as suggested by her receding chin — the powerful personality of her mother. No one claims she was beautiful, but she was good and gentle and admirably brought up as Isabel of Castile's daughter could not fail to be. She was moreover reasonably intelligent and accomplished, and possessed all the qualities required to make a good wife and good queen. D.Manuel could well congratulate himself upon his satisfactory second choice. On October 30th 1500, in the ancient town of Alcacer do Sal, Manuel and Maria became man and wife.

So passed the time awaiting news of India and the dozen ships that had sailed for the Cape from the paradisal Land of the True Cross.

Six only of the twelve ever came home. Four had been swallowed up in the great seas around the Cape, and two had been lost in the Indian Ocean. Another storm-beaten ship had wandered blindly along unknown coasts to the entrance of the Red Sea, where two thirds of its crew had died. Too few in number for manoeuvring the sails, they had secured them to the mast, and unable to tack or furl, by an amazing feat of navigation found their way back around Africa to the Cape Verde Islands.

This was the ship of Diogo Dias, brother of Bartolomeu. But the discoverer of the Cape never returned, nor yet reached India. His ship was one of the four that had capsized and sunk, so that he never crossed the ocean he had been the first to enter.

The captain, Pedro Alvares Cabral, came back with the remaining ships. He told a story of success — and tragedy. At first all had gone well at Calicut. The Samorin had been pleased with the present and seemed favourably inclined. Visits had been exchanged; the Portuguese

had landed and set up their trading post and begun to take on cargo for
their return. The Samorin had asked assistance for the capture of a ship
bearing an elephant he wished to buy and which the owner had insisted
on selling to the King of Cambay. The ship in question was well armed,
but, as a gesture, Cabral sent his smallest unit to bring the vessel and the
elephant to Calicut. The Samorin had been delighted with the prowess
of his new allies and everyone was happy. And then — no one could say
exactly how it came about, the whole atmosphere had changed. The
Arab merchants from the Red Sea, furious to see newcomers on the
pepper market which had hitherto been wholly under their control, had
intrigued and made trouble. Knowing the language and the country and
the ropes, it was easy for them, and they worked to such purpose that
one day a seething mob bore down upon the Portuguese factory, killing
and looting. Some fifty men were massacred, including the factor Aires
Correa, whose small sons, however, were saved by a friendly Moslem.
The others managed to swim out to the ships where Pedro Alvares
Cabral waited in vain for some word from the Samorin. When no apology was made, he had bombarded Calicut by way of reprisals, and
sailed to Cochin further down the coast. The Rajah of Cochin welcomed the Portuguese. He did not love his overlord the Samorin, so
gladly accepted the offer of D.Manuel's friendship and protection. He
placed his port and all the pepper he could find at the strangers' disposal.

The ships were loaded to their hatches at Cochin, with pepper, cinnamon and cloves, nutmeg and ginger. Cochin not only had a splendid
port, but it stood at the fountainhead of the pepper supply. At Cochin
too (at last!) some Christians were found — authentic Christians these,
descendents of the converts of St Thomas. They told of the tomb of
the saint, at Meliapur on the coast of Coromandel, where pilgrims of all
nations worshipped at his shrine.

Two Christian priests from Cranganor had the courage to embark in
Cabral's ship for the long voyage to Lisbon whence they would proceed
to Rome. They brought with them a jar of earth from the holy tomb of
Meliapur — a wonder-working relic for D.Manuel. Other rulers of Malabar beside the Rajah of Cochin had expressed their desire for Portuguese friendship. The fact was that they all disliked the Samorin and
felt a foreign alliance would enhance their prestige. The Rajah of Can-
nanor, whose domain lay just north of Calicut, would have pressed

more spices upon Cabral, who simply could not take them on but promised to come back.

At sea, the captain had established his country hegemony and defined Portugal's position in the Indian Ocean. A richly laden Moslem ship had been challenged and overhauled, but hearing it belonged to Cambay, higher up the coast, it was suffered to proceed unmolested. Let the captain inform his king, explained Cabral, that the Portuguese had not come to India to make war, except on those who broke their faith as had happened at Calicut.

Thirteen ships had left Lisbon—six returned. The proportion might seem disastrous. But what a cargo those few ships had brought! 2000 quintals of pepper and 600 of cinnamon, ginger, benzoin and sandalwood. For all the heavy loss, a profit still remained of 100%.

Venetian merchants in Lisbon were livid.

VI

Repercussions

"Congratulate me!" said D.Manuel to Cretico, the Venetian envoy, on the night of the festival of St. John the Baptist, 1501. The Indian fleet was coming in. One ship had already arrived laden with spices. "And I duly rejoiced with him," writes the ambassador. Bland and smiling, the Venetian witnessed the great feast at the palace that night, while church bells rang throughout the land.

D.Manuel told Cretico he must write to the Doge and tell him that in the future his galleys should be sent to Lisbon for spices. They would be welcome there as in their own home port, and he – the King of Portugal – would see to it that the Soldan of Egypt received no more pepper from India. Then the two beamed on one another like good diplomats, though each was perfectly aware of what the other was feeling.

This is "the worst piece of news that the Venetian Republic could ever have received!" was the comment when Cretico's letter was read in Venice. The city already had difficulties to cope with, owing to war with Turkey which had broken out in 1499 and been signalled by the enemy's sea victory at Sapienza. It was to sue for aid from Portugal that the Doge had sent Cretico to Lisbon. And now this blow! The Indian voyage "mattered far more to the Venetian State than the Turkish war or any other war that might break out." To be told that they should be glad for the Sultan to receive no spices! Why, it was he who had supplied the Venetian market, and Alexandria was much nearer than Lisbon! If this Portuguese navigation were to continue, all merchants must go to Lisbon to furnish themselves, and Venice, which hitherto had controlled the market and retailed the goods, would simply be unable to compete. Already pepper was being sold in Lisbon at a fraction of its former price, and cinnamon at a ducat for a large jar. The

King of Portugal – alas! – would soon be called "the King of Money!"

"Everybody is stupefied," writes the diarist Priuli, "that in our time a route has been discovered, new and unheard of in the days of our forefathers . . . I clearly foresee the ruin of the Venetian city! "

More cheerful persons liked to think the news might be a false alarm, and even if it were quite true, a number of reasons appeared to indicate that this state of affairs could not continue. For one thing, the mighty Soldan of Egypt would have to weigh in to protect his own interests – "for when spices no longer reach Syria and Alexandria, he will lose the great wealth and profit he derives therefrom." And even if he did nothing, which was unlikely, surely the King of Portugal would find he could not persist with this enterprise. The voyage was too long and dangerous. Only consider what had happened already – of thirteen ships no more than six had made a safe return! Financial loss must far exceed the profit, to say nothing about the human element. Ships require men, and obviously "none will be found willing to go, for fear of losing their lives."

Further letters from Lisbon proved all this to be wishful thinking. The King of Portugal, although grieved at the loss of men and ships, was preparing immediately another fleet to sail for India – "saying that he desired these caravels to proceed beyond Calicut." As for man power, the Venetian groans – "there has not been the least difficulty in finding men eager to go," apparently "they do not fear to die! " Facts must be faced. "The King of Portugal will send every year to Calicut." And that was that!

Pathetically anxious to know the worst, Venice lapped up all crumbs of information. Sailors disembarking from Cabral's ships were lured into the palaces of great bankers like Affaitati, and urged to tell their story. The Indian envoys brought from Cochin and Cannanore were waylaid to pump for information and to stuff with propaganda. Let it be known to them that Venice was the greatest sea power of Christendom, who ever since trade had existed in the world had negotiated the spices brought to the Middle East. Portugal was too small and poor a nation to undertake business on such a scale. The Portuguese were warriors, not merchants. It was Venetian capital that backed them up. In fact the Venetian envoys had come to Lisbon for no other purpose than to discuss the loan that the King hoped to raise for the equipment of his fleet. In view of this the Indian princes had been ill-advised to think of exchanging those Arab traders who had always kept them well supplied with Venetian goods for insolvent newcomers!

The Indians listened politely. We do not know if they were such simple souls as not to wonder why people should try to discredit an enterprise in which admittedly they had invested. It seems that during the return voyage to India they told the Portuguese captain about their talks with the Venetians, and thereupon he opened for them to see a whole chestful of Guinea gold, which helped to restore confidence.

Thus Venice tried to hold her own and put on a brave front, but private correspondence registers the sighs and moans. And the eager curiosity — "things have been discovered that for infinite time people have longed to know." If only maps could be obtained of the new ocean route — but how was that to be? "It is impossible," writes Trevisano, secretary of the Venetian embassy at Granada, and secret agent for the Republic — because "the King has condemned to death any person who should reveal the map." But Venetian spies were active and their masters lavish with their money: "If we reach Venice alive," writes Cretico from Lisbon to the Doge, "Your Magnificence will see maps."

Equally interested but far more dispassionate onlookers were the Florentines. Of these were many merchants established in Lisbon. Unlike Venice, Florence had no proprietary interest in the spice trade. Florentine merchants — rich, refined and highly cultured, as befitted the cradle of the Renaissance, dealt in silks, fine woollen cloths, and leather, receiving in exchange cork and salt, fish, slaves and ivory from Guinea, besides the excellent sugar of Madeira, trading with which the banker Bartolomeu Marchione had amassed great wealth. He was perhaps the richest man in Lisbon at the time, but Girolamo Sernigi was not far behind. These financiers were always ready with the capital Portuguese merchants lacked, and so were greatly favoured by the kings of Portugal and granted papers of naturalization. It was in gratitude for benefits received that they had offered to King João II the famous illuminated Bible, known as the "Biblia dos Jeronimos," preserved in Lisbon to the present day.

Marchione wrote home with enthusiasm of the arrival of Cabral's ships. Soon Italy and all western Europe would be furnished with spices from Lisbon. Obviously this would cause great inconvenience to Venice, and perhaps still more to the Soldan, but Marchione plainly is not troubled about this. The King of Portugal, says he, is making ready twenty ships to sail back to India — "may God bring them safely home. They will obtain great treasures and all things good and necessary," besides many curiosities and strange animals of species never known before. Stories about creatures told by Pliny which had been considered as lies were now proved to be true. Even news of the fabled island of Taprobana was expected soon, for it was the King's intention shortly to send his ships there — "May God take them safely there and back that every year we may know new and beautiful things! "

The repercussions throughout Europe were tremendous — far greater than those arising out of Columbus' voyage. The lands discovered by the Genoese might well be connected with Asia — except in Portugal, most people surmised that they were — but if so, what? They did not appear to be in direct touch with India or the Spice Islands. By the same token little notice was taken of Cabral's discovery of the Land of the True Cross, lightly dismissed as the "Land of Parrots," nor yet when, in 1501, Gaspar Corte Real arrived in Lisbon reporting a line of coast in the distant northwest, was there any special excitement. The envoy, Pietro Pasqualigo, writing to Venice at that date, observed it was believed in Portugal "that this land is continental and joins the one discovered in the west by other caravels of His Highness. They supposed it to be also connected with the Antilles discovered by Spain, and with the Land of Parrots, recently found by the ships of this kingdom on their way to Calicut."

A new continent, a fourth part of the world? If that were so, Europe could not care less. What interested most people was not cosmography, but the golden East. Their dreams were all of pepper, ginger, cinnamon and cloves and pearls and diamonds from the glittering oriental kingdoms. When rumour spread from port to port — northward to Bruges, Antwerp and Southampton, and eastward along the Mediterranean shores — that ships of Portugal had actually returned from Calicut, then kings and merchants sat up with a jerk. Could it really be true? Was the pepper they brought the genuine article? It might be only malagueta from Africa as seen before — not bad, but not to be compared with the real thing from India hitherto supplied by Venice. The arrival at Antwerp in 1502 of a shipload of spice dispelled all doubt. The pepper was somewhat small and green, but it was genuine and good; the cinnamon was perhaps a little too large – but what mattered was that spices had come direct to Flanders and were being sold at a fraction of the former price. The market rocked with excitement. The axis of the spice trade was shifting from east to west. No longer were the goods to pass from hand to hand – from India through the Red Sea bottleneck, accumulating duties as they travelled. The future distributing centre would be Lisbon, nearer and more accessible than Venice for the Atlantic peoples. In view of this the canny financiers of Augsburg, the mighty Fuggers and their colleagues the Welsers, who had been considering opening branches in Italy, decided they had better go to Lisbon.

Amid all this, D.Manuel, serene and satisfied and bland, accepted congratulations graciously, and indifferent to envy, planned great things. Material profit was acceptable no doubt, and even necessary to pay for the fulfilment of his dreams, but this, one gathers, never was the first consideration. D.Manuel ruled a nation born of the Reconquista and he came of a crusading house. His great-grandfather, King João I, founder of the dynasty, no sooner had obtained victory over the enemy that threatened the country's independence than he had carried his sword against the Infidel, crossing to Africa and conquering Ceuta. The Infante D.Henrique, Manuel's great-uncle, a seeker after knowledge but also a soldier of the Cross, had received knighthood in a mosque re-consecrated as a Christian church, and thereafter had devoted his life to the discovery of the earth which was to bring lands and peoples yet unknown into the Christian fold. D.Manuel's father, the eager, unstable, impetuous Infante D.Fernando, had spent his short years in the African crusade; D.João II – certainly no mystic stargazer – who had brought up D.Manuel, himself was knighted at the age of sixteen in the conquered town of Arzila, and he was resolved, if he had lived, to renew the Crusade.

D.Manuel had been given by him command of the crusading Order of Christ. The holy war, to which all Christendom was called, therefore loomed large on his programme. The riches of the East must be a means but not an end. Backed by a warrior nation that was first upon the seas, hoping for treasures from the Orient to roll in every year – might not – should not – the King of Portugal persuade Europe to launch upon a vast Crusade – even to the reconquest of Jerusalem?

VII

Latter-day Crusade

Manuel's first idea had gone no further than "to pass over to Africa" as his predecessors had done before him. As early as 1500 we find him writing circulars to different fidalgos, ordering his subjects to make ready to sail with him to Africa in the summer of next year. Preparations were to be strictly military – no money to be spent on outward show, so dear to the contemporary heart: neither silks nor brocades – the proscription imposed by King João II on such things was to be rigidly observed: all outlay was to be devoted to the best arms and the best horses obtainable: no purely ornamental retinues were to accompany their lords, nor pages under military age.

In August that same year the King was calling on the cities of his realm for their support in men and ships and money for the holy war. In January 1501 went forth a further order for a census to be made of all able-bodied men "to pass over with us to Africa, which passage, please God, will be on the 15th of next May." In spite of the entreaties of his newly-married queen, D.Manuel was determined to command the expedition in person. So probably he would have done but for the arrival of the ambassadors from Venice mentioned in last chapter.

As we have seen, these were dual purpose envoys, their function being that of ambassador-cum-spy. The secret mission was the more important, perhaps for Vasco da Gama's voyage was more alarming to Venice than the approaching Turks. This danger, none the less was very real, for at the time it seemed that Venice might lose her Greek islands. The kings of Christendom did not appear inclined to help. Had not Venice, after the fall of Constantinople, entered into an unholy pact with the Infidel? Now that the Turks had turned against her, let her face them alone! Therefore Venice appealed to Portugal, a nation whose crusading fervour was well known and whose relations with the Republic had been always cordial. Early in 1501, Pisani, Cretico, and Pietro Pasqualigo appeared in Lisbon, all smiles, congratulating the King upon his second marriage, and bringing him a Venetian gondola as wedding present from the Doge.

D.Manuel received the messengers with open arms, though well aware of their ulterior motives. His African expedition was far advanced, but how much more to the glory of God, exclaimed Pasqualigo, it would be to turn these armaments against the Ottoman threatening the very heart of Christendom as he drew nearer Rome than to attack Moors in North Africa who, for the present at least, were no serious menace!

D.Manuel thought it over. The Venetian was right. His counsellors agreed. They never had liked the idea of their sovereign leading his armies overseas in person. He had as yet no heir to succeed him and anything might happen. So they weighed in on the Venetian side. Surely the service of the Lord required first the reduction of the Turk, enemy number one of Christendom! "Though we are very sad to give up our expedition already so far advanced," the King wrote to the Pope, "we have decided to postpone our passage and help the Venetians."

D.Manuel selected thirty ships, the best equipped of the fleet he had made ready, and manned them with 3,500 troops. Commanded by D.João do Meneses, created Count of Tarouca in honour of this important mission, the armada sailed for Apulia and the coast of Greece where they were met by the Venetian fleet and guided to the delicious island of Corfu, to be regaled with luscious fruit and many gifts. Commanders on both sides were killingly polite; their followers, meanwhile, quarrelled with each other and with the islanders, like cats. Sailors and soldiers, observes Damião de Gois, are an unruly lot. They gave their captains and the local authorities much trouble. Withal the Turks failed to appear. The Sultan, hearing that help had come to Venice, decided to call off his fleet. The harassed Venetian general begged the no less harassed Count to take no further trouble. Since the Turks had withdrawn, why should the King of Portugal incur more expense? Whenever he would, D.João de Meneses might go home, having earned the undying gratitude of Venice! D.João replied with protestations of his deep regard and sailed. Next year Pasqualigo returned conveying the

Doge's warmest thanks. The envoy was received with overwhelming honours and invited to stand godfather to the little Prince, the future D.João III, born to his happy nation on June 6th 1502.

Thus dearly Portugal and Venice loved each other.

Meanwhile, in greatest secrecy, from 1501 to 1504, a series of embassies from Venice waited on the Soldan of Egypt. Could not the two states between them devise some means to put an end to Portuguese intervention in the spice trade?

The Soldan of Egypt shared their concern. Kansuh-el-Ghauri, who had succeeded to the throne in 1501, was the last of the Mamelukes — a dynasty of Turkish slaves of the royal bodyguard who for centuries had been pushing one another on and off the throne of Cairo by bloodshed and murder.

The uneasy court of Egypt, for the moment at peace with the Turks of Constantinople, had flourished on the revenues it owed to its strategic position. Sitting astride the bottleneck through which the spices flowed from East to West, the Soldan controlled the markets of Alexandria, Damascus and Beirut, and levied heavy tribute on all oriental produce, more particularly pepper. This was bought at an enhanced price by the Venetian merchants who passed it on at a still higher figure to the rest of Europe. The business was very rewarding.

But suddenly the fountainhead had dried. Venetian galleys sent to Beirut in 1502 returned with only four bales of pepper. Of five ships that went to Alexandria the same year, only one came back laden. In 1504 there was nothing at all! Consternation was general.

Not only the Venetians came before the Soldan with their tale of woe, but Arab traders frequenting the Indian ports joined the lament. Did the great Lord of Cairo realise what was the source of all this mischief? Infidels from the West had appeared in the Indian Ocean and were carrying off the spices by their new sea route! More than that, they were holding up Arab ships sailing with their cargoes to the Red Sea! Reprisals of some kind were urgent. Why should not Egypt build a mighty fleet at Suez, and sweep the upstarts from the surface of the waters?

Why not? The Soldan meditated. It seemed to him that less expensive measures might be taken first. Such as blackmail. The holiest places of the Christian world were in his hand. Pilgrims from far and near came every year to visit them. On the crags of Mount Sinai there was the monastery of St Catherine. The Soldan informed the monks of St Catherine that unless they could persuade the Pope to call off the Portuguese ships, he would massacre every Christian who appeared in his domains, and destroy all their shrines, including of course the monastery and every Christian church, leaving the Holy Sepulchre without one stone above the other.

The monks took fright. Hitherto they had lived in peace upon their desert peaks, forgotten by the world. But they knew well that Christians were on sufferance in Moslem lands. The Soldan of Egypt tolerated them because he levied tribute on the pilgrim traffic and the sale of sacred relics. The Holy Sepulchre especially was a gold mine to him – but what if he decided that the spice trade mattered more – as very probably it did?

El Ghauri sent a monk of Sinai, Fra Mauro, with a letter to the Pope, informing him that "the greatest King, Lord of Lords, the noble, excellent, wise, victorious King of Kings, sword of the world, Prince of the faith of Mohammed and his disciples, Executor of Justice, heir to all realms in the world, King of Arabia, Persia and Turkey, Shadow of God on earth," and so on and so forth, would have His Holiness to know how well all Christian pilgrims were treated in his dominions. They came and went and visited the holy shrines quite unmolested. But this could not continue while the princes of the Iberian peninsula persecuted the followers of Islam. Unless the Pope ordered the king of Portugal to call off his navigation to India, the Soldan would proceed to carry out the threat that every Christian in his dominions should be put to death, all Christian churches would be levelled to the ground, and the Holy Sepulchre totally destroyed.

Pope Julius read this letter and he shrugged his shoulders. Let this be carried to King Manuel, he told Fra Mauro. What answer would the King wish him to make?

What answer? D.Manuel chortled. He said he was delighted. His only regret was that there was not more cause for complaint! He hoped soon to remedy that. Let the Soldan wait for the day "when our armies, as by God's mercy we trust will be soon, have reached the House of Mecca where lies the false prophet, and will have taken it by force of arms." After that he could complain!

And this was no vain boast, added D.Manuel, nor even difficult – seeing how with God's help such great and prosperous things have been accomplished. But — "Holy Father, we hardly believe the Soldan to be such a fool as to destroy the Holy Sepulchre to spite the Christians, for that would bring the whole of Christendom down on his shoulders!" Besides, he added to Fra Mauro, El Ghauri was making such a good thing out of the Holy Sepulchre that he would hate to overthrow it. He had more cause to venerate the sacred relics than to scatter them!

His morale completely restored, enriched by generous gifts for the monastery, Fra Mauro went his way, leaving D.Manuel aflame with reinforced crusading fervour. Surely the omens were propitious and the hour was ripe for Christian princes to forget their dissensions and rivalries and march together on Jerusalem!

The King had long talks with his confessor, Frei Henrique of Coimbra, a remarkable and travelled man. A Franciscan of austere life and missionary zeal, Frei Henrique had sailed with Cabral on the momentous voyage of 1500. He it was who celebrated the first Mass heard on the virgin soil of Brazil, while naked Indians gaped in wonder. At Calicut, without either a knowledge of the language or competent interpreters to help, he had set about at once preaching the Gospel, and even made a convert, we are told. A yogi hermit felt that he had found the truth for which he sought, and was baptized by the name of Miguel.

Frei Henrique escaped the massacre of Calicut and returned with Cabral to Portugal, but not to rest from his labours. In constant consultation with the King, Frei Henrique discussed the part the Christian church must play in worldwide politics, and talked over the news from Cairo and Mount Sinai. Perhaps it was he who suggested to D.Manuel the idea of a grand crusade carried out by Christendom united. The omens all seemed propitious, but let us not forget the lessons of the past! Too many heads had wrecked former crusades. Only a few of the most dedicated ought to lead this one. Let soundings be made at carefully selected courts. D.Manuel's father-in-law, the King of Aragon and conqueror of Granada, was obviously indicated as a partner. The King of England, too, might be a good man to approach. The royal house of that country had a most distinguished crusading record, and King Henry VII had every reason to be thankful to the Lord Who had delivered him from all his enemies and led him to a throne to which he had a dubious right. What better than a crusade to express his gratitude and wipe out any guilt incurred upon the way? King Manuel resolved to send a faithful messenger to him — and who more suitable than Frei

Henrique de Coimbra?

Frei Henrique's journey to England followed immediately after the departure of Fra Mauro for the Middle East. The end of July 1505 saw the Franciscan received in audience by King Henry. He told him that D.Manuel "desired and wished above all things . . . to wage war for God upon the Infidels who hold and occupy the Holy Land, Jerusalem and the surrounding country . . . ." If Henry would join in the expedition planned, the King of Portugal was quite prepared to surrender the command to him and march under his banner. D.Manuel proposed to put into the field 1500 men, equipped and maintained at his own expense, for a period of three years.

The historical image of the calculating King Henry VII does not fit well with that of a crusader, yet — surprising though it may seem — the fact is that he responded with enthusiasm. Immediately he undertook to sound King Louis XII of France, and in August of that same year he sent Lord Herbert to Paris upon this subject. King Louis's reply, although polite, was non-committal.

No sooner had Frei Henrique arrived home from England than he had to take the road again. He was despatched this time to King Fernando of Aragon and, weary but pursuant, he plodded overland on foot because his vows of poverty excluded the luxury of travel on horseback. Fernando lent a willing ear and sent back practical suggestions as to men and money.

At the same time the European courts were being canvassed by the King's secretary, Duarte Galvão, another starry-eyed enthusiast, as well as veteran diplomat who, having served under the three last kings, had seen the Quest of Henry the Navigator grow and expand to worldwide ambit. Duarte Galvão was a learned historian. He was also a devout student of the Prophets and saw the fall of Islam clearly foretold in Holy Scripture. All signs indicated this would be soon. If only Christian princes would forget their quarrels they would perceive the passing hour and rally to the banner of the Cross.

Duarte Galvão traipsed from France to Flanders and to Italy. He spoke to Louis XII; at Louvain, as if by accident, he waylaid the King of the Romans, Maximilian, first cousin to D.Manuel, out hunting in the autumn woods and handed him a letter. Burning with zeal, though shivering with fever picked up in unsanitary hostels and draughty anterooms, he travelled in a litter through the January frost to Rome to interview the Pope and obtain his approval for D.Manuel's enterprise. The Portuguese cardinal, D.Jorge da Costa who, though a centenarian, still remained a power at the papal court, presented his compatriot to Julius II, who beamed and blessed, and despatched him with a Brief, by which — the Cardinal wrote to the King after Galvão had left — "Your Highness will see how gracious is the Pope's reply, and what an honour for you and your children!" The Holy Father sent D.Manuel the Golden Rose, and granted Duarte Galvão the privilege of adding the pontifical arms to those he bore upon his scutcheon.

But nothing happened. At the end of the year D.Manuel was writing to the Cardinal indignantly: Words were not enough, the King points out — one would see deeds! He suggests that D.Jorge da Costa has not been pressing the case on the Holy Father, although the honour of the pious enterprise would reflect in great part on him, "for this realm is the country of your birth! "

More satisfactory was D.Manuel's exchange of impressions with his father-in-law, as may be gathered from the glowing letters he wrote to the Archbishop of Toledo, the famous Cardinal Ximenes Cisneros. Nothing had given Manuel more joy than Fernando's adherence to his plan. He tells him that the King of England also has shown enthusiasm. Cisneros could look forward to the day when, as in times of old three kings had journeyed to Jerusalem, three modern kings would kneel before the Holy Sepulchre and there receive the Sacrament from the Cardinal's hands!

These mystical and romantic outbursts did not stand in the way of practical considerations. D.Manuel and Fernando of Aragon discussed resources and ways and means. They and King Henry were to be the sole leaders of the enterprise which they meant to accompany in person. Should other kings be invited to go with them? D.Manuel thought not. He knew sufficient history to remember the squabbles between allies that had wrecked crusades in the past. Others might be pleased to acquire merit by sending men and munitions, but one hoped they would stay at home themselves, for — "great inconvenience can arise from many heads."

The plan of action was to bring a fleet bearing all volunteers through the Mediterranean, to disembark at Alexandria and thence march on the Holy Land. Meanwhile the Indian armada of Portugal would sail up the Red Sea and join the allies near Suez.

Here Fernando the Catholic, always a realist for all his crusading fervour, appears to have conceived a dark suspicion of the singleness of purpose of his dear son-in-law. Might not his crusade be a mere pretext for bringing international assistance to Portuguese expansion in the East? We gather he hinted as much.

Quite on the contrary, Manuel solemnly assured him — "if the affairs of India had for sole purpose the obtaining of spices and acquiring wealth, we willingly would give them up in favour of the present enterprise. But Our Lord knows we labour rather for the hope of winning and saving souls, and the destruction of the Moors than for the profit of spices or any other riches." In a near future one might look forward to see oriental Christendom as powerful as that of Europe! Already D.Manuel had ordered his fleets to enter the Red Sea and make war on Egypt. "Our ships can reach within two days of Mecca, and three leagues from St Catherine of Mount Sinai." The discovery of India had opened the way for the deliverance of the Holy Land.

And Prester John was to come into all this. The legendary Christian king of a vast realm, all surrounded by Moslem lands, that had filled the imagination of the Middle Ages, had only recently become identified with Abyssinia, the mysterious empire south of Egypt whence monks and pilgrims had from time to time appeared at Jerusalem, and even Rome. Some had attended Councils and a few had journeyed west, to Aragon and Portugal, where they had been received with great interest. The information that they gave about their country seems to have been vague, and Pero da Covilham who had been sent there by King João II never returned to tell his story. Nonetheless it was certain that a Christian realm existed far up in the African mountains — a very great and powerful empire, the Abyssinian pilgrims said, and all Europe believed them. Therefore — if in the ports of the Red Sea, the Portuguese could unite with the armies of Prester John — "as I trust in the Lord they will," D.Manuel wrote, the downfall of Islam was certain!

D.Fernando thought that a meeting between him and his son-in-law might be useful, but Manuel said, not yet. Wait till plans were further matured — for the present, ambassadors, sent in great secrecy, ostensibly to treat of other matters, would be sufficient. For the time being meetings on a high level would involve too much publicity.

Fernando, always cautious, not to say suspicious, said the three partners should be bound together by solemn oaths and severe sanctions, lest one without the others should default.

What was the date to be fixed for all this? The sooner the better! said D.Manuel.

The date never was fixed. Diplomatic wheels turn slowly even today, and still more so in that century of tardy communications. Three years later the weighty vows and sanctions had not yet been signed, and Fernando of Aragon had somewhat lost interest. His arguments with Maximilian over the regency of Castile on behalf of his mad daughter Juana, and the affairs of Italy were proving more absorbing than the liberation of the Holy Land. Nor did the kings of Europe seem inclined to sink their differences and pool their resources to favour a crusade. Maximilian, for one, was quarrelling fiercely with the King of France. Of what avail, cried he, was it for Christian princes to make peace and turn against the Infidel, when the worst Turk of all — King Louis XII — continued his nefarious works? Spluttering with rage, Maximilian prepared to march on Italy and turn out all the French, while the Pope at the centre of the trouble spot, was far too harassed and perturbed to think about Jerusalem, though he assured D.Manuel that no one had the Holy War at heart more than himself. However that might be, the crusade he chiefly wished to promote was against the Turks of Constantinople — so much nearer Rome!

As for Henry VII, in 1507 his crusading fervour was still burning bright. In the same vein as Manuel had written to the Cardinal, King Henry told the Pope how beautiful and fitting it would be if, even as three kings from the East once came to worship the Babe of Bethlehem, three kings in this latter day should journey from the West to liberate the Holy Sepulchre!

But in 1509 King Henry died and his hearty young son does not seem to have been inspired by the crusading vision.

D.Manuel must have been disappointed, but he was not cast down — neither he nor Duarte Galvão, nor anybody else in Portugal. What if the Pope and princes showed themselves lukewarm? Perhaps it was the will of Heaven that Portugal should lead the way, putting other Christian rulers to shame and stirring up their emulation.

VIII
India

The atmosphere was full of portents and prophecies. Men talked about three pillars of ancient stone found sunk in the sandy beach below the Sintra heights, under the rock called the "Hill of the Moon." Some letters almost worn away by time and wave were deciphered. The learned read a Latin inscription *Sibilie vaticinium occiduis decretu,* and lower down was a verse which they interpreted:

> The stone will be turned over and the letters set in order
> When thou, O West, shalt behold the treasures of the Orient.
> It will be wonderful to see the Ganges, Indus, and Tagus,
> For each will exchange merchandise with the other!

Some say this prophecy was first unearthed in 1499, shortly before Vasco da Gama arrived back from India. Others have it that the stones were discovered in 1505, which seems more likely, for prophecies, as everybody knows, are chiefly heard of after their fulfilment. What happened to this portentous find? The chronicler says no one bothered to collect the stones — "The Portuguese," he adds, "know better how to fight than to preserve antiques." So these remained abandoned on the beach.

In any case, D.Manuel required no Sybilline utterance to be convinced that Heaven's blessing rested on his enterprise. Results so far had been breathtaking. Vasco da Gama on his second voyage in 1502 had wreaked vengeance on Calicut and chastised those sultans of East Africa who had deceived him when he passed in 1498, seeking the route to India. He had consolidated and rewarded the good friendship of Malindi, Cochin and Cannanore, and returned in 1503 to Lisbon with thirteen shiploads of pepper. He walked to the palace preceded by a page who held a basin filled with 2000 mitkals of gold from Sofala — tribute money offered by conquered Kilwa. First fruits these from the Indian Ocean to be consecrated to the Lord! The King handed the gold to Gil Vicente, his most gifted craftsman, and Gil, with the same master touch he brought to the composing of those *autos* which have immortalized his name, fashioned the precious metal into the famous Monstrance of Belem that we admire to-day as the most perfect specimen of Manueline art.

We are not told what was done with the golden idol captured from a Moslem ship — an idol which weighed thirty pounds, which had two costly emeralds for eyes set in its monstrous face, was wearing a cloak of hammered gold, all encrusted with jewels, and displayed a great ruby on its chest.

Strange things and new! Next year together with the spice came forty pounds of pearls, four hundred of seed pearls and eight pounds of mother-of-pearl shells; a diamond as large as a bean, exotic jewelry, besides two steeds — one Persian and one Arab, both fleet as arrows. Truly the Ganges and India were bringing their treasures to the Tagus and it was wonderful to see!

Quite naturally the Moslem world was not prepared to take this lying down, and resistance was stiffening day by day. The Arab traders of Calicut were urging the Samorin to punish his disobedient vassal of Cochin, who harboured the strangers in his port. The Rajah of Cochin, hating his overlord, and well pleased with his new allies, refused to give them up. Although he saw his lands invaded and himself a refugee in one of his own islands, he yet remained convinced he was not backing the wrong horse. The arrival in 1503 of ships from Portugal, commanded by the cousins Francisco and Afonso de Albuquerque, promptly restored him to his throne, and though after their departure the Samorin returned, Duarte Pacheco Pereira, with ninety Portuguese, defended Cochin and defeated the invader. The grateful Rajah would have loaded him with lands, riches and spices, but Duarte Pacheco refused them all. What he had done, said he, was in the service of D.Manuel, his King and lord, who would reward him. Indeed he was received in Lisbon with tremendous honours: solemn processions issued from every cathedral in the realm, vibrating sermons were preached, and Manuel wrote to the Holy See the tale of the spectacular defence of Cochin. So far as we know, however, nothing more material was done for Duarte

Pacheco. The King perhaps was rather spoiled by having too many heroes at his beck and call!

With all these things, though much was still left of the glamorous haze, the Indian picture was becoming clear. The prospect was quite different from the peaceful walk-over the Portuguese had planned, in which numbers of grateful (and Christian!) Indian princes would welcome their co-religionists from overseas, and gladly close their ports to the obnoxious Moslem traders. The hard fact that emerged was of an almost wholly heathen continent, disliking the Moslem Arab who exploited the natives, but not unmindful of the profit derived from their trade. The principal port of the coast was Calicut, and there the Moslem influence was strongest. The Samorin, of whom D.Manuel had hoped so much, blew hot and cold. He probably would have been willing to negotiate with both parties, but finding they were incompatible with each other, from habit more than love, he chose the Arabs. The lesser rulers of Malabar, who disliked him quite as much as they disliked the overbearing Red Sea traders, welcomed the Portuguese – with warmth that varied according to the number of Moslem merchants frequenting their ports. Thus Cochin received the newcomers with open arms, Cannanore with slightly more reserve, and Quilon, further south where the Nestorian Christians had a church and Moslems were few, was wholly disposed to make friends.

But northward up the coast, most of the ports were firmly held in Moslem hands, while Moslem princes ruled over a Hindu population. The magnificent town and harbour of Goa had been wrested from the Hindu realm of Vijayanagar by the Turkish lords of Bijapur and the Deccan, and the great kingdom of Cambay, whence cotton textiles were exported all over the East, was dominated by a dynasty of Moslem sultans. The Arab lands stretched westwards to the gates of the Red Sea, and Arab sultanates were established down the east coast of Africa, from Mogadishu to Sofala, the most southerly point of Indian Ocean navigation. It was into this almost closed circle of Moslem powers that Portugal, quite suddenly, had broken.

There had been great surprise and even some panic at first, but reaction was bound to follow. How long would it take for the powers of Islam to realise and concentrate their strength? How could a few ships arriving once a year from thousands of leagues away, battered and tempest-tossed during a six months voyage, face organized resistance?

The Soldan of Egypt was the great hope of his co-religionists. A mighty fleet could be built at Suez to launch in the Red Sea. The Moslem ports of India would be open for this navy; Calicut had ships and would also help. At the same time Venice – beloved Venice! – would be aiding and abetting in the background out of sight.

All this was known in Lisbon, but Portugal did not worry. Since it appeared to be a matter of sea-power there was no cause for alarm. The Portuguese were few in number but they were better seamen and had better ships. Their navigators were the most skilled in the world; the charts and maps by which they sailed filled rival powers with envy and Lisbon with spies. Already they had friends and allies in India. As for the Indian Moslems – individuals and native states – if any of these wished for peace, Portugal was prepared to grant it. The enemy, then as always, was the ancestral foe, who from the lands beside the Enclosed Sea where the Prophet arose, had spread in days of old over the western desert and across the narrow Straits to Europe, conquering the Visigothic realms of Christian Spain. That outrage had been recently avenged when Castile thrust the Moors out of Granada. There still remained the Holy Land downtrodden by the Infidel, and the Turkish menace lately had raised its head. But students of signs of the times were quite convinced with Duarte Galvão that the sands were running out and Prophecy about to be fulfilled. When Portugal and Prester John (Abyssinia) should meet by the Red Sea, then the liberation of Jerusalem would be at hand.

That was not all. The whole vast golden East was there to be explored, evangelized – and exploited, why not? The labourer is worthy of his hire and the far fountainhead of spices would reward him. There was Ceylon – Taprobana of the Ancients – whence rubies came, cinnamon grew, and elephants were bred; and further off Malacca glowed like a rainbow at the end of the earth. And what about the Spice Islands in the Far East? The aroma of cloves was wafted across the Indian seas. Earthly paradises all these, destined to become gardens of the Lord, recompensing the warriors of the Faith who were to carry there the banner of the Cross. Thus Manuel lived in an atmosphere of mystic joy, of dreams come true, of having been entrusted with a mission from on high that was to be infinitely rewarding, both in terms of spiritual merit and material profit.

Shortage of means to bring about all this did not appal so great a

faith. Yet Portugal about that date had a population of less than two
million, and half of these at least would not be fighting men. Crews for
a fleet of any size had to be combed out from the highways and hedges,
while fields remained untilled. Lads pressed straight from the plough
were sent on board ships they had never seen before. "Speak to them
language they can understand!" one captain said to his pilot, seeing the
helmsman's wheel turn wildly to the cry of "Starboard!" or "Lar-
board! " Resourcefully, they had a string of onions and another one of
garlic tied respectively on each side of the ship, and this worked like a
charm. To the orders of "Garlic!" and of "Onions!" the ship crossed
the bar and kept her course. Even an inland Portuguese has got salt in
his blood, and landlubbers soon became hearty seamen.

This episode occurred with the fleet sailing for India in 1505 — the
greatest armada yet sent east. In answer to rumours of hostilities preparing at Suez, the King had decided that permanent forces must be
kept in India. Accordingly twenty-four ships were armed with 1500
men, commanded by a Governor-General vested with viceregal powers.
He would remain in India for three years and so would his subordinates
the captains of fortresses that should be built, with men-at-arms and
officials in charge of trading posts. The ships bearing the precious pepper must be sent home every year, but a squadron would remain behind, cruising around the Indian Ocean to protect the bases by the
coast and intercept all Arab shipping bound for the Red Sea.

The first man to be chosen by the King to carry out these measures
was a fidalgo named Tristão da Cunha. The reason of this choice is not
apparent. Tristão da Cunha was an able man there is no doubt, but was
he so outstanding as to impose selection among the many remarkable
men who frequented the court? He was the son of the High Chamberlain of Manuel's father, the Infante D.Fernando, and so must have been
well known to the King, but of his early career there is no record, nor
has he left any deep mark in history. Perhaps he would have done
brilliantly as Governor of India, but that we shall never know, for just
as everything was ready and the fleet about to sail, Tristão da Cunha
was seized with sudden blindness. This state proved only temporary,
happily for him, but though he recovered his sight within the year, it
was too late. The fleet could not be held up, so the great honour passed
him by. At the last moment, hurriedly, the King had sent for D.Francis-
co de Almeida, second son of the Count of Abrantes.

This choice surprised no one for D.Francisco was a brilliant figure, distinguished in camp and court. In his youth he had acquired renown fighting as volunteer in the wars of Granada. On returning to Portugal he had enjoyed the favour of D.João II. In addition to his military exploits, D.Francisco was a skilled seaman, versed in problems of cosmography, and as such had taken part in the delicate negotiations concerning the dividing line of Tordesillas. Experienced as he was on land and sea, accustomed to commanding men and serving kings, such a person was fitted to be Governor of India. That he should only have been thought of as a second choice seems strange. Indeed the King himself appears to have been afraid that D.Francisco might not like being sent for as a stop-gap. Damião de Gois says that he was accorded special favours to make up for any fancied slight, and the chroniclers all spread themselves describing the flattering and almost apologetic reception given him by D.Manuel. He would be distinguished by the title of Viceroy, declared the King, once he had reached the Indian coast and built some fortresses; he was to maintain princely state with a resplendent guard of halbardiers; he would have power of life and death over his subordinates and negotiate at his discretion war or peace with Indian kings. No subject had ever before been raised to so great honour.

D.Francisco kissed his sovereign's hand and made appropriate loyal speeches. On March 25th 1505, wearing a black satin tunic and a frilled tabard, with a rich chain around his shoulders, he rode down to the waterside upon a mule caparisoned in velvet with gold fringes. In front of him marched his viceregal bodyguard of eighty men dressed in black velvet jackets with purple satin sleeves, slashed breeches with coloured stripes, white shoes, caps of satin with white plumes on their head and golden halbards in their hands.

Before them all, prancing on a white horse, came young Lourenço, D.Francisco's handsome son, carrying his father's banner. His French tunic had wide brocaded sleeves lined with crimson satin, slashed and caught up with golden roses. A gold enamelled girdle encircled his waist, his white breeches had a brocade lining; his hat of crimson satin with golden brooches and a white plume was suspended from his shoulders by a blue taffeta band, so leaving bare his curly head to the admiring glances of ladies pressing at the palace windows.

All the fidalgos following wore their most splendid clothes; the ships were all flying their flags; the Viceroy's boat, awaiting to row him on board, was hung with white and purple velvet awnings fringed with gold, and fluttered with crimson damask banners. A thundering salvo of artillery sounded as the ships glided downstream, and anchored at Belem to sail the following morning.

D.Francisco took with him a long and detailed paper of instructions, both concerning the voyage and his mission in India. This must begin by building fortresses on the East coast of Africa — at Sofala, with the agreement of the local sheikh, and at Kilwa where the tribute imposed by Vasco da Gama was to be collected from the Sultan. If possible he was to reconnoitre all that coast as far as Cape Gardafui. Then, crossing over to India, a fortress must be built on the island of Angediva, which should be a convenient base in a central position.

Letters and presents and great friendship were to be offered to Cochin and Cannanore, but war was to be waged on Calicut, unless the Samorin should repent of his past misdeeds and offer compensation for the massacre of Cabral's men and the plundered factory. Ships must be detailed to patrol the coast, visiting Chaul, Dabul, the ports of Cambay, and Ormuz on the Persian Gulf. Peace was to be granted to anyone who desired it, in exchange for a reasonable tribute. Discipline must be rigorously enforced; men must behave themselves ashore, giving the natives "all good treatment." All harbour dues were to be scrupulously paid, and any man who did what he should not must be severely punished. In everthing and everywhere justice should be observed.

Having despatched the pepper fleet from Cochin, the Viceroy was to sail to the Arabian coast and choose a site for a fortress at the entrance of the Red Sea. Then, at the earliest opportunity he must visit Ceylon — perhaps he might even make his headquarters there. Thence he could easily proceed to Malacca. Wonders were told of Malacca, the emporium of the Far East; there ought to be a fortress there if only to keep out Arab traders. Rather a heavy programme to be included in a three years' mandate, it would seem. Of course D.Francisco must be guided by circumstances and conditions found on the spot, but let him remember that Malacca and the Red Sea were priorities!

The fleet sailed. The King waited and wrote enthusiastic letters to Cardinal Ximenes. On the verandah of his royal palace perched aloft he sat, overlooking the broad estuary where tall ships rocked at anchor. His young queen sat beside him, and their baby daughter, the Infanta D.Isabel, played by her father's chair.

But the King's thoughts were not on the domestic scene. Before him stood a captain returned last year from the Indian seas: bearded and bronzed and thin, a man in middle life, with hatchet face and eagle nose, and a compelling eye. D.Manuel and he discussed oriental politics, the Indian Ocean and the map of Asia. Together they were studying a plan that was to cover the known world from Africa to China. To this man everything seemed easy. But, he warned his sovereign, it was no enterprise for swashbuckling adventurers or swelled heads: "India," he said, "was the most dangerous thing in the world for vain men full of wind!"

Did Manuel at that time sense the genius of Afonso de Albu-querque? That is by no means certain. The King was not, so far as may be seen, really a judge of men. Studying his appointments through the years, we cannot fail to be impressed by the hit or miss policy that seemed to govern his selections. His fortune was to have around him many able men, and this he owed in great part to his predecessor. Indeed, throughout the glorious first half of D.Manuel's reign we feel the projection beyond the grave of the tremendous personality of D.João II. All the first acts of the grand drama of expansion in the East had been prepared by D.João and executed by men of his making: Vasco da Gama, as we have seen, was one of these, and Duarte Pacheco Pereira – explorer, cosmographer, mathematician, seaman, and epic hero – was another. D. Francisco de Almeida had also enjoyed D.João's confidence, and so had this Afonso de Albuquerque, of the royal body-guard and equerry to the late king, who had served his apprenticeship of arms in Africa, who was able with equal assurance to navigate a ship, manoeuvre fleets at sea, command armies on land, and cope with prob-lems of diplomacy and statesmanship. Where he had acquired all these skills is not apparent. He first appears upon the scene in 1503, in full use of his many-sided talents.

Though this had been a shared command its success had been largely due to Albuquerque, in great part through the tact he showed in han-dling native rulers. He made good use of his three months in India to take stock of everything and observe all that he could see of local problems – political, military and nautical – studying among other things the direct course from Cannanore to Mozambique, together with a native pilot. "Be careful, he may prove a traitor! " the other captains warned, but Albuquerque, who always knew his man, said this one would be true, and made a record voyage across the Indian Ocean. He had arrived in Lisbon at the end of July and there was very well received, declare the chroniclers – but not at first, we gather from his own account. The petty spite and jealousy that followed Albuquerque's career must have been already at work, for he says he found his deeds and services "effaced before Your Highness, hidden, and attributed to whom they did not belong, before I was heard, or could plead for justice. Without any human intervention, as Your Highness knows, Our Lord was pleased it should be rendered me; you learned the truth and recognized my services, and granted me honour and reward."

This is absolutely all we know of that obscure intrigue. What is certain is that the King, in what must have been a series of interviews, became so impressed by the personality and ideas of Afonso de Albuquerque that he decided this must be the man to succeed D.Francisco de Almeida as governor of India when, in 1508, his three years' commission should have expired. Meanwhile, Albuquerque was to return to the Indian Ocean, bearing with him the Letters Patent of his future appointment, which were, however, to be kept secret till the Viceroy's term of office had elapsed. Present orders were to sail with his cousin Tristão da Cunha, now hale and well, who would command the pepper fleet of 1506. Together they would build a fortress on the Island of Socotra by the Red Sea, then Tristão would depart for India, while Albuquerque remained with five ships and 400 men, patrolling the Arabian seas and visiting the Persian Gulf, particularly the port of Ormuz, which controlled the trade of the Middle East. In 1508 he would sail to India and take over the government from D.Francisco de Almeida.

There is much talk and argument about Afonso de Albuquerque's imperial plan. Was he acting upon his own initiative, or following instructions laid down by D.Manuel before he sailed? The "regimento" he carried with him has not survived. Reading his letters, however, we deduce that he was executing point by point a pre-determined programme. Obeying orders? Quite! But from what we know of the man it would be difficult to doubt that he himself had suggested those orders and drawn up the sequence to be followed, in the King's name. And exceeded sometimes? Of course! When the subordinate is built on a much larger scale than his commander, then opportunity must lead to independent action.

Meanwhile news from India had been gratifying. D.Francisco de Almeida had captured strongholds in East Africa and consolidated positions in India. Ably assisted by his son, who was chief captain of the Indian fleet, he enforced Portuguese naval supremacy by issuing a system of permits – like those called navicerts in modern times – without which no ship was allowed to cross the Indian Ocean. Young D.Lourenço visited Ceylon; father and son together overcame hostilities at Cannanore, where Moslem intrigues had resulted in outbreak of war. No opportunity was found to sail for Malacca or the Red Sea, because of the Egyptian fleet which reached the Indian coast in 1507 – twelve powerful ships and galleys manned by Turks and Levantines – and Venetians – all the most valiant warriors of the Middle East, joined off the coast of Gujarat by forty galleys of the King of Cambay. The Viceroy's son came in for the first clash and died heroically in an unequal fight at Chaul.

"He who has eaten the cockerel must kill the cock, or pay the price!" D.Francisco remarked grimly on hearing the bad news. He gathered nineteen ships and 1600 men and sailed north to meet the Egyptian fleet, which he found and destroyed in Dio harbour. The Sultan's galleys all were burned, his captain, Mir Hussein, fled inland; Malik Ayaz, the Russian renegade who commanded the King of Cambay's fleet and had been careful not to let himself be heavily involved, came off the fence when he saw how the battle turned, and prostrated himself before the Viceroy's feet. This victory was decisive. It was the last serious attempt to challenge Portuguese supremacy over the Indian Ocean.

Afonso de Albuquerque meanwhile, having bidden a glad farewell at Socotra to Tristão da Cunha, his joint commander, sailed for the Persian Gulf. He had a fleet of six ships and 400 men but, after a voyage in tropical waters which various circumstances had prolonged for sixteen months. both ships and men were in a sorry case. Supplies of every kind were exhausted: ropes and sailcloth were depleted; water barrels were cracked; the gunpowder was wet; the crossbows had no arrows left; the lances all were rotten. Out of the crews few gunners had survived; of carpenters and coopers there were only one or two, and half the men were too ill to be of any use, added to which there were only provisions left to last about a week.

With such a fleet Albuquerque swept round the Oman coast, con-

quering as he went by the towns of Kalyat, Kurhat, Muscat, and Orfa-
çan, and anchored before Ormuz — Ormuz, queen of the Persian Gulf,
jewel of the Arab world, into whose warehouses were poured by sea
and land the riches of Persia, Egypt, Turkestan, India and the Far East,
whose harbour bristled with a hundred ships all armed for battle.
Afonso de Albuquerque came and saw and conquered Ormuz with his
few rotten craft, in one conclusive action. He imposed tribute on the
King and with his men began building a fortress.

Was he obeying instructions laid down — or was he acting on his own
responsibility? His captains, very bored and anxious to be chasing Moslem shipping off Bab-el-Mandeb, declared he was exceeding his commission. After some stormy scenes they left him and slipped off to
India, to the Viceroy who, jealous of Albuquerque perhaps, and certainly in need of men, gave them no punishment for desertion but took
them with him to the naval battle of Dio.

Needless to say there was a coolness when Afonso de Albuquerque
arrived in 1508 to take charge of the government of India. The Viceroy,
after a most unseemly show of reluctance, which went so far as to
arrest his successor, in 1509 was persuaded at last to sail for Portugal,
but on the way got himself killed beside the Cape, skirmishing with the
Hottentots.

In India, meanwhile, Afonso de Albuquerque was stepping up the
pace. The Viceroy had been dynamic but the new governor was a
whirlwind. "Men do not eat the bread of idleness with me!" he told
the King. Certainly they did not; it was a thing he himself never tasted.
"He neither slept nor rested day or night!" João de Barros says, and
his men had to follow panting after. Some cursed and some adored, but
nobody had a dull moment. Every year the volumes of letters that went
home — dictated by the Governor to nodding secretaries in the still
watches of the night — told of new triumphs and sensations. In 1510
Goa was taken from the Turks of Bijapur by a force of 1680 men
against some thirty times that number. The Island of Goa, with its
magnificent town and fertile lands around, was the first territorial ac-
quisition of the Portuguese beside the Indian coast. Surrounded by
rivers and therefore highly defensible, it had two splendid ports and,
owing to its central position, its strategic importance was such — says
Albuquerque — that if you lost the whole of India, from Goa you could
win it back.

Between November and April Albuquerque organized Goa — administratively, granting new liberties to the delighted natives who had groaned under the Turkish yoke and now were to be ruled according to their law and customs — defensively, turning everyone, himself included, furiously to fortress building — and diplomatically, receiving with deliberate pomp, ambassadors from Indian princes and the Shah of Persia.

In 1511, leaving in India his best ships and most of the men, the Governor sailed for Malacca, where in the last year of the Viceroy's rule a small fleet had been despatched from Lisbon under Diogo Lopes de Sequeira. The visit had proved unfortunate, owing to the unusual intrigues of Arab traders working upon the treachery of the local ruler. As had happened at Calicut, the factory established ashore was seized and plundered. At least there was no massacre, but 27 prisoners were taken and Diogo Lopes found himself obliged to leave them behind when he sailed.

Afonso de Albuquerque sailed for Malacca with all the forces he could muster. It was nearly a year before he reappeared once more in India.

"You never send me enough men," he told the King, "Malacca would not have given me so much trouble if we had been more than 800 white men, with 200 Malabaris." This exact number the Malays had soon found out. Albuquerque says that they counted the wounded and counted the graves, and knew how many men were sick — "Believe me, Your Highness, they were not three men out!" But Malacca was taken in spite of the accuracy of their arithmetic, their 30,000 men and fighting elephants. The town was found to be replete with treasure like Aladdin's cave.

From Malacca ships were despatched in search of the Spice Islands, an embassy was sent to Siam and to various kinglets of Java and Sumatra, and happy relations were established with Chinese merchants visiting the Straits.

All this accompanied by feverish fortress building, to leave Malacca in a good state of defence: "Never worry about your fortresses," wrote Albuquerque to the King, "even if you hear they are besieged once, or twice, or ten times. So long as there be a few Portuguese upon the battlements with helmets on their heads they never will be taken! " And Malacca, defended by 300 men and a few ships, held firm.

Time was short, for India could not be left too long, but Albuquerque was used to working at top speed and making everybody do the same. The fortress was finished in one third of the normal time. The Governor organized the garrison, appointed officials, built a church, struck coin, and made the natives happy by just government such as they never knew before.

Back to India with three rotten craft, worm-eaten and corroded by years in tropical waters. The flagship struck a rock and fell to pieces on the way; the Governor and crew saved themselves on a raft, and all the gold of Malacca went to the bottom.

Reaching India at last, Goa was found closely besieged by a strong Turkish force, which Albuquerque overthrew in a joint military and naval operation.

1513 saw the conqueror preparing to sail for the Red Sea, where no Christian fleet had yet penetrated . . . D.Manuel, a little dizzy, read his Indian mail. Pile upon pile of letters from the Governor – letters from other people too: shouts of delight, squeals of dismay, paeans of praise, bitter complaints – everybody was seething. We fancy that D.Manuel shook his head. A brilliant man without a doubt, this Afonso de Albuquerque – but was he not moving almost too fast? Might he not be a dangerous firebrand? He certainly was that! wrote cautious spirits who could not keep up. He will lead all your ships and men to ruin, and empty your exchequer!

The King himself, it would appear, when genius and mediocrity stood side by side, could understand mediocrity much better. He was a quiet and steady man. Afonso de Albuquerque, with his superb self-confidence, his disregard for the impossible, made him uneasy. The conquests nonetheless filled Manuel with pride and joy. Surely the Lord looked favourably upon his undertakings! D.Manuel wrote letters full of enthusiasm to the cities of his realm and the Archbishop of Braga, Primate of all Spain. For each victory in turn devout processions of thanksgiving were held in every church. To the man who was winning them in India he was careful not to say too much.

IX

The Dark Kingdoms of Africa

From the intoxicating glamour of the East – the "fumes of India" as it has been called – from subtle complications of oriental politics, D.Manuel could turn for rest and change to the simpler African problems.

This had been the first field of Portuguese expansion and discovery, prolonged over a period of seventy years. During that time extensive relations commercial, cultural and religious, had been established with the kingdoms and tribes of the West Coast. Princes of Senegal and Gambia came to court with embassies, and hailed the King of Portugal as arbiter of their disputes. Portuguese merchants and explorers sailed upriver to the markets of Cantor; they penetrated inland to the desert town of Timbuktu, and wandered over the regions of Futajalon and countries of the Upper Niger. Cosmographers, such as Duarte Pacheco Pereira, journeyed from the coast with compasses and astrolabes, measuring latitudes and drawing maps. Respectful calls were made upon African chiefs in their round huts, with offers of peace and friendship from the great white king.

The little town and fortress of St George by the Gold Coast – St George of the Mine, they called it – first European settlement in equatorial Africa – had been founded in 1482 by D.João II. It was visited every year by twelve small ships carrying supplies for the garrison, and merchandise to barter with the native tribes around for ivory, malagueta pepper, and gold brought from inland, sometimes as much as 70,000 doubloons worth.

And slaves – Alas! – were profitable too. This was the curse of Africa dating from ages immemorial. Since the days of antiquity the Arabs had supplied slave labour to the Mediterranean lands and Christian conscience only very late awoke to the abuse – an abuse at which

Africans themselves connived, for their chiefs made a very good thing out of it. There is no doubt that Portuguese navigation along the West Coast brought an influx of Negro slaves to Europe, but to hold Portugal responsible for the slave trade, as some writers would do, is unfair. It had existed long before they visited those coasts, and when they came to take part in the profitable traffic, other nations, envious and quite unshocked, awaited the first opportunity to join the racket. After all, was it not for the heathens' highest good to be carried off from regions of fetish-ridden darkness to the light of Christian lands where they might save their souls? A most convenient doctrine made to fit the case, but sincerely believed by many.

In spite of all such aberrations the fact remains that Portuguese expansion overseas was largely impelled by the hope of winning souls for Holy Mother Church. The extension of Christendom throughout the world had been Henry the Navigator's dream and the same vision shone before the eyes of his successors. The preacher and the explorer and the trader travelled abreast – indeed they sometimes exchanged functions. We know that Diogo Gomes, a navigator in the service of the Infante, proclaimed Christianity with much success to the chief Nomimansa by the river Gambia. In 1503, the captain of the castle of St. George of the Mine, having made friends with the sheriffs and chiefs of tribes of the outlying country, persuaded them to enter the Christian fold. The factor, Diogo de Alvarenga, in a letter to D.Manuel, describes how the captain's embassy, bearing a cross aloft, walked in solemn procession into the presence of the King of Afuto. When the ambassador had said his piece, the King had been baptized together with six of his lords. Three hundred people were converted on the spot, and parents with children in their arms had struggled for precedence at the font. The Vicar General of St. George had improvised a chapel for them with an altar and a cross – "the which they reverence more than one can say." The King was baptized by the name of João. He sent his son to live with the captain in the fortress, after having him christened as Manuel.

Ships not exceeding fifty tons could reach the river port of Gwato, twelve leagues from the coast, which served the capital of Benin nine leagues inland. When Manuel was still a boy, João Afonso de Aveiro had discovered "the great city of Benin," as Duarte Pacheco calls it. This writer visited the place four times, and he describes it as an unwalled town, a league in length, of clay built houses covered with palm thatch, and a wide trench all round by way of sole defensive work. In the deep forest shades around the men of Benin practised heathen rites and offered human sacrifices. Yet they had a strange elementary culture of their own and they were skilled workers in brass and ivory.

The King of Benin had welcomed the Portuguese as beings from an unknown world. He wanted to find out more about these strangers of mysterious origin, who seemed to be so wise and were apparently so rich. He readily had agreed to send one of his chiefs to Portugal to look into these matters and to bring back teachers.

This envoy, whose dignified repose of manner much impressed the court, was welcomed festively and treated to all of the best. He was amazed by everything he saw. They sent him home dressed in fine European clothes and bearing many rich gifts for his king from D.João II, accompanied by brotherly advice and exhortation. The missionaries delivered this. We are told that the King of Benin listened with delight but always evaded the issue. The chroniclers say conversions were few. The sovereign himself, João de Barros writes, was moved by the wish "for powerful support against his neighbours rather than a desire for baptism."

Which probably was true. The King of Benin was continually at war. Yet, as late as 1516, it seems he still was toying with the idea of conversion. One, Duarte Pires, writing from Benin city, tells D.Manuel that the king "wants to be your friend and never speaks of anything but matters of Our Lord and concerning yourself." The Portuguese were treated with peculiar honour; they had free run of the royal residence and sat at meat with the king's son. The priests enjoyed special favour and accompanied the king to war. Until he had overcome his enemies, the sovereign explained, he had not time to think about conversion. Nonetheless he consented that his son and many of his chiefs should be baptized and that a church should be built in Benin city. The converts, says Duarte Pires, are being taught to read, and "Your Highness must know that they learn very well."

It seems, however, that all this effort petered out. The white men in the swamps and forests of Benin did not last long enough for permanent results to be established by their mission. This witching land of Guinea, João de Barros writes, is a garden of Paradise. It yields all fruits desirable to man, and ivory, gold, leather and wax and pepper in abundance. The people are mostly friendly and ready to accept the Christian

faith. A very Eden in all things, but at its gates as in the days of our
first fathers' fall, the Lord has placed an angel with a flaming sword —
"that of the mortal fevers which prevent us penetrating deep into this
garden from which flow the golden rivers."

But penetration went on nonetheless and some of it was deep. The
wide mouth of the mighty river Zaire which sweetened the salt waves of
the ocean thirty leagues to sea, lured caravels to sail upstream into the
vast kingdom of Manicongo — Mani in local dialect meaning "a king."
Disembarking upon the river shore, the Portuguese had journeyed inland to the capital Congo Ambasse, where, naked to the waist, the King
sat on his ivory throne, a horsetail hanging over his shoulder, an ivory
bracelet on his arm and a tall headdress like a tiara on his brow. Respectfully the strangers kissed the royal hand on bended knee, as they
would have done to a European prince, and friendly relations were at
once established.

The realm of Manicongo was the greatest polity the Portuguese had
found in Africa, and its people were eager for intercourse. Natives of
the Congo were sent to Portugal and returned home dressed to the
nines and with glowing tales to tell of marvels seen and good treatment
received amid the wonders of civilization. The King of Congo was afire
to bring his own kingdom up to standard. He called out for everything
Portuguese. The Congo was to be another Portugal! He sent an embassy
with a list of his needs: he wanted stone masons to teach his people to
build houses like those seen in Lisbon, and master carpenters to show
them how to fashion wood; he asked for yokes of oxen to plough the
fields of Africa, and farmers to teach agriculture; bakers must come to
show African housewives how to make bread, and schoolmasters to
teach people to read, and priests to instruct them in the Christian faith
that everyone might be baptized!

How much of all this it was possible to send is not quite clear, but
we gather that something went of everything. The Congolese ambassador returned a baptized Christian to his native land, a godson to the
King and Queen, rejoicing in the name of D.João da Silva. His followers
had also been led to the font by some of the noblest in the land.

The King of Congo's enthusiasm knew no bounds. The Portuguese
embassy which brought the envoys home was welcomed with flourishes
of ivory trumpets and the clash of cymbals. Fervent speeches were
made. The King would be baptized forthwith and he would be named

João like his brother of Portugal, while the Queen of course must be Leonor! Their eldest son was christened Afonso, after the young Portuguese Prince, and the King's uncle chose the name of Manuel, because he said he was a duke like the King's cousin, Duke of Beja.

There was much feasting and rejoicing; the King embraced everyone all around; a church was erected in haste; the priests and friars preached and celebrated Mass; converts were catechized and taught to read and write — but, only too soon, the angel with the flaming sword manifested his presence. The missionaries died one by one. Already the Queen's baptism had been hastened for fear that no one would be left to celebrate it, and she was christened by a fever-stricken priest before the church was finished.

Four of the friars survived and stayed behind when most of the members of the Portuguese mission went home. A native who had learned to read and write in Portugal continued to help teaching the children. In spite of all set-backs due to the deadliness of the climate, Portugal did not lost interest. In 1504 D.Manuel sent out a new batch of theologians and men of letters and schoolmasters and choirmasters to teach the organ and plainchant. These brought with them church vestments, crosses and chalices, and "all things necessary for divine service."

The King continued to be instructed in dogma and doctrine, but sad to say, the more he heard, the more his enthusiasm cooled. Could a Christian really have no more than one wife? Such a religion could not be for him! Most of his henchmen felt the same way — monogamy could only be a counsel of perfection! There might have been a mass return to heathenism had it not been for the heir to the throne, the Prince Afonso.

This was a most remarkable young man — intelligent and earnest. His conversion had been no matter of mere expediency but a real change of heart. Even when persecuted by his backsliding father he remained firm. As soon as he succeeded to the throne (in 1506, it is presumed) Christianity became the official religion of the land, and the King decreed that all idols would be burnt.

During the whole of his long reign of 37 years, King Afonso I, the Christian ruler of Congo, laboured for the enlightenment and progress of his people. He learned to read Portuguese and studied the Scriptures and lives of the saints, so earnestly that he often forgot to eat by day and at night fell asleep over his books. "He knows the Prophets and the Gospel of Our Lord and all things of Holy Mother Church better than we do . . ." wrote the delighted Vicar General, Rui de Aguiar, in 1516, adding that this king preached to his people "with much love and charity," every day in church after Mass — "begging them for love of Our Lord to be converted and turn to God . . ." He spoke so beautifully that, Rui de Aguiar declares, he seems "an angel rather than a man! "

Of course this fervent and sincere Christianity was cut upon the 16th century pattern. From Europe it had been received entire, with all that period's lofty flights and its intolerance. The words "compel them to come in," from the parable of the wedding feast, were taken literally by Christians of that generation. If people would not see the truth for their own good, it must be forced upon them! In the Congo, therefore, those who kept idols in their home, or who practised witchcraft were punished by sentence of death.

Alongside religion, education flourished. Young Africans were sent to Portugal to learn, and teachers were sent to the Congo where schools were opened, not for boys only, but even for girls. It seems that the King's sister was a pioneer in feminine education. She herself learned to read when already sixty years old, and taught girls in the school that she had founded.

All this effort was backed and blessed by Portugal. Begun by D.João II, it was continued by D.Manuel and carried on later by his son, D.João III. All the young African students in Portugal were maintained at the royal expense, in monasteries or else at court where they might acquire culture and good manners. The King of Congo's sons, Henrique and Manuel, were sent to train for holy orders and to qualify for high ecclesiastical distinction. D.Pedro de Sousa, the King's cousin, who had first come to Portugal with his wife in 1493, remained there for ten years, mostly in the convent of St Eloy, where he studied theology. His wife was often seen at court where she enjoyed the favour and friendship of Queen Maria who, says Damião de Gois, took pleasure in her company and conversation.

With all this there was no attempt upon the part of Portugal at political or military conquest. The intercourse between the kings had begun and was continued on a tone of equality, as brother sovereigns, heads of independent states. Quite naturally, the King of Portugal is seen more often in the part of elder brother and adviser. Many suggestions are offered to his colleague, but nothing like an order. In everything it is assumed that the King of Congo as a Christian ruler, would desire to conform to the usage and ceremonial observed in the courts of Christendom.

Like other Christian kings he ought to have his coat of arms to display on the royal standard. Portuguese heralds therefore got busy devising appropriate bearings for him. Some great victory should be commemorated in this way: D.Afonso had won his throne through a fierce battle in which he had triumphed over his heathen enemies thanks to the intervention of St. James, the warrior Apostle. So, upon a field gules were blazoned five arms, each one brandishing a sword; above was a cross argent and the cockle shells which are the emblem of St. James. Below, a black idol broken in fragments was depicted on each side of a shield bearing the five *quinas* of Portugal − to show, as the delighted king explained to his subjects, how Christianity had come to the Congo through Portuguese action.

The question of the King of Congo's signature was also given earnest thought by D.Manuel and his council. A paper preserved in the National Archives sets forth their findings: "This is the signature which it seems to the King our Lord that from now on the King of Manicongo ought to use: *ElRey dom a°*"

The model is repeated seven times below with a few slight variations. The cross to figure in the middle suggests that though King Afonso read easily, he had not found it necessary − or perhaps possible − to master the art of writing.

All this was debated in 1512, when Manuel sent Simão da Silva with an embassy to the Congo. A list has survived of the many things to be presented on this occasion: six horses with a couple of mares, several donkeys and half a dozen carts, a pair of greyhounds and two hares, also, if possible, a falcon. There was a camp bed for the King with the necessary bed-clothes, and a small tent, curtains and cushions, a golden sword with velvet scabbard, a gaily trimmed hat lined with coloured silk or taffeta, and also a gilt Venetian mirror. Two high-backed silk upholstered chairs and a dining table were included; a dozen torches and a few candles, just "as samples because there is much wax there but they don't know how to use it." Clothes such as shirts and caps were provided, as well as slippers and shoes and cloaks for the royal wardrobe.

Agriculture was not forgotten: grafts of trees were sent to be tried out, fig trees being specially mentioned. Flax seed was also sent and wheat and barley — "a little of each" — peach stones and those of apricots, almonds and hazel nuts and chestnuts to be sown. Possibilities for the kitchen garden were also considered, and seeds were provided of cabbages, lettuce, radishes, pulse of different kinds, beans, melons, pumpkins, cucumbers, onions and garlic.

Artisans were also despatched — the first lot sent by D.João II most probably had died — smiths now embarked, a carpenter, a stone mason, a tiler, to make roof tiles, a shoemaker, a rope maker, and a farmer to break oxen for the plough and teach Africans how to make cheese — "because there all the milk is wasted." A tailor and a barber also went to teach their crafts, and it was suggested as desirable to find a man who knew how to make sugar.

The ambassador, Simão da Silva, was at the same time enjoined by Manuel to see that a fine house of stone and cement with an upper storey were built for his royal colleague. This would be "better for his health and safety. In all things we should like to see him live as a faithful Christian and after the manner of Christians! "

All this betokens a sincere and wholly altruistic wish to raise the standard of living in Africa, for Portugal had nothing to gain from introducing such improvements. There was no idea of settling Portuguese peasants on land of their own in the Congo when even the little farms of Portugal were short of labour.

D.Manuel furthermore felt that his African colleague might like to organize his royal household after the European pattern. Simão da Silva therefore brought with him a list of all the functionaries at court, such as High Chamberlain, Standard-Bearer, Master of Horse, Keeper of the Royal Robes, Controller of the Privy Purse — and so on, down to the humbler offices of porters, butlers, pantlers and cooks, that the King of Congo "should he so wish, may establish the same rule in his realms."

It also seemed important that King Afonso should be shown how justice was administered in Portugal. For his enlightenment Manuel not only sent doctors of law, but a copy of the recently printed *Ordenações Manuelinas* — the latest revision of the code by which his predecessors on the throne had governed. There every crime and offence was set forth with the appropriate punishment for each. The King of Congo listened wide-eyed while each detail was read to him. Such minutiae seemed to the African a counsel of perfection. "Tell me," he cried laughing, "what is the punishment in Portugal for treading on the ground?"

Hardly a legal system that could be transferred wholesale to the African bush, and King Afonso had the sense not to attempt as much.

Wherever possible, however, he was anxious to keep step, and when his brother of Portugal informed him that Christian kings were expected to send ambassadors offering allegiance to the Holy See, he was willing and eager to conform to custom.

D.Manuel suggested that he should send his cousin D.Pedro to Rome, accompanied by twelve persons "of noble birth, discreet and prudent." Six servants ought to be enough to swell his train with dignity, and all would travel in great style from Portugal to Rome, at Manuel's expense.

Under D.Pedro's wing should go the young Prince Henrique, one of the King of Congo's sons. He too had spent some years in Portugal and – "praise be to the Lord, he is well taught and grounded in the Faith ... he already knows Latin and the Oration of Obedience will be given by him in Latin to the Pope." At the same time D.Manuel was petitioning the Holy Father that D.Henrique should be enthroned as first Bishop of Congo.

But the young man was still far from canonical age. Therefore it is not surprising that the petition was only granted six years later. Even then the black prince had to be given a special dispensation to be made bishop – not of the Congo indeed, but of Utica – when only twenty-four years old.

Ruled by a Christian king, protected and instructed by the pioneer nation of interracial intercourse – might not the Congo have been led 450 years ago into the fellowship of Christendom, to share the cultural heritage of Greece and Rome? The vision was bright but it was premature. The vast forests of Africa still harboured in their depths – untouchable, unreachable – the spectres of witchcraft and superstition and deadly disease. To bring the daylight through required more than the efforts of one extraordinary man and a few fever-stricken expatriates.

For centuries still the Angel with the Flaming Sword continued to stand at the gate of the African Eden. The missionaries died one by one and had every few years to be renewed. Envoys succumbed, sometimes even before they reached their journey's end, like Simão da Silva with his carefully thought out instructions and constructive plans, who died on his way to the Congo capital, passing his mission to his second-in-command. Explorers perished in the wilderness, as did João Afonso de Aveiro in the Benin forests, and many more whose names remain unknown.

Only in modern times and with the help of modern science, modern medicine, and modern means of communication and transport, has the West Coast of Africa become a land of promise and no more the White Man's grave.

But 16th century Portugal was full of hope.

X

The Forests of Brazil

Beside the breezy river on a summer afternoon the King was giving audience in a wooden pavilion built right on the quays of Santos-o-Velho. Observant, eager-eyed, the twelve-year-old page, Damião de Gois, stood not far off.

A ship newly arrived from western seas swung in the stream whence Jorge Lopes Bixorda, concessionnaire of the commerce of brazil wood, was rowed ashore. Following him there came three tall brown men, high-cheeked and Mongol-eyed, with ears and lips and nostrils weighted down by heavy pendents. Their bodies, painted and tattooed, were naked except for girdles of brilliant plumes; each man carried a long bow of dark wood, and arrows winged with parrot's feathers. By their side came a Portuguese who spoke to them in a strange guttural language.

Jorge Lopes Bixorda walked up and introduced the party. These men were natives of the land of Santa Cruz, he said, and they were mighty archers of unfailing marksmanship: should His Highness be interested to see their skill, they would be glad to show him.

The tide was running out to sea. Upon the shining surface of the water swam a few pieces of cork floating swiftly downstream. Together each one of the painted strangers raised his bow and shot at the flotsam as it passed, and every arrow flashed straight to the target.

And then — what did they say or do? The writer leaves us with this picture only, fixed by the wondering eyes of youth. What was the fate of those Brazilian savages brought overseas from the primeval forest in that year of 1513? Did they live long in Portugal? One writer tells us that natives of Brazil soon died in Europe — which fact he attributes to the wonderful Brazilian climate. It is the best in the whole world, therefore those who have not been hardened by the rigours of less happy lands are not prepared to face them. People in Brazil die of old age more often than of illness!

Winter was unknown there, nor great excess of heat. It was a fair land of caressing breezes and leafy trees, of mountains bubbling with fresh streams, of tall grass and forests everlastingly green. Anything might be made to grow there, Caminha said. All the same there was no immediate rush to colonize. Portugal had no surplus population waiting for a chance to settle overseas. Only two decades later did emigration to Brazil start upon a large scale, promoted by a government convinced that it was necessary to occupy or lose.

Meanwhile, in the reign of D.Manuel, the problem did not arise. For Manuel in Portugal the case was one of what the French call the "embarrassment of riches." The commitments of Africa and India had been mounting up before this new Land of the True Cross — Land of Parrots — Land of Brazil — had risen from the sea. "Miraculously discovered by the will of Our Lord" — D.Manuel had written joyfully to his parents-in-law — because it was so "necessary and useful to the navigation of India."

Useful it certainly could be to ships that might run short of water or supplies before reaching the Cape, but necessary would hardly seem the word to use when we observe how few of the ships sailing every year from Lisbon to the Orient found themselves obliged to put in at the new continent. Some people have suggested that D.Manuel only said this to make his Castilian kinsmen feel there was no other material interest in the discovery. Delicate issues were involved in exploration of the western hemisphere, owing to the partition line of Tordesillas. In those days and for many years to come, before the invention of the chronometer, precise degrees of longitude were impossible to determine. Exactly how much of the new continent could be included in Portugal's hemisphere? Reconnaissance suggested that the coast, both north and south, soon trailed into the Castilian preserves, so cartographers cooked their maps while small publicity was given to coastal exploration.

Italian observers, panting with curiosity around the wharves of Lisbon, were frustrated at every turn: "The map of this voyage is impossible to obtain," sighed Dominico Malpieri, "for the King has imposed the death penalty on any one who would send it abroad! " But bribery and corruption seldom fail to find a way, as is illustrated by the splendid planisphere which Cantino had copied at great expense for his patron Herdules d'Este. There we see depicted the broken outline of South America, bulging well to the east towards Africa, all glowing with gaudy parrots strutting underneath green trees — the famous trees of brazil wood which were at last to give the land its name.

Many alternative designations had been tried out first. The less known planisphere of Maiollo, drawn at Genoa in 1504, showing further exploration beside a longer line of coast, named the country the "Land of Gonçalo Coelho, also called Vera Cruz." This Gonçalo Coelho was a well-known sea captain, whose son, Duarte, was in after years to be the founding father of the future state of Pernambuco.

As for the name, so differently attributed in various documents, and Manuel's own choice of Santa Cruz, by 1513 we find the King himself referring to "Our Land of Brazil." In spite of all pious protests the material view had prevailed; dye wood being the most useful merchandise found in the country yet, it came to be called exclusively — "Brazil."

The species of this wood that flourished there was a variety of *Leguminosae Cisalpina,* known to Europe since ancient times, but hitherto imported from Asia. That growing in Brazil was of the finest sort. The Indians called it Ibirapitanga, meaning "red wood." It was found in abundance in the forests by the coast — tall trees, some of tremendous girth, with small leaves resembling those of box bushes, and a thorny trunk. In spite of the hardness of the wood, those great trunks had to be hacked through almost to the core to reveal the red vein at the heart. This, even in a gigantic tree, might be no thicker than a man's leg. The wood was very difficult to chop into manageable lengths and very heavy to transport. Without oxen or any other form of animal traction, it might take as much as a year to load a ship.

Even so it seems that the trade was profitable and there was no lack of merchants anxious to embark upon it. Rondinelli, one of those ubiquitous and informative Italian letter-writers to whom historians owe so much, writing from Seville in 1502, says that the King of Portugal has granted a three years concession of Brazilian trade to certain New Christian capitalists, principally one Fernão de Loronha. In exchange for the grant they were to undertake to send six ships every year to explore 300 leagues of coast and build fortresses to defend their discoveries. "The first year they will pay no tax on their profit, but in the second year one fifth, and in the third one quarter. They expect to bring back brazil wood and slaves, and possibly they may find something else of value . . . ." This vague hope shows how far contemporaries were from suspecting the gold and diamonds of Brazil and other mineral riches to be found in the next century.

We gather that the slave trade was relinquished early. It certainly was never brisk. The naked Brazilian Indian, more primitive and fiercer than the African, could not do much to solve anyone's labour problem. Besides, royal orders were to do no violence to the natives. "You will forbid the master and the whole ship's company from doing any harm or injury to the people of the country" ordains the "regimento" carried by Cristóvão Pires, captain of the ship *Bretoa*, which sailed for the Brazilian coast in 1511. A few slaves were brought home nonetheless — we do not know if Bixorda's archers were of the number — but the *Bretoa* carried thirty-five, possibly sold by their own people since kidnapping and coercion were forbidden. Parrots and monkeys and wildcats also figure on the list of marketable goods (the great lords of the 16th century loved menageries!), and cannafistula and other medicinal herbs are included, but certainly for many years to come the principal export of Brazil was dye wood.

At the same time some fortresses had been erected by the coast. Exactly when or how? It would be difficult to say. No record has been found, for instance of the first building of the Pernambuco fortress. We only know that it was there in 1532 and said to have been there already thirty years — which takes us back to the first years of the discovery! It may well be that the fort was built in accordance with Fernão de Loronha's contract of 1502.

Of early settlers in the land there is slight documentary proof. There is of course the famous case of Diogalvares Caramuru, found living with the Indians at Baía twenty years at least after having suffered shipwreck at the beginning of the century; and further south we hear of a mysterious *bacharel* marooned on the Brazilian coast, nor should we forget the famous João Ramalho, patriarch of the future São Paulo, who in 1530 had been living for untold years in the mountains of Piratininga. All these were shipwrecked seafarers, but even in D.Manuel's time we find some indications of deliberate and sustained attempts to people and cultivate Brazil.

Exploration undoubtedly was carried on. It was important to verify the exact limits of the zone assigned to Portugal by the Treaty of Tordesillas. In 1513 a fleet sailed south and reached the River Plate — in debatable longitude and that same year the unhappy Estevão Frois, investigating north of Pernambuco and forced by hostile Indians to leave that coast, found himself sailing in Castilian seas where he was arrested and taken prisoner to Santo Domingo. The kings of Portugal and Castile — beloved son and father-in-law — officially lived in each other's hearts at home, but overseas their subjects showed no mercy to each other. Captivity or death awaited those caught on the wrong side of the dividing line. In vain poor Estevão Frois pleaded that he had only willingly touched lands peacefully owned by Portugal for over twenty years! — a statement which has sparked off endless arguments among historians. Should it be taken literally, and to imply a Portuguese discovery of Brazil in 1493? Or is it only a figure of speech? Unless some document appears to settle the question, it may be argued till the end of time. We gather that Estevão Frois was set at liberty at last, in exchange for another prisoner and not, it would seem, for having proved his case.

There is, however, documentary evidence of definite attempts to colonize from 1516 on. At that date we find D.Manuel ordering officials of the Casa da India to supply axes and hoes and all necessary implements to those who wished to settle in Brazil. The King furthermore desired to find a man "experienced and able to go to Brazil and start a sugar mill." One gathers that the King also appointed captaincies — not on the vast and feudal scale into which his son later carved Brazil, but as an official charge of limited scope and without suzerainty: *capitanias da terra* with authority on land, and *capitanias do mar* to support them at sea.

Little is known about these early settlements or their commanders, but one of them is mentioned as Pero Capico. And it seems that the sugar industry made some progress. In 1519 Pigafetta found indications of sugar plantations round the bay of Rio de Janeiro, and already by 1526, duties were being paid in Lisbon on sugar brought from Pernambuco.

Exasperatingly vague as all these pointers may be, they are sufficient proof that long before D.João III launched his colonizing drive in 1532 Brazil was being taken seriously in Portugal. Henry the Navigator never knew about this "Fourth Part of the World," but his great-nephew and heir refused to be excluded from his share of the new continent.

XI

North African Mirage

Portuguese expansion had started at Ceuta in 1415, when D.João I led his three elder sons across the Straits of Gibraltar to win their knightly spurs fighting the Moors. A century later, when his great-grandson styled himself Lord of the Conquest, Navigation and Commerce of Ethiopia, Persia and India, it might well seem that the Algarve of Africa was purely incidental.

In fact it was far otherwise. The Atlantic shores of North Africa marked the terminus of the great Arab world — the point where western Christendom made direct contact with the vast dominions of Islam that stretched across two continents to the Far East, a dominion which the tiny kingdom of Portugal had braved the unknown seas to challenge.

His predecessors had left to D.Manuel four African strongholds: Ceuta, Alcacer-Ceguer, Tangier and Arzila, commanding the Gibraltar Straits and out to Cape Spartel. There, in the massive castles they had built beside the sea, Portuguese garrisons held firm against every onslaught and practised military exploits in guerilla warfare. Great deeds of valour were performed on either side in raid and counter-raid, spoil exchanged hands, prisoners were taken whose ransom enriched their captors. Skilled captains trained young fidalgos for war, and earned fame as commando leaders. Deported criminals and unemployed adventurers settled in the Algarve Beyond the Sea, in the small towns that grew up within fortress walls, and soon produced a generation of Luso-Moroccans.

To the average young Portuguese of Manuel's reign the African Algarve might be no more than a military school, or even penitentiary where sins could be expiated by crusading merit, but to their rulers the upkeep of these outposts of sovereignty was of strategic and political importance.

The four fortresses were under continual fire. The King of Fez came down to raid them almost every Spring, when pasture land beside the coast was green and luscious for his herds and horses. From the holy city of Chechauen in the grim mountains of the Riff, the warriors of the Prophet swooped to harry Tangier and Arzila. And there was Tetuan – an eagle's nest perched on the rugged heights above a little bay haunted by pirates. Tetuan's sparring partners were Ceuta and Alcacer-Ceguer. Repeated assaults on either side made life exciting.

If all those fierce and valiant soldiers of Islam had lived in harmony with one another, there is no doubt the Christian never could have gained, or kept, a foothold in their country. But as it was the Sheikhs and Alcaides all quarrelled and intrigued and pushed each other out of place and leagued together for the downfall of their rivals. Hence the strange episode of Tetuan, at the beginning of the century.

It is not widely known. No reference is found in the chronicles and documents are scanty: only four of these so far have come to light. The whole affair is like a puzzle with most of its pieces missing.

The principal performers in this little act behind the scenes are familiar enough to students of Luso-Moroccan history. They were no lesser persons than Sidi Ali-ben-Rached, the sanctified Sheriff of Chechauen, and his very well-known son-in-law, El Mandari, Alcaide of Tetuan. Both worthies had played a distinguished part in hostilities against Portuguese fortresses beside the Straits. Then, at the turning of the century, for reasons that we cannot guess, the two decided to pack up and migrate to Tunis with all their families and goods and chattels. For such a major move they thought that Portuguese shipping might be a great help, and in return they offered – Tetuan!

It seems that they approached the captain D.João Afonso de Sousa on the subject and he reported to the King, the draft of whose reply exists: "As for the case of Tetuan," D.Manuel writes on June 13th 1501, "we were glad that you wrote to us in detail on the subject." The King hopes that D.João will give the matter careful consideration and let him know as soon as possible "how the thing might be done, what men you would require and what would be the most convenient time . . . We should welcome your views upon this matter." This is all that may be gathered from a couple of cryptic paragraphs in a letter mainly about other things.

Subsequent messages were certainly exchanged. There is a letter signed in Arabic at Tetuan from El Mandari, dated January 22nd (year unspecified, but probably 1502), acknowledging a missive from D.Manuel delivered by one Afonso Caldeira, to which El Mandari declares he has replied at length, propounding "all my will and intentions so that there remains no more to be said." The envoy, adds the Alcaide, made a most favourable impression – so well bred and courteous was he and so apparently trustworthy! El Mandari had felt no fear to place "our lives and honour in his hands."

We suppose it was in answer to this communication that the King despatched a safe-conduct, declaring to whom it might concern that should Ali ben Rached and the Alcaide of Tetuan "desire to go in person to any of our fortresses of Africa, and enter with their goods and chattels, or – without coming in person, should they send the said things and possessions there, they may do so without let or hindrance." The Portuguese captains have orders to treat them with favour and every honour.

From reference in another letter we gather that this document, of which only the draft, undated and unsigned, has come down to us, must have been despatched on March 13th 1502. This further information is given by a certain Lourenço de Vargas nine months later to his captain – whether of Alcacer or Tangier we are not told – reporting the substance of an interview with Ali-ben Rached. We can form some idea of the profound secrecy surrounding these negotiations from the fact that Ali-ben-Rached swore he did not yet know the gist of the safe-conduct received, because the messenger who had delivered it could speak no Arabic and there was no Moor or Christian captive he could trust to interpret it for him. Would Lourenço de Vargas kindly read and translate it? Lourenço de Vargas, a Luso-Moroccan no doubt, was bilingual: "I read it to him, and declared all that was in the safe-conduct and he was very pleased. I was alone with him and no one else was present."

They talked over the situation and the proposed move to Tunis. Ben Rached felt that eight or ten Portuguese ships might be necessary for him "with all his household, nephews and relations," to say nothing of those of El Mandari, to be transported to Tunis. In exchange D.Manuel would receive Tetuan, all pacified and set in order. The Portuguese could do what they liked with the city – settle there, or if they preferred, raze it to the ground, added Ben Rached amiably.

What happened next? Nothing, so far as we know. Unless new evidence should come to light Lourenço de Vargas' letter to his captain remains the last word we have on this intriguing episode. This letter is undated like so many others written in the African Algarve, but Vargas says that the safe-conduct which he read "was made on the thirteenth of March 1502," and that Ben Rached had had it in his possession for nine months, which brings us to December of that same year. Why matters went no further is not clear. Possibly owing to mutual distrust. Moroccan politics of that period are an unfathomed well.

The episode, although curious, may be dismissed as unimportant for it led nowhere, but it is useful to the picture of Portuguese influence in North African affairs.

Tetuan was supposed to be subject to the King of Fez. His was a vast untidy kingdom. No one seemed certain of its frontiers to the east, and on the west, south of Cape Spartel, it faded out towards the edge of the Sahara and the vague domains of the Hintata dynasty of Marrakesh. The warlike nomad tribes that roamed and fed their flocks on those sparse pasturelands were under no constituted rule. The tribesmen preyed upon the cities of the coast and fought the lords of Fez and Marrakesh. Already in the reign of Manuel's uncle, Afonso V, the mercantile towns of Safi and Azamor had offered tribute in exchange for Portuguese protection. From the teeming waters by Azamor ten thousand shad were yearly shipped to Portugal, while Safi sent 300 mitkals of gold and two fine horses of the famous breed that flourished on those barren hills.

At Safi and Azamor Portuguese trading posts were established through which D.Manuel was informed of all the vicissitudes of internecine intrigue and rivalry that kept the rulers of the cities at continual variance. Those were turbid waters in which the King's agents freely fished, while rival alcaides appealed in turn for Portuguese support. Outside their walls the nomads prowled and sparring politicians called them in at intervals to lend a hand. The King of Portugal, with timely gifts of money, splendid clothes and – duly authorized by the Pope – lances and swords and coats of mail, also made a bid for the tribesmen's friendship. So extended a zone of influence around the towns, while further south, on the fringe of the Sahara, the people of the port of Masa, visited by the Portuguese since Henry the Navigator's time, declared themselves vassals of Portugal. In 1505, the captain João Lopes

de Sequeira, built a castle at his own expense beside Cape Ghir. There
he lived with his family, and fought and·traded with the Berbers
around.

D.Manuel meanwhile, as an experiment, decided to build a fortress
by the deserted shores south of Safi. The little rocky bay of Mogador,
with its chaplet of islands along the beach appeared a likely spot, for it
could receive supplies from Madeira. The veteran captain, Diogo de
Azambuja, was called in for this. He was a man of more than seventy
years, who had served D.João II faithfully on the Gold Coast where he
had founded the first colony and built the Castle of the Mine. True
Portuguese of that unflinching generation, he accepted his new mission
undismayed. By 1506, at Mogador, his *Castelo Real* had risen firm and
strong, in spite of opposition from fierce fanatical Berbers. The shrine
of their holy Mogdul, from which the bay derived its name, was near
the castle and so the presence of the Infidel was bitterly resented. We
gather that the Alcaide of Safi, for other reasons, also disapproved.

The King continued calmly gathering information. The vast interior
of North Africa seemed to him and his counsellors a very useful territorial base for world expansion. True, the Arab kingdom of Fez was
powerful and strongly rooted – but what about the Berber realm of
Marrakesh? The rule of the Hintata Emirs of Marrakesh was weak,
hardly reaching the coast. Might not the Emir welcome Portugal as
friend and protector? Indeed he would! declared Yaya Aziate, the
exiled nephew of the Alcaide of Safi who had been ousted from his
place by a determined cousin. Yaya offered himself as intermediary
between the King of Portugal and the Emir of Marrakesh.

These things, D.Manuel felt, called for careful investigation. He sent
for Lopo Fernandes, squire of the royal household and a man of great
resource.

Lopo Fernandes must have been born in North Africa, for he spoke
Arabic as if it were his native tongue. He knew the Moors intimately
and Moslem customs. Let him go, said the King, to Mogador to ask
Azambuja for guides to lead him through the unknown lands lying
between the coast and Marrakesh – "the further you can penetrate
inland, the better we shall be served" – enjoined the King in a long
paper of instructions. Lopo Fernandes was to find out the names of all
the sheikhs and their respective tribes and the forces that each one
could muster. He was to study the formation of the land, if mountain-

ous or flat, and the means of communication; what villages or towns there were, if any, and the crops they cultivated. Furthermore he was to discover what the rulers of Safi felt about the building of the Castelo Real. D.Manuel knew that the Alcaide was not popular in the city. Might not native merchants be glad to transfer their trade to Mogador where they could count on honest dealing and good faith − "for we have ordered that the Moors trading there should be well treated and have no duties to pay upon the wares they buy and sell." Clearly D.Manuel hoped that Mogador would be a rival market.

On his side Lopo Fernandes was to tell the Moors all about Portuguese victories and fortresses in India. They could now furnish Morocco with oriental goods, and Mogador would be the distributing centre. All of this would be advantageous for the tribesmen.

These things must be touched upon casually, in conversation, and not as if Lopo Fernandes were the mouthpiece of authority above him. In the same noncommittal way he was to ascertain if any of the local chiefs would care to enter the service of Portugal, receiving the King's pay and flying his flag.

Especially if he could find anyone to guide him safely to Marrakesh − "we should be glad if you went there, carrying a letter from Diogo de Azambuja for the ruler, in accordance with the terms I have written to him." And presents would accompany the letter.

Anybody knowing the warlike tribes that roamed the no-man's land between the sea coast and the mountains would be fully aware that this was a tall order. For a Christian isolated amid those fierce fanatical Moslems chances of survival were slight. Lopo Fernandes was a brave man, but he was a realist. He went, says he, feeling "like a lamb among wolves."

He faced them nonetheless, and he got safely home, bringing a full and interesting report. He travelled across the desert lands and he reached Marrakesh − the first Christian perhaps to penetrate at liberty those red ramparts.

The journey had proved as dangerous as he had foreseen. The hazards several times were touch and go, as when the Alcaide Abderraman of Safi had despatched his minions to arrest the envoy on the way. Only the good faith of his guide and the man's dislike of the Alcaide − a tyrant and a drunkard, said he − saved Lopo Fernandes on that occasion. Later on, when they entered a village of holy imams, it was his own persuasive tongue alone preserved him from a violent death. After some such experiences Lopo Fernandes cut his hair and trimmed his beard in the Moorish fashion and dressed as a Moor of Granada. Practising Moslem rites and calling himself Sidi Nassar, he escaped detection till he reached Marrakesh. Danger was over then for the Emir received him well. Moulay En-Nasser, the Hintata lord of Marrakesh, with rebel tribes seething all round, felt he might welcome Portuguese protection. He plied the envoy with questions about Portugal, but more especially on the subject of India. One heard so many things, the Emir said, that were not easy to believe.

So Lopo Fernandes told him all about the triumphs and victories of the last six years, and we may be certain that the account lost nothing in the telling. The Emir was amazed, declares Lopo Fernandes in his report – "and at the same time delighted, saying that now he felt as sure as if he had witnessed these happenings himself that all he had heard of Portugal in India was quite true!"

Consequently the messenger was treated with great favour. He dined on hunks of tender mutton cut by the Emir's own hand, he feasted on cuscus from the royal dish and slept on fine carpets in a tent by that of En-Nasser. He explored the city of Marrakesh, half ruined at the time, it would appear, by nomad incursions, with great open spaces between the buildings. Lopo Fernandes stayed there several days quite happily, feeding on buttered honey cakes, chicken, mutton and cabbages and pomegranates and nuts and almonds.

The return march to Mogador was not without its risks, for once again the Alcaide of Safi tried to waylay and catch him. Abderraman offered for his capture fifty ounces of gold and a fine suit of clothes, because a man like Lopo Fernandes, he said, who could pass as he chose for Christian or Moslem, and knew so much about the Moors, was better dead! The dangerous Portuguese, however, escaped him, and so "the lamb among the wolves" returned to tell his story.

For several years D.Manuel and the Emir of Marrakesh continued to toy with the idea of mutual friendship and alliance. D.Manuel suggested that the Emir might like to pay tribute and have the Portuguese to build a fortress in his capital, but En-Nasser, in spite of all "the pleasure, rest and security" promised him, was not prepared to go so far and negotiations petered out.

Meanwhile, in 1508, the King's agents had been dipping a successful oar in Safi's troubled waters. While rival alcaides murdered each other and called in nomad tribes to bathe the streets in blood, the Portuguese had quietly turned their factory house into a fortress. Among the fighting politicians they supported Yaya Bentafufa, a young Berber chief, whom Diogo de Azambuja had despatched the year before on a long visit to Lisbon. There D.Manuel had charmed him so wisely and treated him so well that, when he returned to Safi, he was a friend of Portugal for life. Yaya was popular in the town and so for many years he ruled Safi as Alcaide, while the Portuguese captain whose right hand he became, was military commander. Together they extended their authority over the nomad tribes around and brought to heel those who refused submission.

With all this it was most regrettable that Nuno Fernandes de Ataide, the greatest of the captains of Safi and the faithful Yaya Bentafufa did not like each other. Complaints to the King poured in from either side. He wisely disregarded them and, continuing to favour the Berber chief, urged the captain to treat him with consideration. Somehow they bumped along together, enlarging their protectate far and wide over surrounding country, till in 1516 the valiant Nuno Fernandes was killed, and some years later the devoted Bentafufa was treacherously assassinated at a banquet by a rival Sheikh — a common fate among the Moorish chiefs, but to the Portuguese a loss beyond repair.

All this time relations with Azamor, the beautiful and wealthy city by the river Um'er'bia, whence the yearly tribute of shad was drawn, had suffered many phases. From King Afonso's time to the end of the century all seems to have run smoothly. In later years the struggles and intrigues of rival sheikhs as well as the undoubted tactlessness — not to say misdemeanours — of certain Portuguese agents, gave rise to a tense situation. The sequence of events is obscure. We know that at some date around 1504 the Portuguese factory was looted and its officials expelled. The outrage was followed by a humble apology, eliciting a gracious pardon from the King. The treaty was renewed — and broken once again, through whose fault is not easy to determine. What with political unrest within the town where leaders quarrelled with each other, and the precarious foothold of the Portuguese, it seemed most likely that the King of Fez would intervene and take Azamor under his direct control, and then — "if he once set foot there," wrote Nuno Fernandes de Ataide from Safi — "all that we have gained will be lost, which God forbid! "

God forbid indeed! echoed the King's council. The military conquest of Azamor was urged and undertaken in 1515 with great crusading fervour under the command of D.Jaime, the Duke of Bragança, D.Manuel's beloved nephew.

A fleet of some four hundred sail was launched to carry 18,000 men, of which the Duke had contributed 3,000, raised in his vast domains, trained in the complicated drill learnt from professional soldiery serving in the Italian wars. All dressed in white, with red crosses upon their chests and backs, they wheeled and turned and executed elaborate figures before the royal palace while Lisbon looked on gaping. The Duke, a splendid figure all in white, bade farewell to the King in the cathedral where D.Manuel was hearing Mass, and laid his flag upon the altar to be blessed. Vibrating to Gil Vicente's stirring "Exhortation to War," the crusaders set sail, and some weeks later Azamor was conquered, albeit not without severe resistance. The defenders fought tooth and nail with every weapon that they had to hand, even hurling skeps full of bees at the assailants' heads — whose helmets, one combatant wrote, actually dripped with honey!

Azamor was taken and fortified, and its vast ramparts along the river front remain today one of the most imposing witnesses to Portuguese dominion by those shores.

Inland the mirage of Marrakesh continued alluring and unattainable. The captains of the fortresses beside the sea urged their sovereign to cross in person with great force, to march over the desert to Marrakesh and crown one of his sons as Emperor of Morocco!

D.Manuel listened and he dreamed, but knew the time was not ripe yet. The captains by the coast continued to make alliances with the wandering tribes around, and with their company to ride on raids inland. They thundered across the stony wastes up to the foothills of the Atlas Mountains. They hammered upon the gates of Marrakesh and young romantics even carved their ladies' names upon those doors as they passed by, while tribesmen cried aloud outside the gates: "Long live D.Manuel, our Lord! "

One thing, however, was certain — it was not light guerilla forces of a few hundred men, operating from bases many desert leagues away, that ever could take and occupy an inland city with immense reserves to draw upon that might be called forth any day to the summons of holy war.

As it was, out of the deep south the Sheriffs from the valley of the Dra, descendants of the Prophet, in his name were moving north over the stony hills towards the Emir's kingdom. The Nazarenes in their strongholds by the coast would yet have to reckon with them, though their approach was slow. These Sheriffs of the Souss, whose shadow was to grow so long in after years, were hardly thought of in D.Manuel's reign.

In 1513 everything still appeared possible. A vast empire in the Algharb of Africa and the Maghreb seemed to open before the King of Portugal to balance his dominion of the golden East. D.Manuel wrote to the Pope a glowing account of his victory at Azamor.

Could there be any limit to his aspirations?

XII

Apogee

". . . Goa is yours; the King of Honawar pays you tribute and obeys you; Batkul does everything that we command; as for the King of Vijayanagar, I think he would give you his realm for the horses that come to Goa from Persia and Arabia" – wrote Albuquerque in November of 1513.

"Your Highness may be assured," declares a later letter, "that from Ormuz to Ceylon all ports are open to you . . . beyond Ceylon all ports and merchandise and gold and silver mines are ready to receive your commerce. Everywhere is quiet and peaceful, so that men may send to Vijayanagar to collect money and merchandise and bring them safely back . . . Your men can wander all over the lands of Malabar and no one asks them where they go, nor whence they come. Throughout the kingdom of the Deccan, they journey and buy and sell and nobody gainsays them . . . Your ships may sail safely even to China . . ." Letters from India sounded like a fanfare ringing from a golden distance.

In Europe, Portuguese prestige was rising to the stars, acclaimed from far and near while Portuguese ambassadors basked in reflected glory. "The lords and people speak of nothing but the conquests of Your Highness," wrote Tomé Lopes from Augsburg. "The Emperor delights to hear about the affairs of India and the kings who are subject to Your Highness! "

These glowing accounts lost nothing in the telling and were often enhanced by rumour. In 1510, the Emperor had been enthralled by a tale that had reached Rome via Alexandria to the effect that "the fleet of Your Highness had gone to Mecca and burned Mohammed (sic), taking much spoil and wealth and on the way had fought a great armada which was defeated and burnt . . ." Maximilian had written about this to his daughter Madame Marguerite in Flanders, and she "and all

the court were very glad . . . Please God it may be true! " concludes the
factor João Brandão who does not appear wholly convinced. As a matter of fact this must have been a garbled version of Almeida's victory in
1509 over the Egyptian fleet at Dabio, enlarged by distance and hearsay
into the conquest of Mecca.

In sober truth, without embellishments, the achievements were
breathtaking enough. The orator, Camillo Porcio, held forth before the
Pope Leo X upon the conquest of Malacca. Camillo Porcio enjoyed
speaking, and the subject gave scope to flowers of rhetoric. Surely all
Christians must rejoice, he cried, that God had granted the fortunate
and invincible King Manuel "so many and such victories and triumphs
over his enemies that we easily believe the Lord is fighting for us! "

Indeed — "could anyone suppose the feats done by the Portuguese
in India under the command of the valiant Afonso de Albuquerque to
be the works of men? Clearly, the hand of God was manifest! " And
now — "after so many victories on land and sea, the rich and fertile
kingdom of Malacca, called by the Ancients the Golden for its great
wealth, has been conquered . . . in which things I know not whom most
to praise, whether the zeal and good fortune of the mighty King Manuel, who with such labour and expense has sought to bear the Christian name to lands so far and people alien to our intercourse . . . or the
effort and skill and valour of the Portuguese who, with boldness unheard of and profound desire to spread the Christian faith, have passed
through so many climates diverse from that of their native land, where
they must fight not only cruel and pitiless foes, but hunger, thirst, and
cold and heat beyond endurance!"

Under the lofty vaulting of the papal hall, the speaker rolled his
silver tongue around the sonorous Latin periods. The Holy Father and
his court of cardinals listened approvingly, while the ambassador Dr.
João de Faria, glowing with patriotic pride, drank it all in.

The spoken word was not enough. Publicists know the value of the
visual aid to drive a message home. So let the splendour of the Orient
be shown at the centre of Christendom! The opportunity occurred
when it behoved D.Manuel, as loyal son of the Church, to make his Act
of Obedience to Pope Leo X. He seized it with both hands.

There was not much that generation did not understand of pomp
and pageantry, but everyone agreed that Rome had never seen, or was
likely to see again, a day such as that of March 12th 1514, when to the

blare of trumpets and the skirl of fifes, the embassy from Portugal marched into the Eternal City.

In front the bugles made the welkin ring. Behind, curveting on a prancing steed caparisoned with solid gold and pearls and precious stones, a Persian rider richly clad held in leash on his saddle-bow a hunting cheetah with a jewelled collar – a present from the King of Ormuz to D.Manuel. Beside the Persian walked a stately Indian elephant bearing a coffer draped in cloth of gold as was also the mahout who sat aloft, directing the great beast by word of mouth.

Next followed the ambassadors with their retinues. Tristão da Cunha, who, nine years before, had so narrowly missed the honour of being first Governor of India, was amply compensated now by command of this glorious mission. He came arrayed in splendid clothes; he wore a hat covered with pearls; he brought with him his three young sons and many knights and noblemen, all dressed in silks and cloth of gold, with weighty golden chains around their necks.

The learned Dr. Diogo Pacheco walked on the ambassador's right hand. Dr. João de Faria was on his left. A purple procession of cardinals came next, followed by the whole diplomatic corps present in Rome – ambassadors of the Emperor and of the King of France, of Poland and Castile and England, as well as the dukes of Milan, Venice, Lucca and Bologna. Like bees around a honey pot they buzzed around Tristão da Cunha, singing the praises of D.Manuel, his grandeur and magnificence, and championship of the True Faith. They talked in Latin, and Tristão – wisely no doubt – left it to Dr. Diogo Pacheco to answer them in the same language. With some relief, perhaps, he turned to the Castilian ambassador who "spoke to him in the Castilian tongue," but though "he understood it very well, he made reply in Portuguese, which he knew better! "

The Governor of Rome stepped forward then and bade the envoy welcome in the Holy Father's name. More speeches followed, as were felt to be appropriate, before the master of ceremonies re-ordered the procession as it was to march into the town and to the Palace of Sant'Angelo where the Pope was residing.

Preceded by the papal mace-bearers and the famous Swiss Guard, all in right sequence as prescribed by protocol, behind the cheetah and the elephant, the radiant beings passed through the gaping crowds that filled the streets and hung from every window and climbed on the roofs. The Pope and cardinals – pop-eyed like all the rest – were watching from the Castle while a thundering salvo of artillery burst forth accompanied by flourishes of fifes and trumpets.

Supremely undisturbed, the lordly elephant arrived below the windows of the castle. Instructed by his mahout, he bowed his great knees three times to the ground, then filled his trunk with water from a basin nearby. Respectfully passing over the lower window where the Holy Father stood, he squirted a shower-bath upon the cardinals and noblemen thronging the upper storey. While everybody rocked with mirth, he turned around and drenched the crowd before continuing his stately march unruffled, under the Pontiff's fascinated stare.

Audience was held at the Palace next day, when Tristão da Cunha presented the letter from his King. Dr. Pacheco made a speech – in beautiful Latin, everyone agreed – the Pope replied, also in Latin, by a glowing eulogy of King Manuel and the Portuguese nation.

Of course the elephant could not be brought into the audience hall, so the Pope repaired to the gardens of his Belvedere on the day appointed for the offering of D.Manuel's present. Once more all the ambassadors crowded to see with eager eyes the opening of the coffer and to hear the King's letter, in which D.Manuel humbly entreated the Holy Father to accept his "little gifts" in the spirit in which they were sent.

The modest trifles consisted of sacred vestments, pontificals, altar frontal and such, all in heavy brocade and cloth of gold, all sewn with pearls and precious stones and uncut rubies. Never such richness had been seen, declared the lords and cardinals, passing the glittering objects from hand to hand in wide-mouthed admiration. The material alone was worth a king's ransom, but the art that went into the execution of the wonderful pieces was valued even higher, declared the Italian Alberto de Carpe, who wrote upon the subject to his master the emperor Maximilian. He specially admired a pomegranate woven in gold and jewels – "a marvellous, sumptuous and magnificent piece of work!"

Another "little gift" was the elephant himself, thrown in together with the hunting cheetah. In the garden the animals were made to exhibit their skills. Game was brought for the cheetah to kill, and panther-like it pounced. The mahout put the elephant through all its tricks. It was much better than a circus and a pleasant afternoon was had by all.

This was "the most honoured and richest embassy that ever entered

Rome!" Tristão da Cunha wrote delightedly to the Secretary of State, on April 11th 1514. "What with this and the great and famous deeds of the King our Lord, he is the most honoured and best-loved prince in the world." Such love, the writer adds, can only be inspired by God.

If not by Mammon! All foreign dignitaries about this time loudly protested their regard for Manuel. The Pope's chaplain, Julian of Medicis, knowing his tastes, sent him a book of music, "to relax his soul from greater cares." The Prior of St. John of Naples wrote a gushing letter to the fortunate monarch who "from Arzila and Tangier and regions of Africa had flown to Taprobana and the Orient." The Prior offered prayers and presents and craved the King's protection for his religious house. D.Manuel's patronage for works of art was keenly solicited by painters and illuminators from abroad, as was also his sponsorship for deeds of arms. Even from distant Poland young noblemen came to Portugal to be knighted by the King's hand – "which honour they desired for his great name," celebrated throughout their lands "for the navigations that he undertook and the wars that he waged against the Moors and Turks, enemies of our Holy Faith! "

In England and in Flanders and in Germany, all Portuguese ambassadors were received with overwhelming honours. In 1511, the Order of the Garter had been given D.Manuel by Henry VIII, "as a token of love." Richmond, the King of Arms in England who died about this time, was a Portuguese it would appear, and Henry wished to have another Portuguese to take his place, because, wrote the ambassador Tomé Lopes, "in this house they have always had a Portuguese King of Arms, and found that he served well." King Henry wished to have a certain Diogo Ribeiro, of the ambassador's household, to fill the vacant post, because this man was a great linguist: "He speaks English and Scotch and French and Flemish as if born in these countries, and German tolerably well." Whether he accepted the post we cannot tell. We only know that Tomé Lopes advised D.Manuel not to let go so valuable a man.

The year 1514 marked culminating points. Never had the spice fleet come in so laden or brought more exotic gifts. From Calicut, once Enemy Number One, but now craving Albuquerque for peace, came a necklace of jewels worth 10,000 cruzados and rich Indian draperies from the Samorin's own wardrobe. From the great realm of Vijayanagar bracelets and anklets were offered, a string of pearls, and a golden dagger set with precious stones. The King of Cambay despatched a couch made in carved mother-of-pearl, and also a tame rhinoceros – a beast that nobody had seen before and whose likeness has been preserved by Albrecht Dürer.

All these things were sensational and they were good. D.Manuel was satisfied with the figure he cut, but it was none of these that caused his cup of pride and joy to overflow. It was a bolt out of the blue that came to fulfil ancient dreams.

Prester John at last! In 1514, the same auspicious year that had seen Tristão da Cunha exhibiting the wonders of the Orient in Rome – the Indian mail from Albuquerque brought exciting news which Manuel hastened to communicate to his good cities. An ambassador from Prester John was on the way and would shortly arrive! – "Wherefore I command you all in general and each one in particular that wherever he [the ambassador] may land, he and all persons who come with him be given lodgings and stabling for their beasts in the best houses of the place where they may be well and comfortably accommodated; he must be given a good bed and abundant fare, as also for his animals, which will be paid for by the person we shall send . . ." The reception must be fitting to "the ambassador of so great a king and coming from so far."

The man duly appeared in anything but splendour. He was an Armenian, about fifty years old, well-spoken and presentable. He had a wife with him and sundry female attendants as well as an Ethiopian youth who, he declared, was a kinsman of Prester John.

He brought a letter from Queen Helena, regent of Abyssinia for her twelve-year-old grandson, written "In the name of the Father, Son and Holy Ghost, Three Persons and One God . . .

"May the Salvation of Our Lord Jesus Christ, son of Our Lady, the Virgin Mary, rest upon our beloved and most Christian brother King Manuel, and grant him victory over his enemies." The writer goes on to speak about the Portuguese in her realm (Pero da Covilham, of course, and a few others) "who have told us many things, asking for men and provisions . . . Therefore we send you our ambassador, Matthew my servant, by leave of the Patriarch Mark, who blesses us and sends us clergy from Jerusalem." She warns D.Manuel that the Lord of Cairo is building ships and galleys "to send against your fleets." But, "we shall give you many men in the Straits of Mecca and Bab-el-Mandeb, or else India or Tor, in order to sweep the Moors from the face of the earth, for we are powerful on land." It had been prophesied that in the latter days a king would rise from among the Franks and he would put an end to all the Moors! "With this ambassador we send a cross of the wood on which Our Lord Jesus was crucified at Jerusalem, which was brought me from thence and of which I have had made two crosses, one to remain with me and we send you the other with our embassy. The wood is black and has a silver ring . . . We could have sent you much gold, but we feared the Moors through whose lands our envoy must pass would take it from him . . .

"If you wish," concludes the Queen, "we should be very glad for you to marry your daughters to our sons and send them here, and take our daughters for your sons, and we shall send them there, richly endowed with gold and silver . . ."

Abyssinia, the Queen explains, has no sea power, nor wood for building fleets, but could provide supplies in abundance for a thousand ships and their men.

This letter overjoyed D.Manuel. He sent a copy to Rome to be shown to the Pope – "as something so new to the world as for an ambassador from Prester John to reach these parts! "

With all this the ambassador, received with open arms, was overwhelmed with every honour.

He needed encouragement, poor man, for he had had gruelling experiences upon his journey. Leaving Ethiopia in disguise, posing as a Moslem, he had aroused suspicions at Dabul where he had been robbed and imprisoned. A stiff message from Albuquerque, whose word was law beside the Indian coast, had brought him to Goa with his property restored. There he enjoyed an enthusiastic welcome. The Holy Cross was encased in a casket of gold. He and his staff had been loaded with gifts by the Governor and given the best accommodation available for the voyage to Lisbon.

His troubles would have been over had it not been for the bumptious young captain of the ship, who would not believe that an Armenian – a white man! – could really be an envoy from dusky Ethiopia. Convinced of his own perspicacity and that the Governor was a fool who had been diddled by a spy, the young man persecuted his passenger in every way he could devise. It must have been a nasty shock on reaching Portugal to find himself arrested for his pains and confined to the dungeon of Lisbon Castle.

Having provided the ambassador with everything that he might need, the King turned his attention to the organizing of a return embassy to Prester John – an embassy the splendour of which was to express his joy at making contact at last with his long-sought African colleague, and set forth before Prester John the prestige of alliance with Portugal.

The head of this exciting mission was selected carefully. No better man could be found than Duarte Galvão who, six years earlier had so fervently canvassed the European courts in favour of the Crusade still hanging in abeyance. Time had elapsed. Duarte Galvão was nearing seventy, if not already past the Psalmist's span, but his enthusiasm was undimmed. There remained for the Lord to show what He could do through Portugal and Prester John! Duarte Galvão would be happy to be sent, he wrote to his friend Afonso de Albuquerque, without a hope of any material gain – "even if I were much older! "

A carefully chosen staff including musicians and skilled artisans would accompany the embassy which carried dazzling gifts of furnishings and clothes and plate. All the luxury known to 16th century plutocrats was included: a bed adorned with artistic paintings, upholstered with six large mattresses stuffed with merino wool, finest linen sheets, bedspreads of velvet and damask, pillows and bolsters of embroidered silk; a dining table of the finest marquetry and several sets of table-cloths besides a complete dinner service with fruit dishes and knives and table napkins embroidered in gold. Added to these were suits of clothes of silk and cloth of gold, dazzling armour and shining swords. The church, of course, had not been forgotten, but supplied with vestments and pontificals and silver for the altar. Seldom had any king despatched so rich a present to another. All this packed in chests with greatest care. Matthew and his companions, all loaded with gifts, were despatched, richly clad.

D.Manuel, serene and satisfied, saw the fleet of 1515 depart. He could not think that things were not going well, but he had decided that year to make changes in India.

XIII

Dropping the Pilot

The captain of Goa, with his horsemen and his halberdiers, pikes flashing in the Indian sun, escorted the ambassador of Vijayanagar. In front a thousand native troops flourished their shining swords to the sound of trumpets and drums, while elephants in single file followed behind. Each one of the great beasts was draped in oriental cloths and the mahout on each one's back carried a silver basin filled with costly gifts of jewels and precious stones.

The brilliant procession wended its way through narrow streets to the governor's residence which once had been the palace of the Adil Khans. From the fortress boomed a salvo of artillery. Portuguese serving-men came forward to unload the elephants, while the ambassador, led by the captain, entered the hall where the Governor sat surrounded by the principal fidalgos.

Afonso de Albuquerque, spare and erect, with snow white beard, severely dressed in black damask, was an impressive figure. He rose up from his chair and stood while the ambassador salaamed, then took him by the hand and graciously received the presents. The King of Vija-yanagar sent him these things, said the envoy; he handed him a letter written on gold leaf, proposing friendship and alliance between the Indian realm and Portugal, and that the horses brought to Goa from the Persian Gulf should be reserved for the great Hindu king. The Governor thanked with diplomatic words, promising prompt dispatch.

The envoy left. The Governor had the present wrapped up in paper and packed in a box, nailed down to be sent to D.Manuel. Such things, he told the fidalgos, belonged to "Our Lord the King." They were the fruits of India.

The ambassador, still with the captain at his side, made his way back to his lodging through the principal street of Goa. Nearing the city gate they had to stand aside to let pass a body of men with pikes upon their shoulders, marching to military music. These were men of the famous *ordenança*, infantry of India, Europeans all and trained by Albuquerque. With swinging step and pennons flying they streamed by in a continuous line, on and on, more and more of them passing through the gate.

The ambassador and all his company waited two hours while still the men filed past. He counted them — ten thousand at the least! Small wonder that Goa was firmly held! They do these exercises every day, the captain explained, to keep up practice in the use of arms. He did not mention that this morning's exercise — which surely must have been rehearsed — consisted in entering the city by one gate, marching across it to another, running around the walls at a quick double, and re-entering again, still in unbroken file.

Did Albuquerque heave a sigh of relief at having once more got away with it? Hardly perhaps. Since he had reached the Indian coast in 1508, he had been repeating that sort of thing. "Give me 3000 men in India for three years," he had written to the King, if all was to be done "as should be for your service! " He never had them. "Did His Highness imagine there were 5000 men in India? ", he wrote in 1513, "Would to God that we were 2500, including those at Malacca! " "You never send me arms nor men, nor any implements of war," declares another letter. Supplies were always short — "in our armadas we embark with a little rice and a few coconuts, and each man brings his arms — if any."

As for the ships so proudly patrolling the Indian seas, before whose flag the navies of the Orient had to strike sail — hardly one of them was sea-worthy. The pepper fleet arriving every year battered and worn, was carefully careened and caulked and cosseted to face the long home voyage; the ships that seemed beyond repair remained in India. And woe-betide the shipwright who, despairing, broke them up! "If they say they are old," writes Albuquerque furiously, "with such as these we sail in India . . . half patched up as they are they do you service . . . I never took charge of a ship here that did not seem more fit to be taken to pieces than for navigation . . . ." A case in point was his old flagship *Frol de la Mar*, which broke in two returning from the conquest of Malacca. Albuquerque suggested to the King that derelict ships dismantled by the Lisbon riverside might with advantage be patched up and sent to finish their career in India. They would come in very useful, and — "it would not cost much to bring them here."

So wrote the conqueror of the East, whose word was law beside the Indian coast, while Indian princes waited on his will.

Was Manuel ever convinced of the inadequacy of means by which his Governor had achieved this amazing prestige? Could he imagine that a man struggling with such shortage of everything would envisage the grandiose programmes that Albuquerque presented to his master. It all appeared so simple! Now that contact had been made at last with Prester John a major offensive could be launched against Islam through the Red Sea: "There are many and good horses in the land of Prester John; with the help of Our Lord it would be easy for 500 mounted Portuguese to disembark at Jiddah, to ride one day's journey to Mecca and burn it to ashes. This seems, Senhor, so easy to achieve that I consider it as done . . . ."

There was another great idea which the alliance with Prester John made possible — why not deviate the course of the Nile? Send for a few of the competent engineers who open irrigation channels in the Island of Madeira and set them to work upon the upper reaches of the Nile. Turn it away from Cairo and Egypt will be conquered by the desert in two years! "I see great things could be done if only the King would support me! "

But D.Manuel did not. He might be pardoned if he found such drastic reconstruction of the map a little staggering. The trouble was not that he failed to follow Albuquerque so far, but that he did not follow him at all. To accomplish Portugal's self-chosen task, the Governor required to be at the same time keen statesman, skilled general, experienced seaman, capable organizer and wise administrator. Afonso de Albuquerque was all these things. What he lacked was a king able to understand him.

To Manuel it doubtless seemed that anybody whose supplies were short would not consider enterprises on that scale. With the means at his disposal the Governor had not managed badly. Should he be encouraged to ask for more? Many prudent people said it might be unwise to give him too much rein.

The Letters of Albuquerque, which even today, after more than four hundred years seem to strike fire from flint, do not appear much to have moved his master. The King had other correspondents in India — verbose and smug and self-seeking — whom he felt to be sound and steady men. On his side, Albuquerque has called these "the poets of India."

Principal among them was Gaspar Pereira, the State Secretary, an inveterate intriguer who already, from 1505 to 1509, had been a thorn in the flesh of the Viceroy D.Francisco de Almeida. For some reason the King liked this man, and sent him back to India in 1512, again to occupy the post of Secretary of India. "When he arrived," writes Albuquerque "he did not approve of me, nor of the way I governed."

Gaspar Pereira always had an excuse not to accompany his chief on any of his expeditions. He had no taste for maritime adventure — "What he would like," said Albuquerque, "are rolls of petitions in his charge to be despatched behind closed doors, and many things for which there is no time in India."

For one of bureaucratic taste Albuquerque was a dreadful trial, He kept no office hours at all, despatching everything that arose upon the spot, on horseback or on foot wherever he might be. One of the half dozen scribes he led around with him would dash off what writing was necessary, and the Governor signed across his knee. Gaspar Pereira thought this highly irregular.

D.Francisco de Almeida seldom wrote or signed reports, and Gaspar Pereira disapproved of that. He disapproved still more of Albuquerque who sat up all night dictating his immortal Letters to the King, but did not show them to Gaspar Pereira. "He complains that I tell him no secrets — I do not! There is no secrecy in him."

Thus Gaspar Pereira was a man with a grievance and he intrigued against his chief with all his might. Things were going from bad to worse in India, according to the letters he wrote home. The Governor was wholly inefficient, dishonest, and not even brave. There he would be skulking behind the lines or sleeping in his tent, while he, Gaspar Pereira, and others performed valiantly. And had not the Governor been seen confabulating most suspiciously with "Moors," and telling him — Gaspar Pereira — to step out of earshot that he might not follow their dark machinations.

The writer moreover draws a touching picture of himself: serving faithfully, discredited by the unworthy Governor who would not listen to advice, terribly ill, ("He is always ill when I want him for anything," was Albuquerque's impression) but ready still to die where duty called.

Lourenço Moreno, factor of Cochin, was another imaginative letter writer, who held forth at great length upon the subject of his own services and the Governor's shortcomings. All that interested Albuquerque, he says, was to wreck ships and sacrifice his men; he had no regard for the royal exchequer. Now Lourenço Moreno at Cochin, were he relieved of this interfering governor, could make his master rich!

He did not add that he himself was growing rich! Lourenço Moreno had lived in India many years and he knew all the ropes. He also knew that the Governor saw through him. Lourenço Moreno hated Albuquerque.

So did Antonio Real, Alcaide of Cochin. This man knew something about ship building and had military experience, having served in the Italian wars. In India, however, he did not mean to overdo it. He dug himself in at Cochin, trading illicitly in pepper and other forbidden merchandise, and railing at the Governor. He came up against a stiff breeze every time Albuquerque passed through Cochin and got his own back sending home diatribes against him. These were worded in his name by his friend Diogo Pereira, clerk of the factory, for Antonio Real, being hardly literate, could not compose a letter. The two between them produced monuments of calumny against Afonso de Albuquerque. He himself has summed up the gist of these letters briefly enough: "He called me a thief and a Moor and a coward, and a man who did not obey Your Highness's commands."

Chance brought this "mine of letters," as he calls them, to the Governor's knowledge at the end of 1513. Characteristically he went straight to the offending parties to confront them with their own assertions. He did not punish anyone. These were personal matters, he said, and should be dealt with by the King. He merely paid them up to date and sent them back to Portugal, with the exception of Lourenço Mareno who was ill at the time and so remained at Cochin, where he went on writing.

The Governor told the others they could go home and prove their lies! "I send you Gaspar Pereira," he told the King, "as he might not think me an unbiassed judge." A man with a guilty conscience does not act like this. If Albuquerque had really been responsible for his alleged misdeeds he might have defended himself better. Tongues that were so dangerous at a distance would not be less harmful at headquarters. Moreover he laboured under one disadvantage with regard to his detractors. They blackened him entirely — he was too fair-minded to do the same by them. Thus we find him writing of a turbulent fidalgo who had given him much trouble — "with all this I assure Your Highness, he is a good man" and of another that, though "he is angry with me and I with him . . . nevertheless he has served well and is deserving of honour and reward." One could cite various instances in which he points out the merits of his opponents — an excellent trait, no doubt, but more help-ful to them than to himself.

It seems incredible that the letters of Antonio Real and company should carry weight. They are so obviously inspired by spite. Yet we gather that the King esteemed the writers and sent them gracious re-plies. He urged the Governor to favour them — "Your Highness recom-mends Antonio Real to me," wrote Albuquerque in 1514 — "but from the letter he sent you about me and the confidence Your Highness has in him, you should rather commend me to him! "

The King's reaction to the campaign of slander had been apparent in the mail reaching India in 1513 — "Your Highness blames me, blames me, blames me! " writes Albuquerque despairingly. Against him were the two factors of time and space — letters written in November or December reached Portugal in June and the answer would only be received in India by September of the following year. The calumnies, writes Albuquerque, would be harmful enough if relating to "things done at Santarem or Sintra, but for Your Highness to remain a year and a half with such information of a man serving faithfully so far away . . ." was unpardonable, and certainly distressing for the victim of the evil tongues.

Despite all his encouragement of the backbiters, the King cannot have been convinced by their assertions. From Albuquerque's answers to mail received at the end of 1514, we gather that he had written on a more encouraging note. Unfortunately, however, the intrigue was not limited to India. For some two years the court had been humming with it and jealousies were rife. The post of Governor of India was the highest in the royal gift, the crown of man's ambition; the conquests of Albuquerque had been spectacular but there were others who felt that they could do as much. Around the throne were rivalries and enmities and old grudges carefully nursed, and there were whisperings upon backstairs.

Many declared the Governor's victories and successes were a good reason for his timely recall. How could they fail to turn his head and make him too big for his boots! There is a letter from Albuquerque, dated December 1514, apparently in answer to one from the King promising future reward. From this document we gather that what Albuquerque most desired was to be allowed to end his days as Governor of India. He asks for reinforcement of authority and money to draw upon to meet public expenses. Can it have been this letter – for we know of no other on the subject – which gave rise to the rumour that Afonso de Albuquerque had petitioned the King to make him Duke of Goa and perpetual Viceroy? Damião de Gois mentions this, but no known document confirms it.

The coil has never been unravelled of the influences at work throughout 1514. Gaspar Correia says the Baron de Alvito was behind them all. He enjoyed favour with the King and it would seem he hated Albuquerque. The line he took was not so much to denigrate as play upon the point that Albuquerque was no longer young and must be tired – he might die any day, and then what would happen to India? Better send a replacement while there still was time – and who could be more suitable than the Baron's cousin and dear friend, Lopo Soares de Albergaria?

Lopo Soares had taken a fleet to India in 1504 and acquitted himself honourably on that occasion. We do not know if he was younger than Albuquerque. Gaspar Correa says he was a great friend of Lourenço Moreno. For reasons we have not found on record, he also hated Afonso de Albuquerque. However that may be, if the idea was to replace an ageing governor whose health might possibly break down, Lopo Soares was a surprising choice – for the man suffered from epileptic fits! The Baron pushed him forward nonetheless, and his faction was powerful at court. Albuquerque still had some friends, who spoke for him – the Queen herself, it seems, was on his side – but he had been away too long, his enemies were on the spot, and they all heaved together.

Of this most puzzling episode not the least puzzling is the attitude of Manuel. He appears to blow hot and cold. In the mail that went to India in 1514, it seems there was a note of confidence and approval, and yet we know that but a few months later the King was signing Albuquerque's recall and the appointment of Lopo Soares as Governor of India. More than that, he was sending back to fill the most important posts some of the worst enemies of Albuquerque! Evidently between the sailing of the pepper fleet in 1514 and the autumn of that same year, when preparations for 1515 got under way, Albuquerque's rivals had done their worst and scored the bull's eye.

Gaspar Correa throws a curious sidelight on the recriminations and heart-burnings that convulsed the court. The Queen, he says, was kept in ignorance till the fatal deed was signed, and when she heard about it she was indignant. Not for nothing was she the daughter of the great Isabel Católica, who never failed as judge of men. She told her husband that he would repent. One did not change a good horse for one whose quality was uncertain! It seems she even wrote to her father the King of Aragon, urging him to remonstrate with his son-in-law.

It is not likely he would trouble to interfere, and anyhow by then the royal word was pledged — the King could not go back on it, though already he began to feel he had made a mistake. Correa says he went so far as to offer Lopo Soares the handsome sum of 20,000 cruzados if he would give up the appointment. Lopo Soares might have accepted, but his cousin the Baron upbraided him. Would he sell honour for money? So Lopo Soares sailed for India. They say the Queen was very angry with the Baron.

All this of course is rumour and hearsay, but it is certain that D. Manuel was seized with grave misgivings. The change might well be for the worse! And tales were circulating from the Middle East — the garbled and distorted facts that reached Europe via Alexandria and Venice. One story said that Albuquerque had taken Aden. Great news! But if he had, and left India at once — who would have the experience to consolidate the conquest? More alarming was the rumour that the Soldan's fleet was coming back to India. His ships were getting underway in the Red Sea and would pass through Bab-el-Mandeb within the next few months.

Then Manuel was seized with panic. Something must be done, whatever Lopo Soares felt about it!

"Afonso de Albuquerque, Friend," he wrote on March 20th 1516, "We have heard through Venice that the Soldan's fleet has sailed for India. In that case it would appear that our service requires above all things that you should remain in those parts, in spite of the message you may have received ordering your return, because from the experience we have of your service and the victories Our Lord has always given you . . . even if the Soldan's fleet has entered India, we shall feel

at rest knowing you to be there! " The letter takes on an almost imploring tone – ". . . in nothing could you serve us better than in this; to
you alone we entrust all these things and feel as certain that they will
be done as if we ourselves were seeing to the matter . . ."

"Lopo Soares, Friend" had his letter too, which must have made
him grind his teeth. D.Manuel trusts he will take his master's change of
plan in the right spirit: Cochin, Calicut and Malacca will remain in his
jurisdiction, with 400 men of his own choice – Afonso de Albuquerque
must have charge of the rest. "Although we have full confidence in
you," the King explains politely, "it did not seem to us you would be
sufficient if the Soldan's fleet came to India." Without the experience
of Afonso de Albuquerque he could not be expected to cope with the
situation!

We wonder how this strange arrangement would have worked. Badly,
no doubt. But it was not put to the test.

Lopo Soares reached India in September of 1515 with thirteen ships,
pleasantly looking forward to his triumph over Albuquerque. He doubtless was sorry to find the Governor was still absent at Ormuz, building a
fortress by the Persian Gulf. At Goa meanwhile he was received politely
but with ill-concealed dismay. At Calicut the Samorin went out of town
to avoid meeting him. If he had known another governor would come
to India, he declared, he never would have signed a treaty with the
Portuguese or granted permission to build a fortress!

The Rajah of Cochin was cold, and reluctant to call on him, consult-
ing augurs and omens to postpone the day. When they did meet at last,
the visit was not a success. Unlike his predecessor, who always knew
how to charm, the new Governor was stiff and proud – "Lopo Soares
treats me as he likes," the Rajah is said to have remarked, "and I shall
treat him as I choose. Afonso de Albuquerque treated me as I liked, so I
did everything he wanted! "

Meanwhile the burning summer of Ormuz trailed to its breathless
end. The pitiless sunlight beat upon the barren salt hills, the scorching
sands, and shimmered on the white walls of the unfinished fort where
all day long weary men were carrying loads of stone. From the noblest
to the least each man had to take his turn at the work, and Albuquerque remained there every day from dawn to dusk. Above, below, all
round, he was everywhere – a driving force of energy unconsumed;
beneath his eye the building grew apace, while daily the men died.

It was early in November when the ship *Frol da Rosa* left the Persian Gulf and slowly crossed the Sea of Oman before a feeble breeze. Afonso de Albuquerque was on his way back to India, but it was evident to those on board that voyage was to be his last. Already he had nearly died at Ormuz, but would not leave before the fort was finished. There had been some hope that he might recover at sea, but a passing native vessel put an end to that. From it they learned the news that another governor had arrived in India, and Albuquerque lost all wish to live.

His friends said that if the King recalled him, it was that he might pass his declining years at ease, and certainly he would receive a title. But Albuquerque did not want to go home and rest. To hang about the court with or without a title could not interest a man accustomed to use princes as his pawns and spread himself across the map of Asia — Portugal is a small country, he said. Besides, he was not even sure of the King's good will. He knew his enemies were numerous and had never been discouraged. "I shall find everyone against me! ", was his surmise.

The weary days crept by while the dying conqueror lay listening to the flapping sails above and wondering if he could live till they reached Goa. At the ship's rate of progress it seemed problematical, nevertheless it was his sole desire.

Slowly they passed around the Gulf of Cambay, and Albuquerque ordered the royal standard to be taken from the masthead, since he was no longer Governor of India. He dictated his last letter to D.Manuel — laconic and unemotional as ever. He announces he is dying in the same matter-of-fact tone in which he might say there was less pepper going home that year:

"I leave my son what property I have, which is very little . . . but I bequeath him all you owe me for my services, and that is much . . . affairs of India will speak for him and me." Not one word of recrimination.

It was the night of December 15th when Goa at last was near. A ship leaving harbour in haste was hailed as it went by. What news of India? The captain answered briefly as he went his way: "Governor, Lopo Soares," and he named the newly appointed officials of the different fortresses — all enemies of Albuquerque — and passed asking no questions.

Albuquerque in his cabin had heard everything. "This is good news for me," said he bitterly, "all those upon whom I reported unfavourably are sent back with the best places! My sins must be great before the King. For the sake of men I have turned the King against me, and for the King's sake I have set men against me – it is time to take refuge in the church!"

This was the end. Albuquerque at the point of death rose from his bed and with support walked to the cabin door. There, leaning against the wall, he looked once more upon his beloved Goa before lying down to die.

They carried him ashore in a boat all draped with black, dressed in the habit of a knight of Santiago. The natives of Goa who had received Lopo Soares so coldly now turned out with wails and lamentations to follow their dead conqueror to his grave in the chapel of Nossa Senhora da Serra, which he himself had built. They said there must be war in Heaven since God had sent for him! For long after they kept his tomb adorned with flowers and carried there all their complaints – to the disgust of Lopo Soares who would have destroyed the chapel if he could.

As usual the Soldan's fleet did not materialize, but Lopo Soares got no pleasure from his three years as Governor of India. He came hoping to triumph over a living man, instead of which he was humiliated by a haunting memory. It followed him to the Red Sea – on that bungled expedition of 1517, when he heard men cursing his incompetence and drawing unfavourable comparisons between him and Albuquerque. It rose to mock him at Ormuz, when the young king, all unsuspectingly filled his ears with praises of his predecessor. And in Goa – haunted Goa – there was never any peace. Every day there were quarrels between his men and those who had served Albuquerque – because, says Gaspar Correa, Lopo Soares' minions "spoke against Afonso de Albuquerque and the men of India could not bear it."

As for the brilliant embassy to Prester John of which so much was hoped, Lopo Soares never got it underway for he took no interest. The ambassador, Duarte Galvão, had died in the Red Sea, the Armenian Matthew in India, awaited repatriation, while the wonderful present they had brought rotted in tropical heat and damp warehouses.

In Portugal, D.Manuel, smitten with deep remorse, read the dignified words of Albuquerque's last letter. He mourned the greatest empire builder that his country ever had. He sent for Albuquerque's only child, a boy about fifteen years old, took charge of him and loaded him with favours, and changed his name from Braz to Afonso in honour of his father's memory.

Lopo Soares never was forgiven. After three undistinguished years in India, he was coldly received at court and soon retired to his quinta at Torres Vedras for the rest of his life.

Neither D.Manuel nor his successor would allow Afonso de Albuquerque's bones to be brought back from Goa. While the body of Albuquerque remained there, Manuel said, he felt that India was safe.

He never realised that more was buried in that tomb at Goa than just the worn-out body of its conqueror. With the passing of Albuquerque a period of the brightest hopes was ended. Heroes continued to go East, great deeds were done, but genius can have no successor. Afonso de Albuquerque had dreamed of empires far too vast for any small country to achieve, yet while he lived they scarcely seemed impossible, and indeed, perhaps they were not. His victories, if they were not fully documented, would be incredible.

In the whole life and reign of Manuel his rejection of Albuquerque is the most inexplicable decision. It demonstrates a vein of weakness in his character hitherto unrevealed. It also shows how much the glorious first years of his reign owed to his mighty predecessor. D.João II had prepared the plan and left behind a team of chosen men ready to carry out and go beyond. D.Manuel had followed on the impetus that D.João had set in motion. But an impetus sooner or later must slow down. D.Manuel, a milder man than D.João, a better man morally, we even must admit, was lacking in the element of greatness that made of his cousin one of his country's most inspiring kings. D.Manuel was swayed by lesser men. D.João never had favourites who could turn him from his purpose.

And Manuel, regrettably, was not a judge of men.

XIV

Afternoon Shadows and Sunshine

During the following years, was Manuel the Fortunate aware that he had passed his peak — the glorious days when nothing seemed impossible and there was but to leap from strength to strength?

At Goa Albuquerque lay in his grave, covered with flowers and scented herbs left there by weeping natives who talked to him as if he were still living.

Duarte Galvão, the ambassador of mystic vision, was buried in the sands of the Red Sea.

Upon the barren hills that roll between Safi and Marrakesh, Nuno Fernandes de Ataide — called "the Unresting" — had met his death in a skirmish with desert tribes of the interior.

The year before North Africa had seen the disaster of Mamora — "the greatest loss of men and munitions the King D.Manuel suffered in his whole reign . . ." according to Damião de Gois.

Yet this expedition had seemed to counsellors and King a sound strategic move and it had been carefully planned. A fortress at Mamora, at the mouth of the river Cebu passing near Larache, would close the line of Portuguese defences by the coast and be a bridgehead for invasion of the hinterland. For Manuel dreamed, and his captains encouraged him, of the conquest of Fez to be firm territorial base for the expansion of his sea-borne empire. His conquests in the East were to be balanced by dominion of the Arab world in North West Africa.

Preparations had been elaborate and methodical. The river mouth was sounded and the best engineers were consulted as to the most suitable site for building the fortress. 8000 men were recruited, 200 ships were manned and — because "what the King desired above all things was to have many towns and strongholds by the sea coast of Barbary" — whole families were embarked in the ships to people the vast empty land.

The Crusade had once more been proclaimed with solemn processions and eloquent sermons had been preached before the altar. Upon a
radiant July day the expedition sailed, commanded by D.Antonio de
Noronha, son of the Marquess of Vila Real.

It all had seemed auspicious, but everything went wrong. We gather
the impression that the fault lay principally in the command. Again we
see that the King was no judge of men! Young D.Antonio de Noronha
was a valiant knight, but does not seem to have been able to impose
discipline or work out operations with method and order.

To begin with, the site of the fortress was soon seen to be ill-chosen
and — worse still, before it was ready, the King of Fez with the Lord of
Mequinez bore down upon it leading over 30,000 men. The half-built
fortress proved untenable — the King sent orders that it should be given
up and D.Antonio had pulled out his men in such disorder that half of
them were killed. As for the unhappy women and children who had
accompanied the fleet, most of them fell into captivity and had to be
ransomed at great expense.

Damião de Gois says that D.Manuel took this reverse quite calmly —
hearing the news "with much patience and giving thanks to God, as he
always did in all events prosperous or adverse that happened to him."
We wonder if the wretched families who were the principal victims met
their fate with the same pious resignation!

However that may be, the repercussions appear to have done little
damage to Portuguese prestige in Europe. So much was left and such
wide horizons still opened every day. The march on Fez obviously had
to be postponed, but in North Africa, thorns in the Moslem flank, were
still Ceuta, Alcacer-Ceguer, Arzila, newly-conquered Azamor, Mazagan
where fortress-building on a vast scale was going on, the mighty castle
of Safi washed by Atlantic waves, the smaller fort of Aguz by the rocky
coast near Mogador and, further south, Santa Cruz do Cabo de Guer,
founded in 1505 by private enterprise and in 1513 taken over by the
Crown.

All these protected the sea way to equatorial lands, below the trading posts of Arguin, Senegal and Gambia. There stood the Castle of the
Mine, first European settlement beside that steamy coast, whence every
year some 170,000 doubloons were shipped to swell the royal exchequer.

More glamorous still was the East coast of Africa — chain of glitter-

ing sultanates beside the Indian Ocean. All these Arab sultans were
tributary. That of Malindi had remained a faithful friend since first he
had been visited by Vasco da Gama. The other rulers – of Mozambique,
Mombasa, Kilwa, Sofala – hostile at first, had all been brought to heel.
Mozambique was the halfway house for Indian fleets on their way out
or returning from India. There ships could be refitted and repaired in
the course of their six months voyage. There was a fortress and a
trading post at Mozambique, and – even more necessary – a hospital
for anybody who might be too ill to proceed, for voyages in 16th
century ships could be a trial of endurance even to the strongest.

Great hopes were centred upon this East coast of Africa. Was not
Sofala the Ophir of Solomon, supplied with gold from the Monomotapa
mines? Many stories were told of the mysterious realm of Monomotapa
far inland, believed to be more auriferous than the mines of Guinea.
The Monomotapa was lord of all this wealth and many princes were his
vassals. He lived up country in a region little known where vast stone
buildings with inscriptions in a writing nobody could read bore testi-
mony to forgotten splendour. The King in his royal village of straw and
adobe was served in solemn state by kneeling courtiers. If he should
cough or sneeze or have a drink, everyone present in the house called
down a blessing on his head, which was echoed from mouth to mouth
throughout the village so that all could know their lord had cleared his
throat or had refreshed himself. The land was abundant in fruit and
corn; there were great herds of elephants – four or five thousand were
slain every year and their ivory exported in vast quantities to India. But
Monomotapa's trade since ancient times was principally in gold – the
river beds were full of the precious metal; one traveller had seen a
basket load of ingots and bars as thick as a man's finger. In that land
everything was paid for by its weight in gold.

The eyewitness who reported these things was Antonio Fernandes –
a carpenter by trade and *degredado* in social status – one of those
useful convicts who for offences, some small, some great, had been
sentenced to deportation overseas. Such might be landed anywhere by
an exploring fleet, and left to overcome their fate or perish in the
wilderness. The number of these who made good and served heroically
proves the wisdom of King João II who used to say it was sheer waste
to execute a man when pioneers were needed for the undiscovered
world!

Antonio Fernandes, left by Cabral in 1500 to his own devices at Kilwa, had learned the language of the country. He wandered up the fever-stricken rivers to Monomotapa's realm and through the domains of his turbulent and rebel vassals. Antonio Fernandes had a way with him. Everywhere he gained such influence over the Kaffirs that – writes João Vas de Almada, Alcaide of Sofala – "they worship him like God, and where he goes all wars are made to cease for love of him!" The Arab merchants who had hitherto enjoyed the monopoly of the gold trade of the interior did all they could to make the natives fear the Portuguese, but the attractive Antonio Fernandes so won the confidence of his Kaffir friends as to persuade them to come with him to visit the foreigners at Sofala.

Antonio Fernandes has left us no written report – he may even have been illiterate – but he came back with many secrets that he hoped one day to tell the King by word of mouth. Meanwhile he would return inland and find out more.

How did he know he ever would get back to tell his tale? Chances were fifty-fifty up those deadly rivers flowing through countries rent by savage wars. It well might be that his knowledge would perish with him. His friend Gaspar Veloso pointed this out and so persuaded him to dictate a few notes, and little else remains today to tell us about Antonio Fernandes' travels. We cannot say if he ever returned to Portugal. We only know that he came and went during several years between Sofala and Monomotapa, wandering around the country, travelling one way and returning another – "only to see more lands."

The African chiefs were taking interest. The great Inhamunda was crying out to see white men – and he wanted a bombard too, he would not ask for any other present! Antonio Fernandes, returning from Sofala, took several men with him, but all of them except himself sickened and fell ill by the way and Antonio Fernandes felt he could not leave them. The chief was angry when the white men failed to appear, and abused roundly his own subjects who had been sent as guides. They should have carried the sick men on their shoulders! he declared. But finally Antonio Fernandes fell ill himself, so got no further upon that occasion.

How many more expeditions returned inland we cannot say, but we know that they were repeated. Antonio Fernandes continued to make friends with the Kaffir chiefs, telling them that his king – the greatest in the world — would make them powerful and rich, and that the things said by the "Moors" about the Portuguese were lies. So it was that the captains of the fortresses established good relations with the chieftains of the interior.

João Vaz de Almada, from headquarters at Sofala, was planning exploration on a larger scale: "If I could have a brigantine," he writes, "with fifteen oarsmen, and a caravel such as there is here, and another one much smaller . . . I should undertake to discover many things. With medicines and a good physician, methinks I could reach Monomotapa by water and thence go on to other parts . . . ." The proviso of "medicines and a good physician" is significant, a grim reminder of the fevers infesting those rivers.

In spite of this there is no doubt that penetration from the coast was carried far inland, thrusting towards the centre of the continent. Antonio Fernandes recognized the copper bracelets sold at the Monomotapa fairs as being identical to those "made on the copper rivers of Manicongo."

The rich mines of East Africa were still a golden dream, a vision for some dazzling future. For the present the spice fleets came and went while Venice groaned, carrying pepper from the ports of Malabar, ivory and cinnamon from Ceylon, and from the far Spice Islands, the Moluccas came at last the precious cloves. Portuguese ships sailed to Ternate; there Francisco Serrão had become the chief power beside the throne, the counsellor and favourite of the native king who never acted without his approval — "he rules the king and the whole country" — Albuquerque had written in his last report, dated 1515. D.Manuel's ambassadors had been welcomed in Siam and others had been despatched from Malacca to China. "We recommend peace and friendship with everyone . . . ."D.Manuel had written in 1514 to Rui de Araujo at Malacca. "Let it be known," he urges in the same letter, "that our people are not just conquerors and subjugators of lands held by the enemies of our Holy Catholic religion, but that in all their dealings they observe truth and good faith."

Venice watched all these things with gloom, but did not yet despair. She hoped to make a contract with the King of Portugal to buy all spices every year for a fixed sum, and so regain the past monopoly. The Captain-General of five galleys bound for England in 1518 was ordered to call in at Lisbon on the way and try to negotiate a deal.

Arrayed in silk and cloth of gold, the General and his officers disembarked on the pier before the royal palace of the Ribeira. Halfway they were met by the King and Queen surrounded by the royal children; the envoy was offered a chair to sit beside the sovereign; all graciousness and charm, the King conversed with the Venetians. He gave them audience a few days later and granted every privilege they asked, but he would make no contract for the spices, and every reason they alleged was turned down with a smile. Frustrated but with fervent mutual assurances of great good will, the envoys retired after presenting to the King and Queen for each a service of finest Venetian crystal. They received in return a rich offering of spices and preserves and silks and brocades and other lovely things from India. Thus Portugal and Venice continued to be beloved friends and cutthroat rivals.

Venice, it seems, was more troubled about the spice trade than the Turkish peril which had flashed up again in 1517 when Sultan Selim took Cairo from the Mamelukes and conquered the lands ruled by Egypt. The rising power of the Ottoman was a menace to Christendom. Surely the time had come for raising once again the call to Holy War! D.Manuel, whose oriental empire touched the Middle East, was quite convinced of this. He wrote to the Pope, exciting him to stir the Christian princes to concerted action. He himself would be weighing in with everything he had, but felt that such an effort should receive support from his colleagues.

The Pope was all sweetness and light. He told D.Miguel da Silva, Portuguese ambassador at the Holy See, that Manuel alone among the princes could be counted on to confirm words by action. But money was difficult to raise, great armies were expensive and times were bad. The princes were unlikely to be forthcoming.

The princes were consulted none the less, and "each one wrote a letter of very good words." The only, however, willing to commit himhimself was Manual's cousin, the aging Emperor Maximilian. At sixty years as enthusiastic as a youth of twenty, Maximilian – "Last of the knights," as he has been called – was the only one to come forward, D.Miguel da Silva writes, "offering his person with great good will." Unfortunately that was all he had to offer. His edifying letter was read out before the Concilium then in session and admired by all, but everybody felt that the Emperor's person alone could not do much – for Maximilian was a permanent bankrupt.

At the same time all were loud in praise of D.Manuel. According to D.Miguel da Silva — "here no one speaks of anything but how you are the only Christian king, for you alone support the Christian cause in truth and word of counsel and when necessary by deed, shedding no Christian blood except in service of Our Lord." The Pope had here the wherewithal to make the other princes blush — is D.Miguel's conclusion. Perhaps, indeed, they blushed but that was all they did about it.

The Portuguese alone defended the gates of the Red Sea, and for the next 400 years Turkey held on to Cairo.

XV

The Little Kingdom

This sea-borne empire of D.Manuel's, a line far-flung half round the world, over two oceans and three continents, was based upon a very small corner of Europe.

The little land of Portugal — a narrow strip beside the western ocean — was peopled by less than two million souls. It had no industries, no special mineral wealth or riches of the soil, its natural fortune was the sea and the sun — the sea that opened the wide world, and the blest sun of Portugal that warms but does not burn, drawing forth corn and fruit and wine out of its rolling hills. Its people were primarily farmers and fishermen. The rocky coast of Portugal, swept by Atlantic storms, had bred a race of seamen that when time was ripe were ready to fulfil their destiny upon the Ocean. Inland the gentle hills and green valleys, watered by pleasant streams, invited cultivation. From Entre-Douro-e-Minho, described by one 16th century writer as "the best garden in the world," to the hot plains of Alentejo where wheat was harvested in June, and the blue and golden Algarve, which from ages immemorial had furnished Europe with dried figs and other fruit, Portugal could be self-sufficing, and had so been in days of peace — "Our neighbours have more need of us than we of them" — Zurara wrote in the euphoria of the 15th century.

A hundred years later the picture was not quite so bright. The bitter sea and distant mirages had begun to absorb earth's kindly fruits; the little fields of Portugal were beginning to feel the lack of arms to till them. The world is very wide and a male population of about 800,000 men are few to spread over the seven seas. While ploughboys were turned into sailors and reached the far ends of the earth, nettles grew in the fallow fields at home. A time could be foreseen when Portugal, far from supplying her neighbours with bread, would have to import wheat from other lands.

But during the reign of D.Manuel the glory and the glamour hardly could be pierced by gloomy forebodings. In this reign writes Jeronimo Osorio, with the wistfulness of two generations later — "it seemed that poverty was banished. Sadness was nowhere to be found, complaints were silent; dancing and merrymaking sounded everywhere...." The good old days of our grandfathers! Who has not heard them praised? We fear, however that to King Manuel's contemporaries, joy was not quite so unconfined as imagined by the good bishop. There were old problems still unsolved and already some new ones cast their shadow. In a small country without industry or capital, and handicapped by shortage of manpower, could it be certain that the treasures of the East would always pay the bill? The cost of bringing them was such and the sacrifice of human lives so great.

It seems, however, that not many people were troubled by this thought in the glorious heyday. Portugal of the early 16th century was a hopeful little country and on the whole well governed. Much local liberty was enjoyed under the administration of its *concelhos,* or free boroughs, subject to the paternal aegis of the King.

This aegis was supreme and absolute, of course. Absolutism was the most up-to-date philosophy of kingship in the 16th century, and Manuel's preceptor had been the learned Dr. Diogo Lopes Rebelo, convinced exponent of the divine right of kings. Upon this subject he had written in 1498 a weighty treatise *De Republica Gubernanda Regem,* dedicated to his royal pupil, then already a reigning king.

Nurtured upon such teaching, Manuel had never dreamed of disputing the will of his cousin, D.João II. A king's mandates were to be judged by God alone, to Whom he was responsible for the people committed to his care. The 16th century Portuguese would not question this concept, the more so that absolutism had not yet degenerated into tyranny. "Our Lord the King" appeared as a father figure rather than an autocrat. Perhaps no European monarch of this period could boast of having such affectionate and loyal subjects as the kings of Portugal: "They all are sons, not subjects! " Queen Isabel of Castile is said to have commented enviously of the people ruled by D.João II, her cousin and rival. There was some truth in the statement. Until the revolutionary 19th century, the Portuguese people prided themselves on loving loyalty to their kings.

D.Manuel, as befitted a ward and pupil of the Perfect Prince, was a

conscientious ruler. He got up early and attended to business most of
the day, receiving ministers of justice, listening to petitions, studying
accounts, while his perpetual orchestra of lutes and flutes and other
instruments discoursed sweet music in his ears. Thus, writes Osório, "he
entertained his spirit in a seemly manner while governing his kingdom."
Which speaks much for his power of concentration!

Assisted by "learned men of his Council," D.Manuel undertook a
total revision of the Code of Law, the *Ordenações Afonsinas,* organized
by the great regent D.Pedro during the minority of Manuel's uncle,
King Afonso V. This work, in future to be known as *Ordenações Manuelinas,* occupied a great part of D.Manuel's reign, although a first
edition was issued in 1512 – the same one which, as we have seen, had
so impressed the King of Congo.

The Archives of the realm also received attention, and many ancient
documents, which time had almost blotted out, were carefully recopied
by the best calligraphers. Utility without beauty is a modern concept.
In Manuel's chancellery prosaic records of money grants and title deeds
are to be seen transcribed on exquisitely illuminated parchment. The
Leitura Nova these books were called – "so great a work" – to quote
Damião de Gois – "that it could not be finished in his [D.Manuel's]
lifetime . . . ." Nor yet, in the reign of his son was it concluded, nor ever
afterwards, though what was done remains today one of the loveliest
works of art to be seen in the Torre do Tombo. Equally beautiful are
many of the charters granted anew during this reign to various municipalities, notably those of Porto, Matosinhos and Lisbon.

Lovely Lisbon, cosmopolitan Lisbon, with more than 10,000 buildings spread over five hills, was a city which – seen through the patriotic, albeit travelled, eyes of Damião de Gois – could hold its own for
beauty and architectural elegance with any other capital of Europe.
There was no shortage there of anything. Its markets were replete with
meat and fish and bread and wine and fruit, and the water supply was
guaranteed by many fountains flowing perennially, especially the
Chafariz del Rei (Fountain of the King) which, under marble arches had
six taps that gushed with pure water sufficient "to give drink to the
world."

And that was good because the whole world came to Lisbon. In the
broad estuary rocked ships from many a distant port, unloading treasures from the far ends of the earth onto its quays, while passengers and

sailors wandered through the town where there was much to see and to admire.

The Rua Nova dos Mercadores, which ran downhill to the river was particularly fine. It measured thirty palms' breadth across and was adorned one either side by noble buildings. There, merchants of all nations chaffered all day long; traders and craftsmen, jewellers, engravers and goldsmiths displayed their wares, and moneylenders held open shop.

On the square opposite the Custom House, in front of tables, letter-writers sat, awaiting clients with pens ready trimmed to indite messages of love, to compose verses or epitaphs, funeral orations, or plain down-to-earth business letters, making their charge according to the subject matter. Damião de Gois declares he never saw the like in other European capitals. Such things, he adds, all go to show "the greatness of Lisbon and the number of its inhabitants," which have been estimated as being at the time close to 85,000.

With the exception of the magnificent Rua Nova, the streets of Lisbon, as in most medieval cities, were narrow and dark, the finest of them seldom exceeding a few yards across. D.Manuel promoted drastic measures to bring in some light and air. The butting out windows and balconies that almost touched each other overhead must all come out – and so they did – "a profitable and necessary decree" – comments Damião de Gois.

It seems a pity that the olive groves within the city walls had also to come down, but with increasing population and consequent housing shortage, the trees were sacrificed for building plots. A wide space was also cleared outside the gates to tether animals, so that they might not clutter up and soil the streets.

Lisbon owes to D.Manuel the vast square by the river – the Terreiro do Paço, which to the present day is one of the chief features of the city. "With great labour and expense" he reclaimed that wide emplacement from the beach and built for himself there a "magnificent and sumptuous palace, the *Paço da Alcaçova,*" on the heights above, where former kings had made their residence, was abandoned. D.Manuel preferred to live by the river, close to his ships. While the building was under way the court removed to the former monastery of Santos-o-Velho, so-called because the relics of the sainted martyrs Verissimo, Maxim and Julia had been enshrined there, before D.João II had them translated to a new building on the hill.

By the river Manuel desired to live, and watch his tall ships come and go, speeding before the wind down to the bar and the great ocean. By this same river he hoped to lie in his last sleep, under the twisted stone cables and shell-encrusted columns sustaining the palmy vault of the great abbey he was building at Belem. The monastery of the Jeronimos adjoined the church, and further down the river stood a lovely little fortress on guard over the bar, all creamy white with crenellated towers, fluted turrets and decorative windows — the prettiest defensive work that anyone could see. Planned, it would seem, by D.João II, the Tower of Belem was built by D.Manuel. One must confess that his taste was unerring.

He it was also who finished Lisbon's great hospital — a work begun by the late king in his last years and bequeathed in his will to his successor.

The Hospital of All Saints — an ever open door for the sick poor — was in all things a worthy monument to the two kings who planned it. "Our hospital," exclaims Damião de Gois, "can be rated above all other royal hospitals, however great and celebrated throughout Spain or other lands of Christendom!" Patriotic exaggeration, perhaps. We gather from D.João's will that the Hospital of All Saints was modelled more or less upon the famous Hospital of Santa Maria at Florence. However that may be, there is no doubt that the great Lisbon hospital of D.Manuel's reign could hold its own with some of the best abroad at the same date. It stood behind the great square of the Rossio, upon land covered today by the Praça da Figueira. There were three hundred beds set out in three spacious wards, two for men, one for women. These opened onto cloistered gardens in which vegetables and fruit were grown and pigeons and poultry kept to supply the kitchen and baking ovens, and several wells ensured abundant drinking water.

Each bed was provided with linen curtains and snowy linen sheets, a woollen cover over the straw mattress, two blankets, a feather bolster and two feather pillows sheathed in pillowcases. These bedclothes and those that the patient wore must, according to the regulations, be changed at least once a week, and more often if necessary, because — declares the *Regimento* of this 16th century hospital — "the patients' health largely depends on cleanliness." For the same reason the floors must all be swept, the patients washed, all plates and dishes scoured, no

evil smells were to offend the nose, against which aromatic scents must
be sprinkled around to purify the air.

The doctor's visit was a solemn rite which took place twice a day,
announced each time by the ringing of a bell. Followed by the pharma-
cist and the head of the nursing staff, he made his rounds, prescribing
medicines and making out diet sheets. The second visit was timed before 2 p.m. and for the rest of the day and through the night, the sick
were cared for by their attendants "with all the charity and love we
owe to God and to our neighbour." Anything else, the kindly *Regimento* observes "would be harmful to the patients' health."

This hospital included wards for infectious diseases and private
rooms for the wealthy. One important department was the nursery for
abandoned babies. All infants left on the steps of the main entrance to
the hospital were taken in and handed over to the care of contracted
wet nurses.

In all the towns of Portugal new hospitals arose during this reign,
and closely connected with them grew up an equally important work —
that of the Brotherhood of Mercy, or Misericordia. This was an association among laymen for helping the poor and carrying comfort to the
sad. Similar charitable associations existed in other European lands, as
had also other *confrarias* in Portugal, but hardly on the scale and with
the scope of the Misericordias, founded during the reign of D.Manuel,
chiefly through the initiative of his beloved sister, the dowager Queen
Leonor.

The widowed queen of D.João II who, with the death of her only
son, had lost all that she held dearest in life, devoted her remaining
years to works of religion and charity. She it was who, assisted by the
saintly Frei João Contreiras, in 1498, had founded the Misericordia of
Lisbon. A hundred laymen "of good reputation, fearing God and keeping his commandments," were recruited to serve in the Brotherhood,
observing the New Testament mandate of "Bear ye one another's bur-
dens." They promised to perform the various works of charity: to feed
the hungry, give drink to the thirsty, clothe the naked and console the
sorrowful, to teach the ignorant, visit the sick and prisoners, and shelter
the homeless. They must forgive those who offended them and suffer
injuries with patience, praying always for the living and the dead. A
high ideal and, with due allowance for poor human nature, worthily
upheld, and that, says Damião de Gois, stimulated the generosity of

nationals and foreigners who, seeing that no money was carried over from one year to another for any other purpose, were glad to contribute to the funds of the Brotherhood.

D.Manuel, when he returned from his frustrated pilgrimage into Castile and Aragon, found and approved the work that his sister had promoted in his absence. There must be more Misericordias in the land, he said, and in 1499, at his order, that of Oporto came into being. Soon every town of any importance in Portugal and many of the smaller ones as well, founded Misericordias. That of Evora was particularly distinguished, counting among its brethren the King himself, his sister D.Leonor, and later on the Queen Maria. The good work was extended overseas. In 1519, at the King's command, a Misericordia was founded at Goa.

The problem of the age, however, before which all social services broke down, was the recurring plague. Bubonic? Typhus? Or even perhaps one of the malignant forms of influenza? Perhaps sometimes one, sometimes another. The vague diagnoses of the period make it difficult to guess. It was simply "the plague" that came and went unaccountably, and disappeared in one place only to flare up in another. Why should this be? the people groaned. Astrologers declared that epidemics might be caused by certain conjunctions of the heavenly bodies. This made all human preventive measures appear useless, but there were practical persons who had observed that where flies multiplied the plague was likely soon to follow.

Many treatises were composed upon the subject and rules laid down – some sensible, others highly imaginative. Keep out of crowds, avoid bad smells, at least they all agreed – do not take many baths in times of plague, the physicians advised – and above all, do not lose heart: confess your sins and cultivate a cheerful spirit! Desirable and even prophylactic though this might be it cannot have been easy to preserve while ambulating evil lurked round every corner.

Someone must be responsible for such a visitation! It was a scourge to castigate the people's sins, pious persons believed, but many simply blamed the Jews. Of course it was their fault! All very well to say that they had been expelled in 1498 – how many had remained under the mask of baptism. New Christians secretly performing Jewish rites! Quite naturally God was displeased, and visited their sin on those who basely tolerated the abuse.

It was the Sunday after Easter 1506. Plague raged in Lisbon and the
city was half empty, for all who could had fled the infection far from
the town. The King was travelling to Beja to visit his mother, when
frightful news arrested him upon the way:

The capital was a blood bath! The population, seized by mass hys-
teria, was slaughtering all New Christians and any person suspect of
being a Jew. Men, women, and children were being hacked to pieces,
houses were wrecked and plundered with the assistance of ruffian seamen from the foreign ships in port, who poured ashore to share the loot
and bear a hand in the massacre.

The principal authorities were out of town. Those remaining could
not – or dared not – check the raging mob. For two whole days the
frightfulness continued.

How had it all begun? As swiftly as a spark can ignite tow. The
melancholy people in the sombre church of São Domingos had been
hearing Mass in the Capela de Jesus. As the solemn notes were intoned a
light was seen to flicker fitfully behind the Crucifix. A miracle – mur-
mured some of the devotees. No miracle at all! a voice proclaimed
aloud. Only a lighted candle in the background. The speaker was a New
Christian! "Heresy! Heresy! " yelled two Dominican friars. The scep-
tic was seized by the hair, forcibly dragged out of church and clubbed
to death. A frenzied mob took up the cry and fell upon everyone who
might possibly have Jewish connections. They murdered in the streets,
they burned the corpses on the beach, they broke into the houses, led
by demoniac monks who screamed that heresy must be obliterated. All
the toughs from the ships in port hastened to join the fray; for two
days Lisbon was a very hell, while brave and merciful Old Christians did
their best to save all those they could. When at last public justice
asserted itself, trying to take control and pacify the mob, already few
victims were left alive.

All this was told the King and Nemesis descended upon Lisbon.
Punishments were applied wholesale. The fierce fanatic friars were de-
frocked and burnt alive, the ringleaders were hanged and property was
confiscated. Of course the foreign crews who had played so conspicu-
ous a part in the disorder were nowhere to be found. They got off
safely with their loot and disappeared on the high seas. Everyone who
might have intervened and failed was relentlessly chastised. The supine
governors and local authorities whose action had been so culpably de-

layed were severely reprimanded. But the whole town was responsible – the King declared – and so must lose its privileges. D.Manuel abolished then and there the *Casa dos 24,* the assembly of free men, freely elected, who governed the borough. Further to this, Lisbon, sunk in ignominy, would forfeit the right to entitle herself officially "Ever Loyal and Noble City."

These terrible strictures, however, were enforced for no more than two years. In 1508, at the intercession of the Queen, the King forgave his capital city – "because of the good will and love she always had and has for it." So the House of 24 held its meetings again and Lisbon once more qualified as "loyal and noble."

In contrast to Lisbon's deplorable conduct on this occasion, her rival in the North, the ancient city of Oporto, was given full marks, as set forth in a letter from the King shortly after the terrible events: "We have been informed how in your city you have behaved towards the New Christians, and that during the disorder and uprising against them and massacres that took place in Lisbon nothing occurred that might cause us displeasure. And we are glad that your city should thus be mindful of what behoves our service ... for it is most essential that these New Christians should be left in peace and that there should be no rioting against them, nor anything small or great to harm their persons or property, and so we enjoin and order you to take good care, as we are confident you will ....'

The cities of Portugal in the days of D.Manuel were few and small, but proud and independent. They were accustomed to rule their local affairs, electing their councillors and aldermen, free from royal intromission. Of course Lisbon where, plague permitting, the court was more often in residence, must have fallen more directly under the royal influence than Oporto – "the Port" – who queened it in the North between the two great rivers of Douro and Minho, exporting the produce of that vaunted "finest garden in the world" – wine, oranges and lemons, chestnuts, almonds and other fruit – to the north of Europe. Oporto was proud of the distinguished part the city had played, always on the national side, during the late dynastic wars, and enjoyed privileges and favours granted by grateful kings, but seldom was honoured – or afflicted – by royal visits. Communications with the hilly north were long and slow and very rough. It was not often that the ambulating court reached higher than Coimbra. The Portuenses did not mind that much. They sent their representatives to the Cortes with their petitions and complaints, but discouraged all interference with the election of their Town Councils. In 1500 they protested to D.Manuel when he required that the list of newly appointed councillors should be submitted to him. The royal reply was tactful and conciliatory: the city must not take it amiss that the King should concern himself with their elections. On the contrary they should feel honoured by his interest – an interest only shown to "very few cities."

We are not told which others were so distinguished. The "cities" of Portugal, in any case, were few. Most boroughs were administered by *vilas* or small towns. Lisbon, Porto, Coimbra, Braga and Evora were the principal cities, the last named being often residence of the court.

The frequency of the royal presence there did not, however, prevent the citizens of Evora from plain speaking. On one occasion, we are told, the councillors refused to pay a tax which they considered excessive. D.Manuel called aside João Mendes Cicioso, an alderman of high rank and influence in the town. The King told him that if he wished to enjoy the royal favour, he must persuade his colleagues to accept what had been consented elsewhere. "Senhor," declared João Mendes, "I do not need your favours. My father left me 250,000 reais revenue, with which I can honourably maintain myself. You cannot very well take this from me, but even if you did, that would not hold me from telling the truth: you cannot in reason and justice impose this tax upon your people, and those who so advise you do not love your soul and honour! "

D.Manuel, the Fortunate, after a spectacular reign of twenty years, would not gladly be gainsaid. He lost his temper: very well, he said, João Mendes would be deprived of his office and sent to prison!

Quite coolly, João Mendes thanked his lord for everything – except the prison, he added, which he did not deserve. On reflection next day the King came to the same conclusion. He sent for João Mendes and declared himself grateful for the candid advice. He wished he had many more such men for the good of the realm.

Between the towns it was a wild country of moor and rock and mountain and forests of chestnut, oak and pine. Rural fidalgos in their little *quintas* hunted the boar, and bears were sometimes seen, while in the winter wolves descended form the lonely hills, ravaging the flocks, attacking cattle and mares with their foals. Things got so bad and the wild beasts so multiplied that the King promulgated a decree for compulsory wolf hunting.

Between Easter and Pentecost, every city and town must organize a hunt; a prize was set on every wolf's head, paid to the killer as a fine by those who had failed to turn up for the hunt. If there were no recalcitrants, the money must be found by the Town Council, and any nest of wolf cubs brought in, living or dead, was to be paid at 50 reais a head.

That was perfectly sound, but the Portuguese people do not like to be regimented. It appears that these compulsory drives brought about so much quarrelling and heart burning that "the profit us not so great as it should be," declares a royal order of 1517. The King therefore ordains that in future there should be no compulsion — only in such places where these hunts were customary should they be organized, without coercion. "And because we wish to do our people favour and that archers and others should strive with care and diligence to kill the said wolves and should have interest in so doing," beyond the 50 reais to be paid by the local authorities for each wolf's head, the slayer would receive a further bounty of 1000 reais from the royal exchequer. Thus, on a purely voluntary base, results were probably more satisfactory.

Another decree affecting the countryside which the King saw fit to modify, concerned the planting of trees. At the beginning of the reign a provision had been issued to the effect that in every district throughout the realm, each dweller in a city, town, or village must plant a certain number of trees within the next four years. These were presumably fruit trees, but the document which has come down to us does not specify. It appears, however, that the execution of the mandate was found onerous — "we are informed that owing to certain difficulties it could not be carried out without oppression to our people." Therefore the King was pleased to prolong the period specified for another year, and all fines hitherto imposed for non-observance of the order were to be remitted and refunded.

This document is of interest as shedding a curious sidelight on the paternalism of the rule as well as indicating a concern for arboriculture one would not have expected in the 15th century.

There is no doubt, however, that agriculture was generally losing interest. The glamour and the glory of wonder-worlds overseas were dazzling everyone in Portugal, from the sovereign himself down to the humblest peasant. Gone were the days when the conquerors of Ceuta rejoiced that after victory they still had time to get home for their vintage. Seed time and harvest had become a dull recurring round set against the yearly return of fleets laden with exotic treasure. At this period all eager youth must embark for the far ends of the earth, or revolve in the glittering ambit of the court where marvels would be constantly renewed.

XVI

The Family and the Court

The ambulating court presided over by D.Manuel the Fortunate was unique in Europe. Glittering with jewels, of course, but that might have been found elsewhere, it was the human element that made it so exotic. It was a multi-racial gathering in which European diplomats rubbed shoulders with black princelings from Congo and Senegal, with pale Persians and brown Asiatics and yellow men from the Far East, even from distant China. There the budding humanist Damião de Gois made friends with the Armenian envoy from the land of Prester John and the future historian João de Barros, still "at the age for spinning tops," became aware of the wide world, while little D.João de Castro, sitting at the sovereign's feet, sharing his fruit, heard pilots and cosmographers hold forth upon the mysteries of the Sphere. These *moços fidalgos,* pages at D.Manuel's court, absorbed an education broader than that of the learned Latinists and grammarians of the University, whose courses the King liked them to follow.

Since D.João II had curbed the independence of the grandees of the Realm, the court of the King had become the hub around which society revolved, the fountainhead of favour and the dispenser of education. The great fidalgos stood around with cap in hand while the King dined. Their sons sat on the floor under his table. When he despatched in public several times a week, his secretaries awaited on their knees on each side of his desk. Yet they say that this king was far from unapproachable. When he went hunting in a happy mood, his pages dared surround his horse and hold him up while they requested favours. He liked to see young people dance, he himself often took the floor; he loved bull fights, tilting and other knightly sports. He was a very cheerful person, writes Damião de Gois, who saw him at all hours, and sometimes held the barber's basin while his brother Fructus, Keeper of the Robes, was combing the royal hair.

Christmas Eve was a great and enjoyable occasion at court. D.Manuel sat publicly in the great hall, surrounded by mace-bearers, heralds and Kings of Arms, with all his orchestra of trumpets, cymbals and pipes braying sonorously behind him. All the lords, knights and noblemen gathered around, and were served with fresh fruit and preserves and confectionary from Madeira. The King then sent the same refreshments to the Queen and her ladies, banqueting modestly apart, after which all the functionaries — chaplains, musicians, physicians, huntsmen, grooms and pages feasted in the guardroom on similar delights. "This was the most solemn and eagerly anticipated festival of the year," declares Damião de Gois.

Intellectual enjoyment at the festive seasons was provided by the "Autos" of Gil Vicente, at least fifteen of which were played before the court in Manuel's time. That same artist-craftsman who had fashioned the Monstrance of Belem from the first Indian gold, was also a forerunner of the modern theatre. His "autos" — written in either Portuguese or Castilian, for the Queen being Castilian, this was a bilingual court — are unique in literature of contemporary Europe. Dramatic art was as yet in its infancy, but Gil Vicente was a star of dawn. There is a warm humanity in all his works, whether devotional, lyrical, sarcastic, or farcical which still has power to move us to emotion or laughter. Encouraged by the patronage of the royal family, especially the Queen Dowager Leonor, Mestre Gil brought forth at each religious festival and on all public occasions his commentary of wit and wisdom. The topic of the day would never fail to draw a comic skit, a song of praise, or biting criticism. His audience listened and laughed and took it all in perfectly good part, untrammelled by the inhibitions of a later period.

Arts were favoured and poetry esteemed at the Manueline court, where poets such as Bernardim Ribeiro and Sá de Miranda spent their youth amid a crowd of enthusiastic amateurs. A gift for turning verses was a prized worldly accomplishment, and at those festive evenings — the celebrated *saraus manuelinos* — young men and maidens vied with one another in the composition of verses, good and bad and indifferent, many of which have been preserved in the Cancioneiro of Garcia de Resende.

On Sundays and holidays in summer time, there were river picnics. The King loved to sail down the Tagus in his galleot, silken-canopied and gaily beflagged, always to the accompaniment of music. By the quays of Santos-o-Velho a halt would be called. There, by the dreamy waters in the cool of afternoon, the King and courtiers sat, while fruit and sweets and wine and water were brought forth for their refreshment, and sounds of melody drifted serenely out to sea.

What must have been a perpetual delight to all youngsters at court, as well, we fancy, as to their elders, was the collection of exotic beasts kept in the royal menagerie. No Christian king before D.Manuel could boast of elephants from India — and he had five of them at one time in his stable: four male and one female. The last was sent him in 1512. The Rajah writes that since the King had liked the elephant previously despatched, he felt "it ought to have as mate this little cow-elephant I am sending you . . . for she is very good and well trained . . ."

To feed an elephant during a six months voyage in a small ship might well have been a problem. A document has been preserved dated December 10th 1512, ordering the storekeeper of the ship *Santa Maria de Ajuda* to lay in 1500 loaves of jaggery and 1500 coconuts and a hundred *paras* of rice for the poor little elephant to eat upon the journey. We hope it was enough!

No European groom could be expected to cope with such exotic charges, so Indian mahouts had to be brought over. We find orders signed in Lisbon for issuing clothes to "Pedro and Tomé, masters of the King's elephants" — baptized Christians these, judging by the names, as probably were not Drama and Draman, described as "servants of the said elephants" and also supplied with clothing.

Damião de Gois saw elephants at work in the Lisbon shipyards. He also was present, an enthralled spectator, in 1513, when the great elephant sent to Rome with the embassy of Tristão da Cunha was embarked. The poor beast was very reluctant, it seems, and would not go on board before receiving through his mahout a personal message from the King, assuring him that he was to enter the service of an even greater lord who would treat him still better. If he were disappointed, D.Manuel pledged his kingly word to fetch him back to Lisbon. On the second hearing of this reassuring message, we are told that the elephant embarked — in tears!

This tale is nothing to those with which travellers returned from India regaled their gaping listeners. Diogo Pereira — a reliable person! — declared that at the court of Vijayanagar he actually had heard an elephant answer questions in a clear voice and articulated speech!

No one claimed such accomplishments for the rhinoceros sent to D.Manuel in 1514 by the King of Cambay. So strange a beast had not been seen before, but was identified with the unicorn described in Scripture. It was said that the elephant and rhinoceros were mortal foes and would fight to the death — when either the rhino would impale the elephant's belly upon its horn or be destroyed by the fearful tusks, and trampled under the great hoofs.

D.Manuel, wishing to put this story to the test, turned out one of his elephants and the rhinoceros together. The rhino charged, but the poor elephant was young with undeveloped tusks. It took to flight and, crashing through an iron gate as through the meshes of a net, ran trumpeting back to its stable through the streets of Lisbon, scattering everything before it.

Such were the delights and distractions of D.Manuel's court. Against this colourful background the Fortunate King made his stately progress, arrayed in splendour like that of Solomon, and put on new clothes every day. His life was calm. The great lords, whose teeth his predecessor had drawn, stood at attention before him, one eye fixed hopefully upon the hand whence favours and promotion flowed, the other watching disapprovingly their peers' progress. The King had no danger to fear from such as these, but they still had nuisance value.

The trouble was chiefly among his own relations. The princely houses of Bragança, Aveiro, and Vila Real stood close on the steps of the throne and multiplied their connections with all the richest and most noble in the land. Questions of precedence were viewed with the gravest concern.

Who, for instances, should enjoy pride of place — D.Jorge, Duke of Aveiro, bastard son of the late king, or D.Jaime, Duke of Bragança, lawful offspring of D.Manuel's sister? The final decision was that D.Jaime was nearer akin to the reigning sovereign and D.Jorge, not unnaturally, was hurt but, being a mild man, he took the ruling quietly.

Far more touchy was the Marquis of Vila Real, whose mother was D.Manuel's niece. The noble marquis was terribly upset when the King's private secretary, D.Martinho de Castelo Branco, was promoted to the rank of Count. But D.Antonio, brother to the Marquis, had no title yet! Why should D.Martinho pass before him? The Marquis wrote a stiff letter of protest to his sovereign lord. He had nothing against

D.Martinho — an excellent person, without a doubt — but neither so noble or deserving as D.Antonio! How humiliating it would be for D.Antonio when at Mass in the royal chapel to have to take a lower seat than one of lesser birth, and to stand with uncovered head before his King, while D.Martinho wore a hat! In face of such indignity — splutters the Marquis — "it would be no wonder if D.Antonio my brother were to lose his reason, or to hang himself!" In Heaven their sainted father must be complaining to the Lord of the affront the King had put upon his son! The tirade goes on thus for over five pages. We gather that the letter was greatly admired.

D.Manuel's reply has been preserved — soothing and wholly noncommittal. He loves the Marquis and his brother dearly, he declares, and the memory of their worthy father is ever present to him. He had done more for that family in general and D.Antonio in particular than perhaps for anybody else. The trouble with D.Antonio was "his great and unreasonable passion" but the King's goodwill towards them all remained unaltered, "nor does it seem to us," he concludes rather crushingly, "that your letter calls for any further reply!"

We suppose that the Marquis had to be content with that, and so far as we know D.Antonio did not go mad, and certainly he did not hang himself. It would have been a pity to do anything so rash, for in 1532 D.Manuel's son, then reigning king, made him Count of Linhares.

Marriages of the great were another princely problem. Noble fathers of many sons and daughters looked to the King to see them suitably settled in life. Hopes, fears, ambitions, clashes of will and temperament involved in this important question raised endless problems for the royal matchmaker. Perhaps the one who caused most worry to his family was the young Duke of Bragança, D.Jaime.

This boy, whose early childhood had been shadowed by his father's execution for High Treason, had returned from exile at the age of seventeen. A brilliant lad, intelligent, adept at games and sports, loving fine clothes as well as any young spark of the court, yet it would seem that the shocks that had destroyed his first sense of security had left him psychologically unstable. D.Jaime was subject to strange fits of sombre melancholy, often amounting to acute neurosis.

D.Manuel, always devoted to his sisters, especially adored this nephew. In consultation with the widowed duchess and the boy's maternal grandmother he had arranged what seemed to all an excellent marriage

THE FAMILY AND THE COURT

for him. The daughter of the Duke of Medina Sidonia, a Castilian grandee of princely rank, was a rich heiress. Hardly of nubile age as yet, whereas D.Jaime was nearly twenty — but did that really matter? Let him be betrothed to the damsel, who would remain in charge of her future mother-in-law for two years before starting married life. Both families applauded. The contract was drawn up and signed. The little bride was welcomed to Portugal — only the bridegroom showed himself wrapped in profoundest gloom, which grew deeper as the date approached for consummation of the marriage.

Parents and guardians did not worry. The little duchess was a sweet child — with wealth to make her even more agreeable. D.Jaime was a good boy. He soon would settle down and learn to appreciate his elders' choice. D.Manuel therefore sustained a nasty shock when, on June 2nd, 1502, he was handed a letter in the Duke's handwriting.

"Your Highness must not take my decision amiss, but I do not feel myself fit for matrimony, nor to rule the household and estate Your Highness has granted me. For love of Our Lord Jesus Christ I therefore beg you to transfer everything to my brother D.Dinis, with the title of Duke. Your Highness will thus serve God and do me a great favour."

And where was the Duke? the King cried in dismay. Nobody knew! He had disappeared the other night from his mother's house at Portel. He was off to Jerusalem, somebody said, and there he proposed to embrace the religious life.

All the royal family was shattered — especially the ladies. For the Duke was already married! they cried. The dowry had been paid and the young bride was waiting for her husband. What right had he thus to shame her and them? What worried the King perhaps even more was that, until a child was born to him, D.Jaime was heir-presumptive to the throne! The Queen indeed was very near her time, but such events are always chancy. D.Manuel in agitation wrote to the Pope. He begged the Holy Father to send Briefs to all convents of Christendom, forbidding them to accept the Duke to their Orders. At the same time he despatched messengers to comb the countryside and apprehend the fugitive wherever he might be.

In the end a certain Febus Moniz ran him to earth — at Bragança, saying his prayers behind locked doors. "He is the greatest theologian I have ever seen . . ." writes the envoy, having at last managed to get himself admitted. All the same, it seemed to the observer, that "melancholy humours" had great part in this devotion.

The long and short is that D.Jaime was persuaded to return and face his marital commitments. Two children were born to the ill-assorted pair, but theirs never became a happy marriage. In fact, ten years later the Duke murdered his wife in an access of jealousy that proved to be unfounded. The royal pardon was easily obtained. The fury of an injured husband was viewed with much understanding by that generation, and if suspicions turned out to be groundless — that was just too bad! Besides, the King adored this nephew. All the same, the remorseful Othello did penance the rest of his life, sitting for hours on end up to the neck in ice cold water. A broken life, one might suppose, but far from that. Following this violent outburst D.Jaime appears to regained his mental balance. He lived another twenty years, a respected figure at court. He fought the Moors and conquered Azamor. In 1520 he married again, a charming wife to whom he was devoted and who gave him sons and daughters.

Happily for the kingdom, perhaps, his position as heir-presumptive did not last, for soon a bevy of royal children were growing up around the throne.

The Queen's first child, the Prince D.João, appeared on June 7th 1502, upon a day of pouring rain and growling thunder. As the King wrote triumphantly to the good cities of the realm — "it pleased Our Lord God by His mercy to deliver the Queen, my well-beloved and cherished wife, of my well-beloved and cherished son, the Prince," for which fortunate event loyal citizens were all invited to rejoice.

A year later the Infanta D.Isabel arrived, and at the end of 1504, another daughter, D.Beatriz, was added to the nursery. The King was disappointed — he wanted more sons, but it was early days to be discouraged. Fifteen months later he was able to announce jubilantly to the King of Aragon, his father-in-law, the birth of the Infante D.Luis — adding:

"If the Queen, my best beloved and cherished wife, had brought forth a daughter, we should have announced this to you more modestly, as befitted the birth of a daughter, but because last night, between two and three hours after midnight, Our Lord delivered her and she gave birth to a son, we wished to let you know this by letter, whereby you may also know that the fear we had lest it should be a daughter like the others, which we felt would shame us both, has increased our pleasure and satisfaction! "

During the following years, only once did the Queen disgrace herself and him by producing another daughter, whose date of birth is not found on record although we know that she died in 1513, but meanwhile a series of sons was growing up to flatter the parental pride.

In 1507, the Infante D.Fernando was born, and two years later D.Afonso. D.Henrique came into the world in January 1512, and D.Duarte three years later. Finally, in 1517, there was the baby D.António, who died at birth.

That left six sons and two daughters whose future must be planned. The problem of marriages, with all the dynastic questions involved, was quite enough to give headaches to a royal father.

Following the tradition of recent generations, D.Manuel looked to Castile, where his nephew, the young king Charles V, was expected shortly to arrive from the Netherlands, together with his sister, Madame Leonor. Here were two marriages, all ready-made! At Brussels in 1517, the ambassador Pero Correa cast an appraising eye upon these two grandchildren of the Emperor Maximilian, and reported his findings to King Manuel.

The boy-king of Castile did not impress him much, although he says he is a fine upstanding youth, not bad looking in spite of a defective mouth, but he is very tongue-tied and unforthcoming. It is also regrettable that he speaks no Spanish language and seeks no companionship except with Flemings.

His nineteen year old sister, "Madama" Leonor, sounds more attractive. Not beautiful to Pero Correa's eyes, but neither, says he, is she ugly — "she is graceful and has pleasant manners and seems to be gentle and wise." It is a pity that she has bad teeth, and she is small of stature, appearing more so that women in Flanders wear low shoes. She is, he adds an enthusiastic and accomplished dancer. Unlike her brother, she can understand and speak a little Castilian. We suppose that her aunt, Madame Marguerite, had taught her, for Madame Marguerite had lived some time in Castile as bride of the unhappy heir of Fernando and Isabel, and Pero Correa says she spoke Castilian very well.

Between the families it was more or less assumed that "Madama" Leonor would marry the heir to the Portuguese throne, whose sister, D.Isabel, might be suitably betrothed to Carlos V. Certainly that was what the young lady herself intended. The Infanta D.Isabel was beautiful and she was proud. She felt that none but the greatest lord in

Christendom should aspire to her hand. Her cousin Carlos V might be a half-baked youth, according to Correa's description, but he was none the less King of Castile and Aragon, Naples and Sicily, Archduke of Austria, Duke of Milan, Count of Tyrol, Lord of the Netherlands and the West Indies, as well as successor presumptive to his grandfather's imperial crown.

D.Manuel was all for Carlos as a son-in-law, but on the diplomatic backstairs of the European courts there were currents and counter-currents. The young King of France, François I, had an infant daughter already — a useful pawn for negotiating with the House of Austria. Moreover, his Queen Claude was far from healthy. He himself might soon be on the marriage market, when Madame Leonor could be considered as possible Queen of France.

Of all these things the observant Pero Correa kept his master fully informed by suitably cryptic allusions. Crowned heads and their offspring are discussed in his letters under various code names. The Emperor Maximilian is called "Cinnamon." In him, writes Pero Correa — "there is neither certainty nor peace. Nor do I like the condition Cardomom [Carlos V] : he is too retiring and lacks many of the qualities he should already display if it be true what farmers say, that the calf shows the sort of ox it will become." In a previous letter "I have written what I think of Malagueta [Madame Leonor], and it appears that Copper [the King of France] is displeased by what is said of her and Rhubarb [Prince D.João] and the reason of this might be that they wish to dispose of her elsewhere." Perhaps, however, "Copper" only desired to interfere with the alliances of "Cardamom," but the ambassador had been informed that, because "his partner is in bad health, he thinks it might be well for Malagueta to be kept for him."

As for D.Manuel's younger daughter, D.Beatriz, at twelve years old she had already been requested in marriage by the Duke of Savoy. Who was this Duke of Savoy, anyhow? The King replied politely that his daughter was still too young, and secretly despatched an envoy to find out the exact state and status of the Duke.

The useful Pero Correa, on his side also made enquiries. His report is not enthusiastic — "Concerning Sulphur [the Duke of Savoy], I have heard that he is ill-conditioned, and so I had gathered from those who came to Portugal before I left, and in my opinion there are other drawbacks to this affair."

While parents and diplomats discussed their future fate, the young Infantes were carefully brought up at court. Their mother, Queen Maria, grave-eyed, self-effacing, virtuous, always busy about the works of religion and charity, plying her skilful needle in most beautiful embroidery, kept a close watch on all her children, guiding them in the way they should go, nor sparing to punish them when they deserved it.

They formed a group of which parents might well be proud – the six sons and two pretty daughters. The heir, Prince D.João, was handsome in a heavy way, with dark blue eyes and fair complexion. They say he was a conscientious but not really enthusiastic student. Helped by a prodigious memory and the best humanists available, he learned Latin and even some elementary Greek. Mathematics also figured on his curriculum and cosmography – for he must know about this wide world of which he was to rule so large a part. It was his father who taught him history. Every afternoon writes Damião de Gois, he had to read to D.Manuel from the Chronicles of the Realm. His early training gave the future D.João III a great respect for letters, though he himself never became a scholar.

In learning he was easily outdistanced by his younger brother, the Infante D.Luis. This was perhaps the most brilliant of all D.Manuel's sons. He studied all the liberal arts, and mathematics and cosmography; he was the friend, patron and pupil of the famous Pedro Nunes, and admiring companion of the learned D.João de Castro. Good-looking and always beautifully dressed, he cut a fine figure at court, showing a ready wit in conversation and sound judgment in council. At the same timy he excelled in every manly sport; in the bull ring and in the tilting yard he always carried off the prizes. Added to these more showy qualities, it seems that D.Luis was the perfect son and subject, always obedient to his father and his elder brother.

The Infante D.Fernando came next. Born in 1507, from the age of ten he became a firm friend of Damião de Gois. Outspoken, hot-tempered and impulsive, all that he undertook was done with enthusiasm. And he loved history above everything. He sent abroad for chronicles in any language that could be found, and from these sources he compiled a genealogy of all Hispanic kings – from Noah down to his father D.Manuel! A drawing of this tree was illuminated by the best master of the art at Bruges.

D.Afonso, two years younger, was from earliest childhood destined for the Church. D.Manuel dreamed of the highest dignities for him, and the King had great influence at the Holy See. Even so, the Pope was taken aback when Manuel proposed that his three year old son be created Cardinal. But such a thing was without precedent! the Holy Father protested. Never had an infant so young been raised so high. Ah! but, said the ambassador, João de Faria, never before was the son of so great a king suggested!

The Pope said that he esteemed and he admired D.Manuel. All the same he could not do that. Eighteen was the minimum age – or fifteen by special favour. But the king did not drop the matter, and D.Miguel da Silva, the next envoy sent to take it up, was a very able diplomat who well knew how to "wangle" – there is no other word for it. In 1517, when D.Afonso was but eight years old, he obtained the privilege desired – on sole condition that the little cardinal was not to use the hat before he was eighteen. Even that the omnicompetent D.Miguel did not take as final – "I shall shortly send you a Brief," he wrote to the King, "that he may wear it if he likes, although," he adds, "this is not really so desirable, for it will be most unbecoming to him! " As well it might be to a child of eight.

The little cardinal grew up in virtue and wisdom. He became a great Latinist and protector of scholars, besides a kindly pastor to his flock. His life was short – he died at thirty-one – but it was happy and harmonious.

He was more fortunate than his younger brother Henrique, also a cardinal, born in Lisbon on a snowy day of January 1512. Alone of Manuel's children he lived to be old and to survive the tragedy of Alcacer-Quibir, which left him sole heir to his childless nephew Sebastião. The Cardinal-King D.Henrique spent two distressful years upon a throne to which he could give no successor, and died seeing his country's darkest hour.

He had outlived by many years his youngest brother, little Duarte, who in days of childhood was his henchmen and ardent admirer. Born in 1515 the Infante D.Duarte was brilliant at his lessons; in three days André de Resende, the humanist, polished his schoolboy Latin to the point of fluent conversation. His memory, like that of his eldest brother, was prodigious, even more so perhaps. They say that not only could he recite a chapter of Cicero's *De Officiis* by heart, word for word, but added to this the not so useful feat of declaiming the same

text backwards! In spite of such literary tour de force D.Duarte was an
enthusiastic sportsman, who stalked the wild boar day and night, sleeping fully dressed on the ground. His charm made him beloved by all,
even his childish pranks were found endearing. Though full of life and
gaiety, he had a strange presentiment of early death, but nobody believed him. His foresight was correct. Duarte died at twenty-five after
four years of happy marriage with his cousin, daughter of the Duke of
Braganca.

These were the children born to Manuel the Fortunate and Maria his
Queen. In a wonderful picture painted by an unknown artist of the
Flemish school, hanging today in the great hall of the Misericordia of
Oporto, we may see the whole family gathered around a fountain filled
with the blood of the Crucified. Before this *Fons Vitae* the King, with
outstretched hands and trailing cloak, is kneeling by the Queen, a slender figure, frail and worn, clasping her long thin hands. On her right are
two slips of girls – the Infantas Isabel and Beatriz – on their father's
left in order of height, we see six little boys – all the royal children
with their red gold hair.

All but one – still to come – D.Antonio, who died at birth in 1517,
two months before his mother's death. Poor Queen Maria, exhausted by
continuous childbearing over fifteen years, never recovered from her
last ordeal, and racked with pain, died on the 6th of March, apparently
from cancer. The blow shook the King out of his Olympian calm. With
the loss of the woman who had been his faithful companion for so
many years, he felt the world crumbling about him. He retired to the
monastery of Penha Longa in the Sintra woods and there he made his
will. What did he care for pomp and show and all the treasures of the
East? He longed to abdicate and finish his days serving God.

His counsellors protested and D.Manuel had a new idea. He proposed
to withdraw into the kingdom of Algarve, and with its revenues and
those of the Order of Christ, he would wage war upon the Infidel in
Africa and succour all his fortresses along that coast. The Prince, his
son, could reign in Portugal.

The counsellors did not like that any better. Could the young
man be trusted? they asked. He was only fifteen. Would he be content
with what his father offered him and let himself be guided by the
counsel of his elders? D.Manuel also wondered. Relations with his
eldest son had not been too happy of late. The boy apparently was

submissive and always respectful, but the King did not care for his favourite companions. There was that young coxcomb, Martim Afonso de Sousa, who had left the service of the Duke of Bragança for that of the Prince. This haughty youth, who could stand up and answer back to any of the great ones of the earth, was hand-in-glove with the heir to the throne as was also Martim Afonso's cousin, D.Antonio de Ataide, a milder and more diplomatic character, but therefore perhaps still more suspect. The three, of almost the same age, were inseparable and the Prince did nothing without them. Infatuation such as this, the King feared, almost looked like witchcraft! He did what he could to break up the fraternity by banishing Martim Afonso and keeping D.Antonio at a distance from the court; but the intimacy, it seems, was carried on by letter.

These things gave D.Manuel much food for thought — and also to his counsellors, who felt they might be relegated in a near future. The King had still his son in close control. Since he became a widower he made the Prince and the Infante D.Luis sleep in his bedroom beside him, and every night young D.Jo͞ao had to read to the three of them the prescribed portion from the history book. All very well so far, but the King was uneasy. This was not the time to retire and he must think again. Some months had passed since the Queen's death. The pang of sorrow was already less acute. All the same D.Manuel, essentially a family man, felt lonely. The best solution, he decided, would be to get married!

XVII

Mainly Matrimonial

In the autumn of 1517, when young King Carlos of Castile arrived in the Peninsula, bringing his sister Madame Leonor with him, nobody doubted that "Rhubarb" would soon get off with "Malagueta."

"The marriage of the King, my brother, and that of the Infanta D.Leonor his sister, ought to be with my children, as being most expedient to the welfare of both parties, and likely to promote peace in all things that concern them." So wrote King Manuel on December 4th, in his first year of widowhood, to his ambassador in Rome.

Already in October he had sent his chamberlain and confidant D.Alvaro da Costa to visit the young king of Castile, conveying greetings and congratulations on his happy arrival in the realms of his forefathers.

Everyone expected a double marriage shortly to be announced, and everyone was happy about it.

Time passed. Nothing was said. D.Alvaro lingered the whole winter at the Castilian court. There were mysterious meetings with Guillaume de Croy, Seigneur de Chèvres, the boy king's omnipotent minister. there were whisperings and confabulations. Only towards the end of April did a strange secret begin to leak out, and, says D.Alvaro — it was letters written from Portugal that first gave it away! Only then did he feel that it was time to inform "Madama" Leonor that the King her lord and brother, was negotiating a marriage for her indeed — but not to her young cousin D.João. She was to wed his father! How the Infanta took this news is anybody's guess. These poor little princesses were so disciplined that very likely she raised no protest. People assured her eagerly that she had everything to gain by exchanging a bridegroom of sixteen for one of forty-nine. D.João was a foolish youth, they said, awkward and ugly — rather an oaf, in fact. Upon the other hand, his

father was good-looking, graceful, accomplished and very well preserved, adorned with every virtue that could make a woman happy.

So said the negotiating parties, but one gathers that scathing remarks
were made by Leonor's contemporaries and those who had no axe to
grind. As for her ex-bridegroom, it seems that he was furious although
he refrained from unfilial comment.

In both countries the news fell as a bombshell and people were
profoundly shocked. In Portugal, except by flattering courtiers, many
hard things were said. What could the King be thinking of – a widower
of recent date and nearly fifty years old, and with eight children on his
hands – to propose marrying a girl of twenty? What an expense such a
marriage would bring about, for the father could not expect to receive
the dowry that would be given to his son! And then – moaned practical persons – what might not be the future cost for the nation? It had
already eight young princes to set up in life. There well might be
another eight. The country would be ruined!

In spite of everything the contract was drawn up in May 1518,
entirely to the bridegroom's satisfaction. The canny ambassador put
through the deal, supported by the all-powerful favourite Guillaume de
Croy, who later on received a handsome present from D.Manuel in
recognition of his services. King Carlos endowed his sister with two
hundred thousand doubloons. On his side the bridegroom made her a
settlement of fifteen thousand for her maintenance till the death of his
sister, the Dowager Queen, when his young wife would have possession
of the lands bestowed on the elder Leonor at the time of her marriage
to King João II.

A highly urgent matter was the papal dispensation, for Leonor was
Manuel's niece by his previous marriage, as well as being several times
his cousin. The time had come, therefore, to mobilize D.Miguel da
Silva, the very wide awake ambassador to the Holy See.

The Pope received the news without surprise – his *nuncio* in Lisbon
had already slipped a hint – but he showed such delight – says
D.Miguel, that – "I thought he would despatch me then and there and
pay me for it into the bargain!" A dispensation? By all means! The
Holy Father would be charmed to issue one but – he warned
D.Miguel – it was going to be expensive! Let him be prepared with
many thousands of ducats! D.Miguel tried to pass this off as a joke,
and so they fenced a while until His Holiness came down to brass tacks:

"He asked for fifteen thousand ducats, and so seriously that he alarmed me! " They haggled up and down and on and off for hours on end, until the Pope named ten thousand as his lowest figure, and — writes D.Miguel — "I thought it better then to have the Bull made out, and later return to the charge, and I did not leave the palace till the draft was ready." By then it was quite dark, but "fearing what may occur in matters of such weight," the canny diplomat would leave nothing to chance or the next morning. He sought the Pontiff once again that same evening and opened his batteries with such effect that in the end the Holy Father had reduced his price to 4000 ducats —and that, he said, was rock bottom; he could not do it for one *real* less! D.Miguel, seeing that further bargaining was of no use, despatched a courier to Portugal that very night of June 15th. Well might D.Manuel congratulate himself on his expeditious diplomats!

Delighted that all was going well, but none the less a little shame-faced before his people, the King assembled the whole court and made a speech setting forth the many and important reasons why he had decided upon this marriage. The courtiers hastened to applaud. As was the custom every one in his turn stepped forward to kiss the royal hand, beginning with the Prince D.João — but he, observes Damião de Gois, while making the correct motions, never expressed any pleasure at all.

Meanwhile at Saragoça, the proxy marriage was celebrated with feasting and pomp and preparations speedily got under way to bring the bride to Portugal.

D.Alvaro da Costa, much preoccupied, wrote a letter of anxious advice. Having discharged his mission with so much success, he hoped to see everything concluded without a hitch. Especially he desired that the bride should be given a warm welcome. It is unlikely that he did not know how much this marriage had been criticized in Portugal, and "here," he says, "there never was a person of such good intention as to speak well of her marriage to the Queen, and many who spoke badly and told many lies." D.Alvaro would like her to feel happy and contented from the first — "aware of the blessing that God was conferring upon her." She ought to be received with special honour, for she was worthy of it all and more. He seems afraid lest the King should not travel far enough to meet her. From Evora it would be well to ride at least a day's journey to her encounter. D.Alvaro hopes he will cross the frontier and advance some way into Castile. He had done as much for his first queen, the Princess D.Isabel, whom he had met at Valença, "where you stayed I know not how many days." No less should be done for the present bride. The Duke of Alba was escorting her with his sons and other noblemen, all eager to enter Portugal, but that – D.Alvaro appears to feel, was less desirable. The King might meet the Duke upon his way, and in the course of pleasant conversation dissuade him from crossing the frontier. At the same time it would be good to make much of the Duke, because the almighty Seigneur de Chèvres esteemed him very highly and this favourite of the young king could be a useful friend and very inconvenient enemy.

D.Alvaro's letter is illustrative of Luso-Castilian relations at their most cordial. Even at such a time as this, when officially friendship was fervent, there always ran beneath a note of mutual distrust.

In spite of these suggestions D.Manuel did not cross over into the neighbouring kingdom. He took up his stance at Crato with the reluctant Prince, and there they awaited the bride.

At the frontier, the Duke of Bragança with bishops and fidalgos were ready to receive her. Escorted by the Duke of Alba and a brilliant retinue, the young queen came courageously to meet her middle-aged bridegroom and bevy of stepchildren. On each side of the little river Sever dividing the realms, both parties halted looking at each other while fifes and drums and trumpets made the welkin ring.

The Count of Vila Nova passed the stream to kiss the hand of his new Queen, who stood between the Duke of Alba and the Bishop of Cordova. The Count of Tentugal was the next to cross, followed by the Bishop of Oporto and the Archbishop of Lisbon.

Then, escorted by more than 300 horses and a hundred halberdiers, Queen Leonor entered her husband's kingdom. The waiting Duke of Bragança leapt from his horse and did her reverence. The Duke of Alba asked him if he was authorized to take charge of the Queen on the King's behalf. A document to that effect was exhibited and read aloud for everyone to hear. The Duke of Alba then led the Queen forward by a golden chain she wore about her arm and thrust the end of it into the hand of his opposite number. The Castilians then went home, leaving the bride to take a day's rest at Castelo de Vide before proceding to Crato to meet her groom.

He came at nine o'clock in the evening, all smiles. By his side walked the Prince, solemn and glum, but still a likely lad and fair to look upon. Poor Leonor started. "Is that the fool?" she whispered just a little sadly to her ladies. But her training was perfect and it did not fail her now. She greeted the King with dignity and every sign of pleasure.

On his side he was delighted with Leonor. She was much prettier, we gather, than poor Queen Maria. Several contemporaries declare that she was beautiful, which is as may be. Beauty, we know, is in the eye of the beholder, especially when the person beheld happens to be a queen! But Leonor was not yet that at Brussels when she came under Pero Correa's inspection, and as we have seen, all he said is that she was not ugly and had a pleasant face. However, it is only natural that a girl in the bloom of her twenty years would be much easier on the eye than a woman of thirty-six, worn out by fifteen years of childbearing. There is no doubt that Manuel was charmed. Perhaps he even fell in love.

His children, all well disciplined, welcomed their stepmother – the Prince punctiliously polite and stiff, the daughters rather shyly. The two young girls, aged fourteen and fifteen, were preparing to run downstairs and curtsey to the Queen, but she, leaping impulsively from her palfrey, met them halfway and hugged them both, refusing to let them kiss her hand. As for the younger brothers, Luis, Fernando, Afonso, Henrique and Duarte, she made much of each one, especially the little cardinal Afonso – "as owing to his dignity."

Beaming, D.Manuel introduced the ladies of his court – dressed in their best and looking very beautiful – observes Damião de Gois. Together they all went to say their prayers in the chapel of St. Andrew, whose festival it was, and next day the King was invested with the collar of the Golden Fleece, sent him by his brother-in-law, King Carlos V.

A happy New Year dawned, and on January 6th 1519, D.Manuel sent a messenger to his cousin, the Emperor Maximilian, informing him how "it has pleased the Lord to conclude our marriage with the Queen, my best beloved and cherished wife, his granddaughter." He thanks the Emperor for the pleasure he has shown in this happy event.

"Praise God, the Queen, my wife, his granddaughter, is already in our house, which has given us great satisfaction, owing to the many virtues of her person and condition, and moreover because she is his grand-daughter than which nothing could have given me greater or so much joy!" Henceforward Manuel will love the Emperor more than ever.

In spite of the conventional and repetitive phraseology, we sense a note of genuine happiness. D.Manuel, nearing his fiftieth birthday, felt rejuvenated. When summer came, he made a garden for his young queen, and sent the Valencian gardener a retable to adorn the sylvan shrine.

The King had got away with his unexpected marriage, but his family problems were not at an end. There were many much younger people on his hands whom he had to settle in life, beginning with his own children.

In the case of his lovely daughters he saw no reason for hurry, remembering the late Queen's entreaty in her will: "I beseech the King my Lord on no account to marry our daughters except to kings or legitimate sons of kings, and if this cannot be, let them be nuns — whether they like it or not, for it would be better for them to serve God than to marry in this realm. His Highness knows well how much his sister suffered who married in Portugal." (She was thinking of her unhappy sister-in-law, the Dowager Duchess of Bragança, whose husband had been executed for High Treason, leaving her many years a widow, with her children in exile.) D.Maria had evidently been deeply impressed by this family tragedy and feared lest her daughters be exposed to such misery. If they would have their mother's blessing, "they must not marry except as I say." Not even at their father's orders!

D.Manuel, however, had no intention of marrying his daughters to any of his vassals, great or small. The elder Infanta D.Isabel, he meant to keep for her cousin, Carlos V, when the time came for the young man to wed. Meanwhile it seemed that Beatriz would go to Savoy after all. The Duke had not been put off by the first show of reluctance to negotiate, but had renewed his suit a second time, more urgently. D.Manuel then asked for six months to think it over, during which interval, as has been seen, he made enquiries. The findings were quite satisfactory: The Duke ruled over wide domains, cities and towns and castles and vassals; he was descended from emperors and kings. D.Manuel graciously informed the Duke that his ambassadors might be permitted to walk up and conclude the contract.

They came as quickly as they could — eager to obtain for their master that which — says one contemporary — he desired above everything: "the most beautiful princess that could be named" — not to mention the by no means negligible dowry of the said beautiful princess, amounting to 150,000 ducats, "good value and just weight," with precious stones, silver and jewels thrown in. The contract was concluded in the spring of 1521, as the King wrote to his ever-loyal city of Oporto:

"Because of the great pleasure it will give you, we would have you know that, praise be to Our Lord, we are marrying the Infanta D.Beatriz, our well-beloved and cherished daughter to the Most Serene Duke of Savoy." The citizens were well aware, the King goes on to say, that it is customary for loyal subjects of a realm to contribute towards the dowry of their sovereign's daughters, but in this case he will hold them excused, although the marriage is to be very expensive, not only in dowry but the cost of the fleet that will escort the bride. "In this marriage," declares D.Manuel magnificently, "we ask of you nothing more than the great pleasure we know it will give you! "

So it was that, upon the 5th of August 1521, the pretty Beatriz embarked in the great ship *Santa Catarina do Monte Sinai,* a luxurious 500 tonner, with the royal cabin all painted in gold and lined with silk brocade. The King and Queen saw her on board; her sister spent the night with her before she sailed, and many tears were shed at the farewells. A fleet of galleons, caravels and galleys went to escort the bride to Nice where she would meet her unknown husband — "a short man of long face and fair complexion, and altogether ugly" — is the discouraging contemporary report on his appearance. The Portuguese retinue was dismissed and went home while the poor little bride, weeping and surrounded by rude Savoyards, rode away to the wild Piedmontese mountains. At least it seems her husband loved her, as well he might, and she it was who came to hold the reins and rule his policy — not always perhaps to his best advantage.

Not all of Manuel's young wards gave him so little trouble as his daughters. The chief cause of anxiety seems to have been his eldest son. Whatever chroniclers may say about the Prince's good behaviour, one gathers that a coolness existed between him and his father. Was it to spite his parent for stealing his bride that young João struck up a desperate flirtation with his pretty cousin, Beatriz, granddaughter of the King's late brother D.Diogo, Duke of Viseu, executed for treasonable conspiracy in 1484 by D.João II?

The Prince must have known that his father had his eye upon this girl as a suitable match for one of the younger Infantes. Beatriz had been left an orphan at an early age; the King as her great-uncle and guardian felt, he says, "he would like to do her favour."

Other suitors were in the field besides the Infantes. The haughty Marquis of Vila Real had requested her hand for his son, the Count of Alcoutim. At the same time the great Duke of Bragança put in a proposal for his own heir. D.Manuel, who rarely denied anything to his beloved D.Jaime, gave him a written promise that if Beatriz did not marry one of the Infantes, she would be kept for the Duke of Bragança's son.

While matters stood thus, the King, profoundly shocked, discovered that the Prince was making ardent love to D.Beatriz, nor was she attempting to freeze him off. D.Manuel was furious, for he had been wholly unsuspecting. How long had this affair been going on under his very nose before he knew of it? he demanded. And how far had it gone? He feared the worst. "It caused much displeasure between me and my son," declared the King in a message in his own writing sent through the Secretary of State to the Duke of Bragança. We well may imagine the stormy scene! As for the little baggage who was at the centre of the turmoil, the Secretary must tell the Duke that "this woman, who is so different from what I supposed and so regardless of her honour," was no longer worthy to marry any son of his, nor was she fit for the son of the Duke of Bragança. Perish the thought! Marry she must of course, forthwith, as best she could — and to the Count of Alcoutim, if he would have her!

He had an interview with the young lady and found her very meek. She begged him sweetly to marry her as he thought fit, with any dowry he might choose to give her — but "I believe from what I saw and have been told," the King went on to say — "that it is her deliberate wish to marry the Count of Alcoutim."

And marry the Count of Alcoutim she shall! declared the King, with only a fraction of the dowry he had intended to give her! He cannot suppose the Duke would care to hold him to the promise previously made, for Beatriz was not the wife to be a credit to his son.

Unfortunately we have not the Duke's reply to this, but from the King's next letter we gather that he demurred. Perhaps he did not think so badly of poor Beatriz. The King expresses surprise that D.Jaime should not agree to his most reasonable suggestions. Better to meet and talk the matter over!

However that may be it is a fact that Beatriz married the Count of Alcoutim, as evidently they both wished. We wonder if the whole affair was not a put-up show staged by the three young people most concerned? And what did the proud Marquess of Vila Real say to all this? We have not a clue. It seems, however, that the marriage was a happy one and blest with many children.

As for the Prince who had incurred his father's wrath, we gather that the estrangement continued. It is significant that about this time the young man's favourite D.Antonio de Ataide was also in disgrace and the King's sister, D.Isabel, Dowager Duchess of Bragança, put in a plea on his behalf, only to receive a chilling reply:

Lady Sister,
We saw the letter you wrote us about the matter of D.Antonio de Ataide and, although we always like to please you in everything reasonable, this is a matter concerning justice in which, as you know, we are obliged only to do what is right. We should be glad if we could comply with your request, nevertheless we shall see that he is justly treated.
Written at Evora, 31st of October 1520.

The whole affair remains obscure. It only reminds us of the many missing pieces there must be in the reconstruction of lives in History. All we can add to this is that D.Antonio was banished from the court, but never lost the Prince's friendship. He reappears in the next reign and fills the scene as the all-powerful minister and King's confidant — the Count of Castanheira.

XVIII

1521

"Oh, year of 1521! When shall we see you out? " D.Manuel was
heard to sigh on more than one occasion.

Wherefore such weariness about this time? It was not old age creep-
ing on. D.Manuel indeed was fifty-two, but so healthy and well-pre-
served, they say, as to appear no more than thirty. He had found
happiness with his young bride and though their first child − a son −
had died in April, 1521, in June that year the Infanta D.Maria, future
muse of Camões, was born and showed no sign of premature mortality.

The country over which D.Manuel ruled was at peace with itself,
untroubled by the feudal problems that distressed its neighbours. His
prestige abroad was higher than ever, the more so doubtless that, adher-
ing to the traditional policy of his country, the King of Portugal
avoided carefully all European entanglements. Consistently he had refused to enter into any league or confederation with other European
powers, for all the pressing invitations he received, for all the close
relationship existing between him and other royal houses. The independence and nonalignment of Portugal were invariably emphasized,
and peace among the nations of Christendom always the avowed aspiration. Manuel frequently offered himself as arbiter between contending
parties, but never would get off the fence on either side. And he would
suffer no confusion with regard to Portugal's position in the Iberian
Peninsula. When King Fernando of Aragon, in the joy of his heart at
having added Navarre to his other realms, entitled himself King of
Spain, D.Manuel protested to his well-loved father-in-law. What did he
mean by that? The term Spain had no significance apart from geog-
raphy, including as it did several independent kingdoms − and Portugal,
he pointed out, was one of these, and subject only to her native
sovereigns!

On his side he abstained from all encroachment. Though in Castile, after the death of the great Queen, there was considerable unrest in her dominions, D.Manuel refused to fish in troubled waters. When the *Gran Capitan*, Gonçalo de Cordoba, quarrelled with King Fernando and asked leave to pass through Portugal on the way to Flanders, D.Manuel persuaded him to go home and make peace. He took the same line with the Duke of Medina Sidonia and D.Pedro Giron, who offered to transfer their allegiance to him. The King of Portugal received them honourably, but once again he acted as peacemaker. He reconciled them with D.Fernando and sent them back to their country laden with gifts of jewels and mounted on fine horses.

In 1511, D.Fernando had tried hard to persuade his son-in-law to enter with him into a league against France, including the Swiss, the Emperor and the Pope. A personal interview, he felt, might overcome resistance, and so he wrote to Portugal, telling the King how much he longed to see his daughter, Queen Maria, and to know his grandchildren. Might he not come to Lisbon with a very small escort and there invest his grandsons with the Masterships of Castilian Military Orders? D.Manuel politely but firmly discouraged the paternal longings of Fernando's heart. Fernando, frustrated, foamed with rage when he heard how just at this time six French galleys, much battered by the sea, had entered Lisbon to refit. The King had made them very welcome and had furnished all their needs!

D.Manuel of Portugal was entertaining schismatics, enemies of the Holy See! Fernando spluttered. Ought one not to declare war upon that country? But the lords of Castile flatly refused. Queen Isabel was dead and they had no love for her widower, nor did they want to comply with his wishes.

The death of D.Fernando in 1516 did not put an end to trouble in Castile. The young king Carlos was a foreigner — more German than Spanish, more interested in succeeding to his grandfather's imperial crown than in his realms of Castile and Aragon. In 1520 these rebelled and offered the crown of Castile and Leon to D.Manuel of Portugal.

This would have touched off a Peninsular and civil war, but happily D.Manuel had the sense to decline the honour. He advised the free cities to remain loyal to their natural king, and supported the legally appointed regency with money and munitions.

Times had changed since the end of the last century when Manuel had dreamed of the Iberian throne. That was before Vasco da Gama had returned from India. From that time on expansion overseas became the only real interest. And what was the position as to this at the end of the second decade of the 1500's?

The picture was of light and shadow – light lingering on from early years, shadows already lengthening but not yet very dark.

Expansion still went on though at a slower pace. The fortress of Colombo on the island of Ceylon was the only progress registered during the three years of Lopo Soares' inefficient rule, for what this governor chiefly had sought was to undo the work of Albuquerque. Under Diogo Lopes de Sequeira who arrived in 1519, matters improved. The embassy to Abyssinia – the Land of Prester John – at last got under way. Account of this had not reached Portugal by 1521, but out of the Far East from time to time came news of penetration into enchanted lands at the world's end.

In 1514 a Portuguese junk had reached the perfumed sandal forests of Timor. From Malacca in 1513 and 1515, Jorge Alvares had carried merchandise to the Chinese coast and erected a stone *padrão* with the royal arms of Portugal upon the beach of Sanchuan. Rafael Perestrelo, who had sailed with him, had come back to Malacca rich, reporting that the Chinese were good people. And Tomé Pires, the apothecary – a man of wide interests and an enquiring mind – in 1516 was left by the captain, Fernão Pires de Andrade, on the mainland of Canton, to travel to Peking as first ambassador of Portugal to China.

At Evora, three years later, D.Manuel and his young queen had welcomed Fernão Pires newly returned from the Far East. He came bringing wonderful silks painted with images of heathen gods, and much to tell his sovereigns of the Chinese empire.

Canton, he said, was a city as big as Evora, built by the riverside, encircled by a great stone wall five cubits wide with battlements and eighty towers, each with its own flagstaff. Seven iron-lined doors, each one shaded by a leafy tree, gave entrance to the town. Its streets were wide and very clean, on either side paved with flagstones; the houses, one storey high, were adorned inside with panelling of carved and painted wood; the population within and without the gates thronged by the thousand. The countryside around was well watered, lush and green, bringing forth fruit and vegetables abundantly to feed the city.

The Chinese, a light-skinned race, attired in silk brocade and cotton cloth cut in the Tartar fashion, took their meals sitting before tables in the European style, with tablecloths and napkins. They ate off dishes of finest porcelain, and were so fastidious that they never touched their food with their fingers. Instead they used a curious kind of little fork, manipulated with the greatest skill. Their banquets were frequent and splendid and the guests prepared for them by days of abstinence.

These people were perfect in all the arts and crafts. They had their artillery and they knew gunpowder. As for the printing press, the Portuguese were told, it had been used in China for uncounted ages.

Strangers were received with extreme reserve, and tact was needed for a foreigner to make his way without offending bureaucratic regulations. In all things Fernão Pires had walked warily; he entertained good hopes for future intercourse. The ambassador Tomé Pires had been set ashore at Canton with a Chinese escort to guide him to Peking. Nothing dismayed, he had ventured to travel deep into that enigmatic land which was destined to absorb him forever.

From the Moluccas the King of Ternate wrote to D.Manuel: "Thy power and state are so great that there is no country that has not heard of it — God has been pleased to favour thee above all others!" The island sovereign had learnea all this from Francisco Serrão, who remained at his court as friend and oracle and understudy.

East of the Moluccas the Unknown Ocean rolled. Here were the far ends of the earth, the extreme meridian set forth in the Treaty of Tordesillas. But just where did that pass? All the hemisphere of the East belonged to Portugal, the western half was the Castilian share. But where did East turn into West? How to measure the longitudinal degree? Astronomers argued and shook their heads. For over twenty years after the signing of the famous treaty the problem had hardly arisen. The Portuguese sailing the seas of their monopoly in time reached the Spice Islands. Were these outside the limits of their hemisphere? Nobody could say for certain and, while the Portuguese alone were able to get there, no one really cared.

But cosmographers wondered. The world was round without a doubt — therefore might there not be a western route to the Far East? If that were so, and if the Portuguese had sailed beyond their demarcation line, then Castile might weigh in and lay claim to the Moluccas!

The idea had occurred to Portuguese cosmographers. A fiery and restless fidalgo, Fernão de Magalhãis, discussed the problem with his friend Ruy Faleiro. Both were keen students of the sphere and the science of navigation. Their interest in the Moluccas question might however have remained purely academic if Magalhãis had not incurred the displeasure of his king.

Exactly why this should have happened is not clear. Magalhãis had good service to his credit. He had fought in India under Albuquerque and taken part in the conquest of Malacca. Returning to Lisbon in 1512, he subsequently fought the Moors at Azamor and was wounded in battle. Dragging a game leg he waited on the King, feeling he was due for promotion. He therefore put in a petition that his *moradia* be increased by the amount of half a cruzado.

This seems quite a modest request, but it was one that meant more in prestige than money. The *moradia* was granted at birth to all the sons of noblemen, the sum of which varied in accordance with the status of each one and would pass on to his descendants. Any increase of *moradia* therefore implied a step up in rank. Why did the King refuse this small reward to Magalhãis? D.Manuel, as we have seen, was not a judge of men. For some reason – or none perhaps – he disliked Fernão de Magalhãis. A difficult man there seems no doubt this was, and one with whom it was easy to quarrel. He was no courtier obviously and Manuel, raised high upon an unexpected throne, had been for nearly twenty years absorbing adulation. They say that he was obstinate and Magalhãis' persistence irritated him. The answer was no! he said. And that was that! Magalhãis felt outraged. Then had he leave to go where he might earn a better living? He could go where he liked! the King replied coldly. Magalhãis bowed himself out, and would have kissed the sovereign's hand, as etiquette demanded, but Manuel angrily turned his back. The rupture was complete – a clash of temperaments destined to have wide repercussions.

As we have said, and say again, D.Manuel was no judge of character and his choices were hit or miss. We cannot be surprised if the same king who had so recently turned down an Albuquerque – the man who had cast empires at his feet – should suffer a Fernão de Magalhãis, whom he hardly had tested yet, to walk out of his sight. The next news to be heard of him came from D.Alvaro da Costa, then at Saragoça negotiating D.Manuel's third marriage.

Fernão de Magalhãis was at Seville, arming and equipping a fleet to sail to the Moluccas by the western ocean! He and his friend Faliero had told Carlos V that the Spice Islands lay within the Castilian hemisphere. Without offending Portugal or breaking any treaty, the King of Castile had a perfect right to send his ships to claim them, and Magalhãis undertook to take them there without trespassing upon Portuguese sailing routes.

Here was a coil! Expert cosmographers were not agreed as to the exact site of the Moluccas in terms of longitude. Meanwhile the Portuguese were there and did not propose to move out. For the Castilians to butt in would be most inconvenient!

Much agitation seethed in diplomatic corridors. D.Alvaro da Costa, more in sorrow than in anger, remonstrated with Carlos V. How could he authorize an undertaking which he must know would be against the interests of his well-beloved uncle, about to become his even better beloved brother-in-law? Sebastião Alvares, Portuguese agent in Seville, expostulated at length with Fernão de Magalhãis. Did he care nothing for his duty to his natural king and country and his honour? But Magalhãis refused to be moved. Talking of honour, he said, he was already in honour bound to Carlos V, whose vassal he had become. And he would do no harm to Portugal, for he would not encroach upon Portuguese waters.

Among D.Manuel's counsellors the matter was discussed with grave concern. Magalhãis was a dangerous man to have let go! He was too versed in cosmography and the science of navigation. The Bishop of Lamego was for offering him a free pardon and good prospects should he return, or else — suggested this prelate of the Renaissance — could he not be quietly bumped off? That would put an end to all the bother! The King and the Duke of Bragança disagreed. To recall Magalhãis by alluring offers would be a great mistake and bad example to all those inclined to place too high a value on their services. He had gone — let him go! His enterprise was most unlikely to succeed. Sebastião Alvares had visited his ships and said he would not care to sail to the Canaries in such vessels — let alone circumnavigate the globe! They probably would never be heard of again.

So nothing was done and, on the 10th of August, 1519, Magalhãis sailed from San Lucar on that amazing voyage, the story of which does not belong here.

Upon the 23rd of August, 1520, the Captain of Malacca, Garcia de Sá, wrote: "Senhor, I have just had news that from the far coast of

Java, on the way to the Island of São Lourenço, three ships have been seen; they say they are Portuguese, which cannot be. If the report be true, it seems to me this must be Fernão de Magalhãis. Your Highness will know more certainly the truth."

This letter may have reached D.Manuel by the summer of 1521. However that may be, it is most probable that this vague and wholly inaccurate surmise was all he ever heard about the voyage of Magalhãis.

The court had spent most of 1520 at Evora, but the King was anxious to return to Lisbon, a better place for receiving ambassadors from the Duke of Savoy and celebrating the wedding of the Infanta D.Beatriz. The ambulating plague appeared at last to have petered out — "Please God," the King wrote on October 16th to his architect Afonso Monteiro, he hoped to be in Lisbon "in this coming month of January, for we have a good report of the health of the city and that of its surroundings." He orders therefore that redecoration and repairs should be made to his palace by the river.

There the court took up its residence in the New Year, and thence D.Manuel despatched his younger daughter to her unknown bridegroom. Her elder sister still remained unwed, waiting for Carlos V to make up his mind. The Emperor Maximilian had died in 1519 and Carlos was his successor elect. The young man, already nineteen years old, was the most eligible parti in Europe and his matrimonial prospects were discussed in every court.

It seems that Madame Louise, mother of the King of France, desired to make a match between him and her son François I's small daughter, aged about five. At this news D.Manuel anxiously put in his spoke: Point out to Madame Louise, he instructed his ambassador, "that the disparity of age between the Emperor and her granddaughter, the daughter of the King of France, is so great . . . that it would seem such a marriage should not take place! " Surely she and her son must see how much better it would be for the Emperor to marry D.Manuel's daughter! Their respective ages were exactly right. As for the little French princess, the King of Portugal had in mind a very satisfactory match for her. What about his own son, the Prince D.João? "Thanks to the Lord, his qualities and aptitudes are most desirable, both as regards his great inheritance and the merits of his person. Please God, this marriage would do much to promote the peace and safety of Christendom! "

We have not Madame Louise's reply to these suggestions, but it is certain that the young emperor inclined more to his beautiful cousin of Portugal, though several years would pass before the marriage actually took place.

Carlos and his uncle-brother-in-law, also prospective father-in-law — were best of friends as fitting to so complicated a relationship. D.Manuel advised his junior how to manage the Iberian end of his heterogeneous empire, and as we have already seen, made peace between him and his disgruntled lords, when during his many absences they rose against him. And always he exhorted him to live on peaceful terms with France — for "that is the greatest service you can render to Our Lord."

Recognized by the Holy See as the champion of Christendom, the arbiter of differences and peacemaker in Europe, ruling a kingdom without territorial problems, receiving every year tribute and treasure from afar, absorbing daily new knowledge of distant worlds, heir to the fulfilment of the hopes and dreams and labours of an earlier generation and holding the answers to their questionings — in 1521 what could D.Manuel lack?

Only the exaltation of a personal achievement, of having overcome by his own strength and climbed the steep ascent to glory. The Infante D.Henrique had toiled and planned and dreamed and died leaving his work half done; D.João II had had to struggle and fight tooth and nail to carry on his great-uncle's quest and pass it to his successor at the point of fulfilment. Neither of these two ever could have known the weariness of satiety. For Manuel the Fortunate remained the tedium that will settle like a chilly fog on human beings who have everything for which they never laboured.

"Oh! Year of 1521! When shall we see you out? "

No slower nor faster than in other years the seasons flowed into the gulf of Time. The drought and dearth that had blighted the countryside that summer were giving place to autumn rains as the dark days of December closed in. The court lingered in Lisbon though the bill of health was no longer so clear as when they had travelled there from Evora in the New Year. Not the bubonic plague this time, but a new form of infection was abroad, and many people were laid low with a kind of lethargic fever which often proved fatal.

The hunting season had begun. D.Manuel's three eldest sons were tempted by the autumn woods of Almeirim. It would be fun to go and chase the boar, and stay in the royal lodge till Christmas. So cheerfully the brothers fared forth one morning and reached Almeirim in the evening. They turned in only to be aroused by a loud knocking at midnight. A messenger who had come galloping from Lisbon, urged the young men to return to the capital at once. Their father, whom they had left hale and well, was smitten with the infection and his doctors were taking a grave view.

A furious ride brought the three princes to their parent's side at dawn. They found him very ill and from the start it seems that the physicians despaired of his life. The fever never left him for nine days during which time his young wife and his daughter the Infanta D.Isabel, and the Prince D.João nursed him devotedly, and all the greatest of the realm gathered around. At least three bishops and the noblest fidalgos seethed in and out − "and other persons ecclesiastical and secular" − records Damião de Gois, who himself was present all the time.

The patient slept for hours on end, but was quite lucid in his waking moments. So much so that on the seventh day of his illness he dictated a codicil to the will made in 1517 at Penha Longa, after the death of his poor Queen Maria. What now seemed to preoccupy him more than anything was his young wife. First and foremost he tenderly commends her to his son: "I very especially entrust to you, my son, the interests of the Queen, my wife, which are my pleasure and to which you are in duty bound, not only because she is your father's wife, but for her great virtue and merit."

Next to this, he enjoins the Prince to bear in mind and to conclude the marriage of his sister Isabel to the Emperor, because − "he knows how hitherto I have worked to bring it about, and how much I desire it, not only for the great pleasure it affords me as for my daughter's sake whom I dearly love." She must be given a dowry worthy of the match − so long as the kingdom was not unduly burdened.

Already on the fifth day of his illness the King had confessed and taken the Sacrament. He gathered all his children round his bed and blessed each one. They remained by his side till evening, but that night he steadily grew worse and they were led away. On the eighth day everyone thought the end had come, but he rallied before nightfall and drank a whole jugful of water. The Queen came to his side and for an hour and a half they conversed, but next morning, Friday the 13th of

December, he said that he felt very ill and asked for Extreme Unction. His dear Duke of Bragança came to him that afternoon and the King knew him still.

Perfectly conscious to the last, his voice was clear and strong when, with the bishops and priests round his bed, he recited the many Psalms he knew by heart. His wife and children, plunged in grief, waited in the next room amid the growing shadows of the winter night.

The end came between ten and eleven o'clock. Through the chill darkness of December, before dawn, King Manuel the Fortunate was carried in his coffin to Belem, escorted by 200 horse and lighted by a hundred torches. With lamentations and with mournful chant, they lowered him into the vault, and the fidalgos all seized hoes and covered up the grave. His great abbey of Belem was unfinished still, so Manuel was laid to rest in the old church awaiting translation.

On December 16th a horseman swathed up to the eyes in black, mounted on a black charger covered with black draperies out of which the eyes and ears only emerged, rode forth after a solemn Mass in the Cathedral. He grasped a linen banner dyed all black fastened to a black staff, and held it downwards almost dragging on the ground. Three judges of the law courts walked beside. At the Cathedral door was placed a bench covered with mourning cloth. One of the judges stepped upon it holding a black shield. In a loud lugubrious voice he cried out to the thronging crowd: "Let us mourn and weep and make lament for the high and illustrious and virtuous Prince and King Dom Manuel, deserving of great memory for the benefits that he conferred on all his people and especially on the city of Lisbon. Let us weep and mourn the death of him who has departed this life and gone to reign in another! "

So saying, the speaker struck the shield a thundering blow, smashing it to smithereens, while a great howl arose from all around.

The same speech and same ceremony of destruction were repeated halfway along the Rua Nova, principal artery of the city and on the Rocio, the wailing multitude, men, women, and children, the courtiers and the people following all the way – "I cannot imagine any human heart that would not have wept! " writes a contemporary observer.

Back to the Cathedral once again they trailed, and sadly dispersed. The "Breaking of the Shields" – the tragic rite marking the death of kings – had been accomplished.

A wild December storm blew up with floods of rain.

The weary year of 1521 at last was ending!

The reign of Manuel the Fortunate – 26 glamourous years – was the most brilliant in Portuguese history, with repercussions that sounded throughout the world. An amazing period that was which saw one of the smallest, poorest and least populous realms of Christendom unaided by any outside resources, develop into a great power, projecting itself across three continents and two oceans, dictating to the princes of the East, a menace to the Turks, and courted by the crowned heads of Europe!

Should Manuel the First of Portugal therefore be counted a great king? Great in outward appearance, certainly. He was a symbol and a figurehead before whom heroes bowed, but when we come to look into the radiant aura in which he basked, we find it is all reflected glory. Manuel wholly lacked creativeness, but his at least was the merit to understand the greatness of the hour ne lived and the intelligence to carry on with a programme outlined and prepared by his predecessors.

The plan was there, the men were also there, carefully trained and chosen by a master-hand, ready for the word of command. The great names of that age are nearly all D.João II's men: Vasco da Gama, Albuquerque, D.Francisco de Almeida, Duarte Pacheco Pereira, Pedro Alvares Cabral, and their colleagues, had all been educated at the court of D.Manuel's predecessor. They were the men whose brilliance lit the first half of his reign; the years that followed under leaders of his own choosing shone less brightly. D.Manuel was lacking in the fundamental quality that marks a great ruler – the faculty of judging and selecting his collaborators.

Where he showed real talent, perhaps, was as a diplomat. Amid the discord rending Christendom – France, Austria and Aragon and Italy and papal Rome – all threatening and fighting and barking at each other – we see the King of Portugal sitting serenely aloof, politely but firmly refusing to grind an axe in the imbroglio on behalf of any beloved brother against any esteemed ally, and remaining on the best of terms with all. He had the sense to understand that Portugal had no interests in Europe. Her destiny was on the sea and in the worlds beyond.

At home D.Manuel was on the whole an able and conscientious ruler. Administratively his government was sound. He upheld justice and reformed the laws; he founded hospitals and protected the poor; his charity was lavish, both publicly in the endowment of Misericordias, and in private also, for we are told he always kept gold coins in his pocket especially to give to beggars.

He embellished the country with beautiful buildings: churches and monasteries and towers, in that graceful fantastic style known as Manueline – a tangle of twisted cables, seaweed, sea-shells and creatures of the deep – around his personal device, the armillary sphere. When Manuel remained awake at night, instead of counting sheep, he planned new buildings. Sleepless nights came expensive, he was wont to say. They often resulted in ten thousand cruzados to be laid out on churches, fortresses or bridges!

That Manuel was a spendthrift should not surprise us. Dazzled by the treasures that seemed to flow from everlasting sources he splashed vast sums on pomp and show and splendour of his court. The adding up of accounts was left for his son. It was to make D.João III very thoughtful.

Was Manuel beloved of his people? Being their king, of course he was. At that period in Portugal *El-Rei Nosso Senhor* would be taken for granted as the objective of passionate loyalty and affection – a sentiment to be transferred from every king to his successor. What was the feeling for D.Manuel as an individual would be more difficult to say. His personality is so elusive and so strangely colourless. Damião de Gois was a page at D.Manuel's court and seems to have liked him well as a pleasant and kindly master. "Liked" is the word. Damião de Gois nowhere gives evidence of the adoring devotion with which D.João II inspired young Garcia de Resende.

We gather that D.Manuel's household was fond of him, and naturally they mourned his unexpected end. "His servants were very sad" – writes an anonymous contemporary, but adds surprisingly – "up to now I do not see that his death has been widely felt."!

CHRONOLOGY
Of Principal Events of the Life and Reign of Dom Manuel

Birth at Alcochete. May 31, 1469.

Created Duke of Beja and heir to his brother Diogo, late Duke of Viseu. August *or* September, 1484.

Death of Prince Afonso. July 13, 1491.

Death of D.João II. October 25, 1495.

Accession of Manuel. October 26, 1495.

Council of Montemor and decision to send Vasco da Gama to India. December, 1495.

Return of Braganças. April 1496.

Expulsion of Jews. December, 1496.

Vasco da Gama sails for India. July 8, 1497.

The King marries the widowed Infanta D.Isabel. October, 1497.

Journey into Castile and Aragon to be received as Prince and Princess. March, 1498.

Vasco da Gama reaches India. May 17, 1498.

Death of Queen Isabel in childbirth. August 24, 1498.

D.Manuel returns to Portugal. October, 1498.

Arrival of Nicolau Coelho from India. July, 1499.

Arrival of Vasco da Gama. August, 1499.

Cabral's fleet sails for Brazil and India. March 9, 1500.

Official discovery of Brazil. May 3, 1500.

Death of Manuel's baby son Miguel at Granada. July 11, 1500.

King's second marriage to Infanta D.Maria. October 30, 1500.

Manuel plans North African expedition. January, 1501.

Expedition postponed. March 1501.

Fleet sent to succour Venice. June 15, 1501.

Birth of Prince D.João. June 6, 1502.

Preachers and teachers sent to Congo. Early in year 1503.

Albuquerque's first voyage to India. April, 1503.

Building of first fortress at Cochin. September, 1503.

Defence of Cochin by Duarte Pacheco Pereira. February *to* September, 1504.

Death of Queen Isabel of Castile "La Catolica." November 24, 1504.

Birth of Infanta D.Beatriz. December 31, 1504.

D.Francisco de Almeida sent to be first Viceroy of India. March 25, 1505.

Arrival of Fra Mauro in Lisbon with Soldan's letter. June, 1505.

Frei Henrique sent to England to invite Henry VII to join a crusade. July, 1505.

Duarte Galvão travels across Europe to canvas princely adherents for same. Summer *and* autumn, 1505.

Duarte Galvão arrives in Rome and the Pope sends Golden Rose to D.Manuel. February, 1506.

Birth of Infante D.Luis. March 3, 1506.

Albuquerque sails for the second time to Indian Ocean. April 6, 1506.

Massacre of New Christians in Lisbon. April 19, 1506.

Birth of Infante D.Fernando. June 5, 1507.

Conquest of Oman and Ormuz by Albuquerque. August *to* September, 1507.

Arrival of Egyptian fleet at Dio. End of year, 1507.

Naval battle with Soldan's ships at Chaul, Viceroy's son killed.January, 1508.

Desertion of Albuquerque's captains from Ormuz. February, 1508.

Albuquerque arrives in India. December, 1508.

Viceroy defeats and destroys the Soldan's fleet at Dio. February 2, 1509.

Diogo Lopes de Sequeira arrives in India on way to Malacca. April 21, 1509.

Unsuccessful visit to Malacca. *From* September 11 *to* end of the year, 1509.

Albuquerque governor of India. November, 1509.

Conquest of Goa. November 25, 1510.

Conquest of Malacca. August, 1511.

D.Manuel receives Order of the Garter. 1511.

Birth of Infante D.Henrique. January 31, 1512.

Embassy of Simão da Silva to Congo. 1512.

King of Congo's embassy to Rome. 1513.

Tristão da Cuha's embassy to Rome. March 12, 1513.

Afonso de Albuquerque's exploration of the Red Sea. February *to* September, 1513.
Conquest of Azamor by Duke of Bragança. September, 1513.
China first visited. 1513.
Arrival in Lisbon of messenger from Prester John. February 24, 1514.
Albuquerque's final conquest of Ormuz. March *to* September, 1515.
Lopo Soares sails for India to replace Albuquerque. April, 1515.
Disaster of Mamora on river Cebu. August, 1515.
Birth of Infante D.Duarte. September 7, 1515.
Death of Albuquerque. December 16, 1515.
Death of Nuno Fernandes de Ataide. May 16, 1516.
Lopo Soares with ambassador Duarte Galvão sails for Red Sea. February, 1517.
Death of Queen Maria. March 7, 1517.
Death of Duarte Galvão on Kamaran Island. June 9, 1517.
Ambassador D.Alvaro da Costa sent to Castile. October, 1517.
King Manuel's third marriage to Leonor, sister of Carlos V. June, 1518.
Her arrival in Portugal. November 23, 1518.
Desertion of Fernão de Magalhãis. 1518.
Death of Emperor Maximilian. January 19, 1519.
Fernão Pires de Andrade returns from China. 1519.
Infante D.Carlos born. February 18, 1520.
Death of Infante D.Carlos. April 15, 1521.
Diogo Lopes de Sequeira from Massawa despatches embassy to Prester John. April 30, 1521.
Infanta D.Maria is born. June 8, 1521.
Marriage of Infanta D.Beatriz to Duke of Savoy. August, 1521.
Embassy from Venice desiring monopoly of spices, Autumn, 1521.
Illness of D.Manuel. December 4, 1521.
Death of D.Manuel. December 13, 1521.

BIBLIOGRAPHY OF PRINCIPAL WORKS CONSULTED

Original Sources

First and foremost among these of course are the thousands of contemporary documents, many of them still unpublished, preserved in the National Archives in Lisbon, and a rich harvest may also be gleaned in various Municipal Archives about the country, notably those of Oporto and Evora.

At the "Torre do Tombo," as the National Archives are called, the most important collections concerning this reign are the ones known as the "Corpo Cronológico," the "Coleçčao de São Vincente," and that of the "Gavetas," which last named is at present in process of publication by the Centro de Estudos Históricos Ultramarinos, 7 volumes having already appeared. Some valuable documents from these and other collections have been published by Antonio da Silva Rego in the series entitled *Documentação para a História das Missões do Padroado Português do Oriente*, 12 volumes, and also by Antonio da Silva Brásio in *Monumenta Missionária Africana*. An indispensable work for the study of D.Manuel's reign is also the edition by the Academia das Ciências of the letters of Afonso de Albuquerque, entitled *Cartas de Afonso de Albuquerque seguidas de documentos que as elucidem*, 7 vols. published between 1884 and 1935.

Rebelo da Silva in his *Corpo Diplomatico Portugues*, vol. 1, has published a great part of the correspondence of the period with the Holy See. William B. Greenlee, in his book *The Voyage of Pedro Alvares Cabral* has collected and translated all the principal documents bearing upon this subject, and there is also a valuable series of *Documents on the Portuguese in Mozambique* in course of publication by the Archives of Rhodesia, in collaboration with the Centro de Estudos Históricos Ultramarinos, in which the original Portuguese appears side by side with an English translation. 5 vols, 1496-1518, have already come out.

Contemporary Writers

Damião de Gois: *Cronica do Felicissimo Rei D.Manuel.* First published in 1556. Most recent edition Coimbra 1950

Ruy de Pina: *Croniqua DelRey Dom Joham II.* Written early in the 16th century published for the first time in 1792. Latest edition Coimbra 1950

Garcia de Resende: *Vida e Feitos delRei D.João II, and Miscellanea.* 1545. and Coimbra 1902

Diário da Viagem de Vasco da Gama. Original manuscript of 16th century, preserved in Oporto Municipal Library and attributed to Alvaro Velho. First published in 1858. Latest edition 1950

Pero Vaz de Caminha: Letter describing discovery of Brazil, dated May 1,1500, published with preface and notes by Jaime Cortesão, Rio de Janeiro 1943

Gaspar Correa: *Lendas da India.* Written between 1512 and 1560. First published in 1858 by Academia das Ciências. (Gaspar Correa was one of Albuquerque's secretaries.)

Fernão Lopes de Castanheda: *História do Descobrimento e Conquista da India pelos Portugueses.* Written before 1538. First published 1551. Latest edition. Coimbra 1924

João de Barros: *Decadas da Asia.* published between 1552 and 1563. Latest edition, Coimbra 1944

Bras de Albuquerque (son of the great Afonso) Comentários do Grande Afonso de Albuquerque" compiled from his father's papers, first published 1557. Latest Edition 1922.

Jeronimo Osório: *Da Vida e Feitos de El-Rei D.Manuel, Lisbon 1571.* Original in Latin. Most recent Portuguese translation, Oporto 1944.

Duarte Pacheco Pereira: *Esmeraldo de Situ Orbis.* Written in 1505. Latest edition Academia da História, 1954

More Recent Works

Frei Luis de Sousa: *Anais de D.João III, Vol. 1.* Written about 1630, First published 1844

Antonio Caetano de Sousa: *História Genealógica da Casa Real Portuguesa* 18 vols. Publishes many documents dating from Manuel's reign and period. First published 1735. Latest edition, Coimbra 1946

Modern Writers

The list of names mentioned below does not pretend to be exhaustive. It only includes some of the principal works consulted. Apart from numerous articles which have appeared from time to time in Academic journals and other learned publications such as the *Anais da Academia de Historia* the *Revista Brotéria, O Instituto de Coimbra*, etc. there are excellent general histories in which the period and reign of King Manuel are the subject of very satisfying studies. Principal among these we may cite those below.

História de Portugal Ilustrada, 8 vols, published at Barcelos between 1928 and 1937, under the direction of Damião Peres.

História da Expansão Portuguesa no Mundo, 3 vols. published in Lisbon under the direction of Antonio Baião, Hernani Cidade, and Manuel Múrias 1937-1940

Jaime Cortesão: *Os Descobrimentos Portugueses*

Damião Peres: *Descobrimentos Portugueses*. Barcelos 1961

Costa Lobo: *Historia da Sociedade Portuguesa em Portugal no seculo XV*. Lisbon 1944

Fernando Correia: *Origens e Formação das Misericordias Portuguesas*. Lisbon 1944

Luciano Cordeiro: *Questoes Histórico Coloniaes*. Lisbon 1936

Bouveignes, Olivier de: *Les anciens rois de Congo*. Namur 1945

Robert Ricard: *Etudes sur l'histoire des Portugais au Maroc*. Coimbra 1955

Conde De Ficalho: *Viagens de Pedro da Covilham*. Lisbon 1898.

There are many others bearing on one or another more specialized aspect of Manuel's reign, such as art and architecture, economics, etc. which are too numerous to be listed here.

INDEX

Abyssinia, 15, 55, 60, 100, 101, 158
Abderraman, Alcaide of Safi, 90, 91
Abrantes, Count of, 61
Aden, 110
Adil Khan, dynastic name of kings of
  Bijapur, 32, 103
Affaitati, Italian banker, 43
Afonso, Dom, Infante, son of D. Manuel,
  141, 143, 144, 155
Afonso V, King of Portugal, uncle of D.
  Manuel, 3, 4, 5, 10, 17, 88, 92, 124
Afonso, Dom, Prince, only legitimate
  son of King João II, 1, 6, 8
Afonso, son of King of Manicongo, and
  later king, 74, 76, 77, 78
Africa, 2, 8, 12, 13, 15, 30, 40, 46, 47, 48,
  49, 57, 59, 63, 64, 66, 70, 73, 81, 82,
  85, 99
Africa (East), 116
Africa (North), 88, 89, 115, 116
Africa (West), 79
Afuto, King of, 71
Aguiar, Rui de, Vicar General, 75
Aguz, fortress in south of Morocco, 116
Alba, Duke of, 150
Albergaria, Lopo Soares de, governor of
  India in succession to Albuquerque,
  109, 110-114, 158
Albuquerque, Afonso de, Governor of
  India, 58, 64-69, 95, 96, 100-115,
  119, 160, 166
Albuquerque, Braz de, son of Afonso de
  Albuquerque, 114
Albuquerque, Francisco
  de, cousin of Afonso, 58
Alcacer-Ceguer, fortress in North Africa,
  85, 86, 87, 116

Alcacer-quibir, in Morocco, 144
Alcacer do Sal, town of Portugal, 40
Alcaçova, royal palace, 125
Alcochete, small town near Lisbon, 3, 28
Alcoutim, Count of, son of Marquis of
  Vila Real, 154, 155
Alenquer, Pero de, famous pilot, 14
Alentejo, 122
Alexandria, 30, 32, 43, 44, 50, 54, 95,
  110
Alfonso (Prince), son of Fernando and
  Isabel "La Católica", 141
Algarve - Algarves - in Portugal and
  Africa, 34, 36, 85, 88, 94, 122, 145
Ali ben Rached, Sheriff of Chechauen,
  86, 87, 88
Almada, João Vaz de, Alcaide of Sofala,
  118, 119
Almeida, D. Diogo de, Prior of the
  Hospital of St. John of Jerusalem, 2
Almeida, D. Francisco, first Viceroy of
  India, 24, 61-66, 106, 166
Almeida, D. Lourenço de, 62, 66
Almeirim, 164
Alva, Duke of, 22 (see also Alba)
Alvarenga, 71
Alvares, Jorge, early traveller to China,
  158
Alvares, Sebastião, 161
Alvaro, Dom, brother of beheaded Duke
  of Bragança, 7
Alvito, Baron of, 109
Andrade, Fernão Pires de, 158, 159
Anfa, in North Africa, 4
Angediva, island off the west coast of
  India, 32, 65
Antarctic, 14

Antilles, 13, 46
Antonio, son of D. Manuel, died in
    infancy, 141, 145
Antwerp, 46
Apulia, 49
Arabia, 51, 95
Aragon, 13, 17, 18, 20-24, 55, 110, 128,
    142, 156, 157, 166
Araujo, Rui de, captive at Malacca, 119
Arguim, in West Africa, 116
Arzila, fortress in North Africa, 47, 85,
    86, 99, 116
Asia, 12, 15, 39, 46, 64, 82
Ataide, Nuno Fernandes de, captain of
    Safi, 92, 115
Ataide, D. Antonio de, future Count of
    Castanheira, 146, 155
Atlantic Ocean, 4, 12, 13, 15, 27, 31, 85
Atlas Mountains, 93
Augsburg, 47, 95
Austria, Archduke of, 142
Austria, House of, 142
Austria, country, 166
Aveiro, João Afonso de, explorer, 71,
    79
Aveiro, ducal house of, 137
Aveiro, Duke of, (D. Jorge), 137
Azambuja, Diogo de, 89, 90, 92
Azamor, town on west coast of North
    Africa, 13, 88, 92, 93, 94, 116, 140,
    160
Azores, islands, 12, 27, 31

Bab-el-Mandeb, Straits of, 67, 100, 110
Badajoz, 22
Baía, 83
Barbary, 115
Barcelona, 23
Barros, João de, historian, author of
    Decadas 67, 72, 134
Bartholomew, St., Apostle, 36
Batalha, Abbey, 34
Batkul, in India, 95
Beatriz, Infanta Dona, daughter of D.
    Manuel, 140, 142, married Duke of

Savoy, 145, 152, 153, 162
Beatriz, grand-daughter of D. Diogo,
    Duke of Viseu, 153, 154, 155
Beatriz, Infanta Dona, mother of D.
    Manuel, 4, 5, 7, 129, 138
Beja, 129
Beja, Duke of, D. Manuel, 1, 6, 9, 11, 12
Belem, 31, 33, 38, 63, 165, Monstrance
    of, 58, 126, 135, tower of, 126, abbey
    165
Bemoi, Prince of Senegal, 11
Beirut, 50
Benin, 70, 72, 79
Berrio, ship, 16, 26, 31
Bethlehem, 56
Bijapur, Indian kingdom, 32, 59, 67
Bixorda, Jorge Lopes, concessionnaire of
    commerce of brazil wood, 80, 83
Black Sea, 32
Bologna, Duke of, 97
Braga, Archbishop of, 69, Town, 121
Bragança, Duchess of, 7, 138, 152, see
    also Isabel
Bragança, Duke of, 4, 5, 7, 10, 93, see
    also D. Jaime, 137, 138, 145, 146,
    150, 154, 161, 165, House of, 137
Bragança, town, 134
Brandão, João, 96
Brazil, 52, 80-84
Bretoa, ship trading with Brazil, 83
Bruges, 46, 143
Brussels, 141, 151

Cabral, Pedro Alvares, 37, 42, 44, 45, 52,
    63, 118, 166
Cairo, 50, 52, 100, 105, 120, 121
Caldeira, Afonso, Portuguese agent in
    North Africa, 87
Calicut, port on Malabar coast, 15, 29,
    30, 32, 33, 34, 36, 37, 40-43, 46, 52,
    57-60, 63, 68, 99, 111
Cambay, Indian kingdom, 32, 41, 59,
    63, 66, 100, 137
Cambay, Gulf of, 112
Camões, 156

Cannanore, 41, 44, 57, 59, 63, 64, 66
Cantino, planisphere of, 82
Canton, on Chinese mainland, 158, 159
Canton, 70
Cape Catherine, in West Africa, 12
Cape of Good Hope, or Cape of Storms,
    12, 15, 27, 31, 38, 39, 40, 67, 81
Cape Guardafui, 63
Cape Ghir (modern Agadir), 89
Cape Spartel, near Tangier, 85, 88
Cape Verde, 27, 31, 40
Capico, Pero, early settler in Brazil, 84
"Cardomom", Code name for Charles V,
    142
Carpe, Alberto de, 98
Casa da India, 84
Caramuru, Diogalvares, saman wrecked
    on Brazilian coast, 83
Cascais, 26
Castanheira, Count of, 155, see also
    Ataide, D. Antonio de
Castelo Branco, D. Martinho de, D.
    Manuel's private secretary, 137, 138
Castelo Real, fortress at Mogador, 89, 90
Castelo de Vide, in Alentejo, 20, 150
Castile, kingdom, 7, 12, 13, 17, 18, 20,
    21, 22, 23, 24, 25, 31, 56, 60, 84, 97,
    128, 141, 147, 150, 157, 159, 161
Castile, king of, 142, Queen of, 5, 12,
    23, Prince of, Alfonso, son of
    Fernando and Isabel, 20, 21
Castro, D.João de, 134, 143
Cebu, river of North Africa, 115
Ceuta, Bishop of, 11
Ceuta, town and fortress, 47, 85, 86,
    116, 132
Ceylon, 60, 63, 66, 95, 119, 158
Charles V (Carlos V), 141, 142, 147,
    148, 151, 152, 157, 161, 162, 163,
    164
Chaul, Indian port, 63, 66
Chechauen, sacred city of North Africa,
    86
Chèvres, Seigneur de, see Croy,
    Guillaume de
China, 34, 64, 95, 119, 134, 158, 159

Christ, Order of, 3, 38, 47
Cicioso, João Mendes, alderman of
    Evora, 131
"Cinnamon", code name for Emperor
    Maximilian
Cisneros, Cardinal Ximenes, 54, 56
Claude, queen of France, 142
Cochin, Indian port, 41, 57, 58, 59, 63,
    106, 107, 111, 136
Coelho, Duarte, founder of Pernambuco,
    82
Coelho, Gonçalo, father of Duarte and
    explorer of Brazilian coast, 82
Coelho, Nicolau, companion of Vasco da
    Gama, 26-29, 31, 32, 37
Coimbra, city, 130, 131
Coimbra, Frei Henrique de, Franciscan
    friar, 38, 52, 53
Coimbra, João de, pilot accompanying
    Vasco da Gama, 14
Colombo, town in Ceylon, 158
Columbus, Christopher, 12, 13, 46
Congo-Ambasse, capital of Manicongo,
    73
Congo, see also Manicongo, 75, 76, 77,
    134
Congo, Bishop of, 78
Congo, King of, 12, 73-77, 124
Conquest, Navigation and Commerce of
    Ethiopia, Persia and India, 34
Constantinople, 48, 50, 56
Contreiras, Frei João, founder of
    Misericordias, 127
"Copper", code name for King of
    France, 142
Cordoba, Bishop of, 150
Cordoba, Goncalo de, "el Gran
    Capitan", 157
Corfu, 49
Coromandel, 41
Correa, Aires, factor of Calicut, 37, 38,
    41
Correa, Gaspar, author of "Lendas da
    India" and one of Albuquerque's
    secretaries, 109, 110, 113
Correa, Pero, ambassador to the

Netherlands, 141, 142, 161
Corte Real, Gaspar, lost navigator, 46
Costa, D. Alvaro da, Chamberlain and confidant of D. Manuel, 147, 149, 150, 160, 161
Costa, D. Jorge da, Cardinal, 32, 33, 34
Covilhã, Pero da, traveller to Abyssinia, 11, 15, 100
Covilhã, town in Portugal, 3
Cranganor, Indian port, 41
Crato, 150
Cretico, Venetian envoy, 43, 45, 49
Croy, Guillaume, Seigneur de Chèvres, favourite of Charles V, 147, 148, 150
Cunha, Tristão da, ambassador to Holy See, 61, 65, 66, 97-100, 136

Dabul, 63, 101
Damascus, 50
Deccan, 59, 95
Dias, Bartolomeu, discoverer of Cape of Good Hope, 12, 13, 14, 37, 40
Dias, Diogo, brother of Bartolomeu, 37, 40
Diniz, Dom, second son of executed Duke of Braganca, 7,139
Dio, 66, 67, 96
Diogo (Dom) son of Infante D. Fernando and brother of D. Manuel, Duke of Viseu, 4, 5, 6, 155
Dionisio, Jewish physician of D. Manuel, 19
Doge of Venice, 43, 45, 49, 50, 97
Douro, river, 130
Dra, valley south of Morocco, 94
Drama and Draman, servants of the King's elephants, 136
Duarte, Infante Dom, son of D. Manuel, 141, 144, 145, 151
Dürer, Albrecht, 100
Egypt, 28, 43, 44, 55, 67, 105, 120, Soldan of, 46, 49, 50, 51, 52, 60
Egyptian fleet, 66, 96, 110, 111, 113
El Mandari, Alčaide of Tetuan, 86, 87
Elvas, 22

England, 52, 53, 99, 119
England, King of, 54, 97, 99
En-Nasser, Emir of Marrakesh, 91
Entre-Douro-e Minho, province of Portugal, 39, 122
Escolar, Pero de, pilot, 14
Este, Hercules d', patron of Cantino, 82
Ethiopia, 101
Evora, 11, 18, 21, 128, 131, 149, 158, 162, 163

Faleiro, Ruy, friend of Magalhãis, 160
Faria, Dr. João de, ambassador, 96, 97, 144
Fernandes, Antonio, East African explorer, 117, 118
Fernandes, Lopo, squire of royal household and North African explorer, 89, 90, 91
Fernando, Infante Dom, father of D. Manuel, 3, 4, 11, 47, 61
Fernando, Infante Dom, son of D. Manuel, 141, 143, 151
Fernando, King of Aragon, 17, 18, 22-25, 39, 40, 52-56, 140, 145, 157
Fez, 86, 89, 115. King of, 88, 92, 116
Flander, 47, 53 99, 141, 157
Florence, 45, 126
Fons Vitae, picture, 145
France, kingdom, 157, 163, 166
France, King of, 56, 97, 142, 162, Queen of, 142
François I, King of France, 142, 162
Frois, Estevão, 84
Frol de la Mar, Albuquerque's flagship wrecked returning from Malacca, 34
Frol da Rosa, ship on which Albuquerque died, 112
Fructus de Gois, Keeper of the Robes, brother of Damião, 134, 135
Fuggers, bankers, 47
Futajalon, region in Africa, 70

Galvão, historian and ambassador, 35, 37, 53, 54, 56, 60, 102, 113, 115

Gama, Gaspar da, converted Jew, 32, 33
Gama, Paulo da, brother of Vasco da
  Gama, 14, 27, 31, 33
Gama, Vasco da, 14, 15, 16, 26-35, 37,
  38, 39, 48, 57, 63, 64, 117, 158, 166
Gambia, 70, 71, 116
Ganges, 57, 58
Garter, Order of, 99
Genoa, 82
Germany, 99
Gibraltar, 13, Straits of, 60, 85, 86
Giron, D. Pedro, grandee of Spain, 157
Goa, 32, 59, 67, 68, 69, 101, 103, 104,
  111-114, 128, Duke of, 109
Gois, Damião de, chronicler of D.
  Manuel's reign, 19, 25, 49, 62, 75, 80,
  109, 115, 124, 125, 126, 127, 134, 136,
  143, 149, 151, 164, 167
Gold Coast, 89
Golden Fleece, Order of, 151
Golden Rose, 54
Gomes, Diogo, navigator in the service of
  Henry the Navigator, 71
"Good People", River of, on east coast
  of Africa, 27
Granada, 13, 18, 40, 45, 52, 60, 62, 91
Greece, 49
Guadelupe, 22
Guinea, 2, 13, 27, 32, 45, 72, 117, King
  of Portugal, Lord of Guinea, 34, 36
Gujarat, in India, 66
Gwato, river port on Senegal, 71

Helena, Queen of Ethiopia, 100, 101
Henrique, Infante Dom, Cardinal-King,
  141, 144
Henrique (Henry the Navigator) Infante
  Dom, 3, 4, 6, 10, 11, 13, 34, 36, 47,
  53, 71, 84, 163
Henrique, son of converted King of
  Congo, 75, 78, 151
Henry VII, King of England, 52, 53, 54,
  56
Henry VIII, King of England, son of
  above, 99

Henry the Navigator, see Infante D.
  Henrique
Herbert, Lord, envoy of Henry VII to
  France, 53
Hintata dynasty, of Marrakesh, 88, 89
Holy See, 78, 120, 144, 157, 163
Holy Sepulchre, 51, 52, 54, 56
Honawar, Indian kingdom, 95
Hospital of All Saints, Lisbon, 126, 127
Hospital of Santa Maria, Florence, 126

India, 11, 13, 14, 15, 26, 31, 32, 35, 37,
  39, 40, 43-47, 51, 55, 57, 58, 60, 61,
  62-69, 81, 90, 91, 100, 102, 103, 104,
  112, 114, 117, 136, 160, "Poets of
  India", 106, men of India, 113
Indian Ocean, 12, 28, 30, 33, 35, 40, 42,
  50, 58, 59, 61, 64, 65, 66, 117
Indies of Castile (West Indies), 12, 142
Indies, 57
Inhamunda, East African chief, 118
Isabel "la Catolica", Queen of Castile,
  12, 17, 18, 22, 23, 24, 25, 46, 110,
  123, 141, 157
Isabel, Infanta, Princess, and Queen of
  Portugal, daughter of the above, first
  wife of D. Manuel, 6, 18, 20-24 39, 40,
  150
Isabel, Duchess of Bragança, sister of D.
  Manuel, 5, 6, 7, 155
Isabel, Infanta and later Emperess, wife
  of Charles V, daughter of D. Manuel,
  63, 140, 141, 145, 154, 162, 164
Isabel, Queen of Portugal, mother of D.
  João II, wife of Afonso V, 5
Italy, 45, 47, 53, 56, 166

Jaime, Dom, Son of beheaded Duke of
  Bragança, who inherited the title, 7,
  93, 137, 138, 139, 140
Java, 162
Jeronimos, abbey at Belem, 126, 165,
  Jeronimos Bible, 45
Jeronimos, convent outside Saragoça, 24
Jerusalem, 47, 52, 53, 54, 60, 100, 101,
  139

Jews, 18, 21, 40, 128, 129
Jiddah, port of Mecca, 105
João, African king of Afuto, 71
João, king of Manicongo, 74
João I, King of Portugal, 47, 85
João II, King of Portugal, 1, 8, 10-13,
  17, 18, 19, 45, 47, 48, 55, 62, 64, 70,
  72, 75, 77, 89, 114, 117, 123, 125, 134,
  148, 153, 163, 166, 167
João III, Prince and King, son of D.
  Manuel, 50, 75, 84, 138, 140, 143,
  145-151, 153, 154, 155, 162, 164,
  167
Jorge, Duke of Aveiro, illegitimate son
  of D. João II, 1, 2, 3, 137
Juana "la Louca", Queen of Castile,
  daughter of Isabel and Fernando, 56
Julia, martyr, 125
Julius, Pope, 51

Kalyat, port on the Gulf of Aman
Kansuh-el-Ghauri, last of the Memelukes,
  Soldan of Egypt, 50, 51, 52
Kilwa, sultanate of East Africa, 58, 63,
  117, 118
Kurhat, port on the Gulf of Oman, 67
Lamego, Bishop of 161
Land of the True Cross, 39, 40, 81, Land
  of Parrots, 46, 81, see also Brazil
Larache, in North Africa, 115
Lemos, Gaspar de, 39
Leo X, Pope, 96, 99
Leon, kingdom, 21, 24, 157
Leonor, 12,Madame, sister of Charles V,
  third wife of D. Manuel, 141, 142, 147-
  153, 164
Leonor, Queen of Manicongo, 74
Leonor, Dowager Queen, widow of King
  João II, sister of D. Manuel, 1, 2, 4,
  5, 6, 9, 34, 127, 128, 135, 137, 148
Linhares, Count of, D. Antonio de
  Noronha, brother of Marquis of Vila
  Real, 138
Lisbon, 11, 26, 27, 28, 31, 33, 34,
  41-45, 47, 58, 60, 73, 81, 93, 119,
  124, 125, 129, 130, 131, 136, 157,

Lisbon castle, 101, Lisbon riverside, 104,
  Lisbon Hospital of All Saints, 126,
  Shipyards, 136, Lisbon, 137, 160-165
Lisbon, Archbishop of, 150
Loronha, Fernão de, Concessionnaire of
  Brazilian trade, 82, 83
Louis XII, King of France, 53, 56
Louise, Madame, mother of king of
  France, Francois I, 162, 163
Louvain, 53
Lucca, Duke of, 97
Luis, Dom, infante, son of D. Manuel I,
  140, 143, 145, 146, 151

Madame Marguerite, daughter of
  Emperor Maximilian, 95, 141
Madeira, 45, 89, 105, 135
Magalhães, Fernão de, 159, 160, 161,
  162
Maghreb, in North Africa, 94
Maiollo, author of planisphere, 82
Malabar, 29, 41, 59, 95, 119
Malacca, 60, 63, 66, 68, 69, 96, 104, 111,
  119, 158, 161
"Malagueta", Code name for Madame
  Leonor, 142, 147
Malemo Canaqua, Arab pilot, 28
Mali, kingdom, 12
Malik Ayaz, vassal of King of Cambay,
  66
Malindi, 28, 30, 57 Sultan of, 28, 34,
  117
Malpieri, Dominico, Italian in Lisbon, 81
Mamelukes, slave dynasty of Egypt, 120
Mamora, in North Africa, 115
Mandinga, African kingdom, 12
Manicongo, or Congo, kingdom of, 73,
  119, King of, 76
Manuel, son of King of Congo, 75
Manuel, Dom, King of Portugal,
  ancestry, childhood and accession,
  1-7, character and appearance, 8, 9,
  decides to send Vasco da Gama to India,
  13, marriage to widowed Infanta Isabel,
  17-21, journey into Spain, 22, 23, birth

of son Miguel and death of Infanta
23-25, return of Vasco da Gama, 26-33,
rejoicing, and foundation of abbey of
Jeronimos at Belem, 33-34, takes title of
Lord of the Conquest, Navigation and
Commerce of Ethiopa, Persia and India,
34, writes letter to Samorin and
despatches Cabral to India, 35-38,
reaction on hearing of discovery of
Brazil, 39, 40, attitude towards Venice,
43, plans for Holy War, 47, renounces
North African expedition in order to
succour Venice, 48, 49, reaction to
Soldan's letter, 51, proposes crusade to
European princes, 52-56, sends first
viceroy to India, 61-63, interviews
Albuquerque, 64-65, relations with king
of Congo, 74-78, policy regarding Brazil,
80-85, North Africa and case of Tetuan,
86, 87, sends Lopo Fernandes to
Marrakesh, 89-91, conquest of Azamor,
93, peak of prestige and dreams of
empire of Morocco, 93, 95, gorgeous
embassy to Rome, 95, gifts and honours,
99, 100, embassy from Prester John,
100, distrust of Albuquerque, 165-168,
recalls Albuquerque and sends Lopo
Soares, 109-110, repents and heaps
honours on Albuquerque's son, 114,
dreams conquest of Fez and prepares
disastrous Mamora expedition, 115,
receives Venetian fleet, 120, revives idea
of the crusade and is praised by Pope
and princes who do nothing, 120, 121,
D. Manuel as king, 123, 124, Leitura
Nova, 124, embellishment of Lisbon,
125, Tower of Belem and Hospital of All
Saints, 126, 127, patronage of
Misericordias, 129, dealings with the free
boroughs and Cicioso, citizen of Evora,
31, reward for wolfs' heads, 131, 132,
the Manueline court, 134-137, elephants
and rhinoceros, 136-137, the courtiers,
137-138, trouble with the Duke of
Braganca, 138, 140, grief at death of
Queen Maria, 145, 146, third marriage,

147-152, arranges marriages for
daughters, 153, 154, policy of
non-alignment in Europe, 156, welcomes
Fernão Pires de Andrade back from
China, 158, 159, rejection of Magalhãis,
160, trouble with son, 153, 154,
pressentiment in 1521, 156, falls ill and
dies, 164, 165, his funeral, 165,
summing up his character and reign, 166

Manuel, uncle of King of Congo, 74
Manuel, son of King of Afuto, 71
Marchione, Bartolameu, Florentine
    banker, 45, 46
Maria (Dona), Infanta, daughter of D.
    Manuel by third wife, 156
Maria, younger daughter of Fernando
    and Isabel, Queen of Portugal, second
    wife of D. Manuel, 17, 18, 39, 40, 48,
    63, 75, 109, 110, 120, 128, 130, 135,
    139, 141, 143, 145, 146, 151, 152, 157,
    164
Mark, Patriarch of Ethiopia, 100
Marrakesh, capital of kingdom of
    Morocco, 88, 91, 93, 115
Masa, port on the fringe of the Sahara,
    88
Matosinhos, 124
Matthew, Armenian ambassador from
    Prester John, 100, 101, 102, 113
Mauro, Frà, monk of Sinai, 51, 52, 53
Maxim, Christian martyr, 125
Maximilian, King of the Romans, later
    Emperor, 53, 56, 95, 98, 120, 141,
    142, 151, 162
Mazagan, 116
Mecca, 51, 55, 95, 96, 100, 105
Medicis, Julian of, chaplain to Pope Leo
    X, 99
Medina Sidonia, Duke of, 22, 139, 157
Meliapur, 41
Mendoça, D. Ana de, mistress of King
    João II, mother of D. Jorge, 1
Meneses, D. João de, Count of Tarouca,
    49
Mequinez, in North Africa, lord of, 116

Miguel, son of D. Manuel by first wife, 24, 25, 40
Miguel, yoghi hermit converted by Frei Henrique, 52
Milan, Duke of, 97, 142
Mina, São Jorge da, 13, See also St. George of the Mine
Minho, river, 130
Mir Hussein, captain of the Egyptian fleet, 66
Miranda, Sä de, poet, 135
Misericordias, 127, 128, 166, of Oporto, 128, 145
Mogadishu (East Africa), 59
Mogador, in Morocco, 89, 90, 91, 116
Mogdul, moslem saint, 89
Mohammed, Prophet, 51, 60, 94, 95
Moluccas (Spice Islands), 119, 159, 161
Mombasa, 28, 117
Moniz, Febus, 139
Monomotapa, kingdom of East Africa, 117, 118, 119
Monteiro, Afonso, architect, 162
Moon, Hill of, rock near Sintra, 57
Monchique, baths of, 2
Moreno, Lourenço, factor of Cochin, 106, 107, 109
Morocco, 93
Moulay en-Nassar, Hintata emir of Marrakesh, 11
Moura, town in Portugal, 3
Mount Sinai, 50, 52, 55
Mozambique, island, 28, 35, 64, Sultan of, 28, 117
Muscat, port on Gulf of Oman, 67

Naples, Prior of St. John of, 99, king of, 142
Navarre, 156
Netherlands, 141, 142
New Christians, 128, 129, 130
Nice, 153
Niger, Upper, 70
Nile, river, 105
Noah, biblical patriarch, 143

Nomimansa, African chief, 70
Noronha, D. Antonio de, brother of Marquis of Vila Real, 116, 137, 138
Nossa Senhora da Serra, chapel founded by Albuquerque at Goa, 113
Nunes, Pedro, mathematician and cosmographer, 143

Oman, coast of Arabia, 66, 112
Ophir, 117
Oporto, bishop of, 150
Oran, 29, 32
Orfacan, port on the Oman coast, 67
Ormuz, town on the Persian Gulf, 63, 65, 67, 95, 97, 111, 112, 113
Osorio, Jeronimo, bishop of Silves, 123, 124

Pacheco Pereira, Duarte, 12, 58, 59, 64, 70, 97, 98, 166
Paris, 53
Pasqualigo, Pietro, Venetian envoy, 46, 49
Pedro, (Dom), cousin of King of Congo, 78
Pedro, Infante Dom, regent during the monority of Afonso V, 124
Pedro, master of the King's elephants, 136
Peking, 159
Penha Longa, monastery at Sintra, 145, 164
Pereira, Diogo, clerk of Cochin factory, 107, 136
Pereira, Duarte Pacheco, see Pacheco Pereira, Duarte
Pereira, Gaspar, Secretary of India, 106
Perestrelo, Rafael, 158
Pernambuco, 82, 83, 84
Persia, 51, 67, 95, Shah of, 68
Persians, 134
Persian Gulf, 63, 65, 66, 67, 103, 111
Pigafetta, companion of the voyage of Magalhäis, 84
Pires, Cristóvão, captain of the ship Bretoa, 83

Pires Tomé, apothecary and
    ambassador to China, 158, 159
Pisani, Venetian envoy, 49
Placencia, bishop of, 22
Pliny, 46
Poland, 97, 99
Pope, 33, 49, 51, 54, 78, 88, 94, 96-99,
    101, 120, 121, 139, 144, 148, 149,
    157, see also Julius II, 54, 56
Porcio, Camilo, orator, 96
Portel, town in Portugal, 139
Porto - 124, 130, 151, 153, (see Oporto)
    Misericordia of, 128, 145
Portugal, kingdom, 12, 13, 17, 24, 25,
    44, 46, 47, 48, 49, 51, 55, 56, 59, 60,
    61, 80, 84, 85, 100, 112, 122, 123, 127,
    158, 161, 166, King of, 82, 84, 94, 119,
    vassals of, 88, cities of, 130, 131, policy
    of neutrality, 156, 157, 166
Praca da Figueira, Lisbon, 126
Prester John, 11, 55, 60, 100, 101, 102,
    105, 113, 134, 158
Priuli, Venetian diarist, 44

Quilon, kingdom on Malabar coast, 59

Ramalho, João, patriarch of São Paulo,
    83
Real, Antonio, alcaide of Cochin, 107,
    108
Rebelo, Dr. Diogo Lopes, preceptor of
    D. Manuel, 123
Red Sea, 28, 30, 32, 40, 41, 47, 50, 54,
    55, 59, 60, 61, 63, 65, 66, 69, 105,
    110, 113, 115, 121
Resende, Andre de, humanist, 144
Resende, Garcia de, historian and poet,
    24, 25, 135, 167
Restelo, village near mouth of Tagus, 16
"Rhubarb", code name of Prince D.
    João, 142, 147
Ribeira, royal palace of, 120
Ribeiro, Bernardim, poet, 135
Richmond, King of Arms, 99

Riff, mountains, 86
Rio de Janeiro, 84
River Plate, 84
Rome, 1, 32, 41, 49, 53, 55, 56, 78, 95,
    96, 97, 99, 100, 101, 136, 166
Rossio, Lisbon Square, 126, 165
Rua Nova dos Mercadores, Lisbon, 125,
    165

Sá, Garcia de, captain of Malacca, 161
Sá, João de, secretary of Vasco da
    Gama, 31, 32
Safi, town of Morocco, 12, 88 -92, 115,
    116
Sahara, 13, 88
Saint Catherine, monastery of, 51, 55
Salamanca, 14, 20
Samorin, of Calicut (Lord of the Sea)
    15, 29, 30, 32, 34, 35-38, 40, 41, 58,
    59, 63, 99, 111
Sanchuan, in China,158
San Lucar, 161
Santa Catarina do Monte Sinai, ship
    153,
Santa Cruz, Land of, (Brazil), 80
Santa Cruz do Cabo de Guer (Agadir),
    116
Santa Maria de Ajuda (ship), 136
Santarem, 108
Sant'Angelo, Palace of, 97
Santiago, Order of, 3,113
Santo Domingo (in Castilian Indies), 84
Santos-o-Velho, royal residence, 80, 125,
    136
São Domingos, church, 129
São Gabriel, ship, 16, 27, 31, 32
São Lourenco, Island of (modern
    Madagascar), 162
São Miguel, ship, 16
São Paulo, city in Brazil, 83
São Rafael, ship, 16, 27, 31
Sapienza, 43
Saragoça, 22, 23, 149, 160
Savoy, Duke of, 142, 152, 153, 162
Sebastião, King, 144

Selim, Sultan of Turkey, 120
Senegal, 11, 12, 70, 116, 134
Sequeira, João Lopes de, founder of fortress at Cape Ghir, 89
Sernigi, Girolamo, Italian merchant, 31, 45
Serpa, town in Portugal, 3
Serrão, Francisco, discoverer of Ternate, 119, 159
Setubal, 4
Sever, river in Portugal, 150
Seville, Archbishop of, 23, port of, 82, 160
Sicily, 142
Sidi Nassar, assumed name of Lopo Fernandes, 91
Silva, D.João da, Congolese ambassador, 73
Silva, D.Miguel da, bishop of Viseu, ambassador to the Holy See, 120, 121, 144, 148, 149
Silva, Simão da, ambassador to Congo, 76, 77, 78
Sintra, 26, 27, 57, 108, 145
Soares, Lopo, see Albergaria, Lopo Soares de
Socotra, island, 65, 66
Sofala, 58, 59, 63, 117, 118
Solomon, King, 117
Songhoi, kingdom in Africa, 12
Sousa, D.Afonso de, captain of Alcacer-Ceguer, 86
Sousa, Martim Afonso de, intimate friend of Prince D.João, future founder of São Paulo, 146
Sousa, D.Pedro de, King of Congo's cousin, 75
Southampton, 46
South America, 82
Souss, Sheriffs of, 94
Spain, 26, 46, 60, 69, 126, 156
Spice Islands, or Moluccas, 46, 60, 68, 119, 159, 161
St. Eloy, 75
St. George, of the Mine, 70, 71, 89, 116
St. James, 76

"Sulphur", code name for Duke of Savoy, 142
Suez, 50, 54, 60, 61
Sumatra, 68
Syria, 44

Tangier, 4, 85, 86, 87, 99
Taprobana, name given by the ancients to Ceylon, 46, 60, 99
Tarouca, Count of, see Meneses, D.João de, 49
Tartary, 32
Tentugal, Count of, 150
Terceira, island of the Azores, 32
Ternate, in the Moluccas, 119, 159
Terreiro do Paco, in Lisbon, 33, 125
Tetuan, 86, 87, 88
Thomas, St., Apostle, 15, 36, 41
Timbuktu, 12, 70
Timor, 158
Toledo, Archbishop of, 54
Tomé, master of the King's elephants, 136
Tor, on the Sinai peninsula of the Red Sea, 100
Tordesillas, Treaty of, 12, 62, 81, 84, 159
Torre do Tombo (Lisbon National Archives), 124
Torres Vedras, Lopo Soares' quinta at, 114
Trevisano, Venetian agent at Granada, 45
True Cross, Land of (Brazil), 81
Tunis, 32, 86, 87
Turkestan, 67
Turkey, 43, 51, 121
Tyrol, Count of, 142

Um'er'bia, river that flows by Azamor, 92
Utica, Bishop of, son of King of Congo, 78

Valença, in Spain, 20, 23, 150
Vargas, Lourenco de, Luso-Moroccan agent and interpreter, 87, 88
Veloso, Gaspar, clerk of the factory of Mozambique, 118
Venice, 30, 43-50, 60, 97, 110, 119, 120
Vera Cruz (True Cross), alias Brazil, 82
Verissimo, martyr, 125
Vicente, Gil, playwright and possibly goldsmith, 58, 93, 135
Viceroy of India, 62, 63, 65, 66, 67, 109
Vijayanagar, Indian kingdom, 32, 59, 95, 99, 103, 136
Vila Nova, Count of, 150
Vila Real, Marquis of, 116, 137, 154, 155, house of 137
Viseu, 3, 153
Vizinho, José, pupil of Abraham Zacuto, 14

Welsers, international financiers, 47

Ximenes, Cardinal, 63, *See also* Cisneros, Ximenes

Yaya Aziate, nephew of Alcaide of Safi, 89
Yaya Bentafufa, Berber chief at Safi, 92

Zacuto, Abraham, cartographer and mathematician, 14, 19
Zaire, river, 73
Zipangu, 12
Zurara, chronicler, 122